The Valuation and Sale of Residential Property

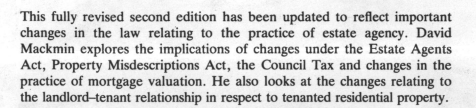

This fully revised second edition has been updated to reflect important changes in the law relating to the practice of estate agency. David Mackmin explores the implications of changes under the Estate Agents Act, Property Misdescriptions Act, the Council Tax and changes in the practice of mortgage valuation. He also looks at the changes relating to the landlord–tenant relationship in respect to tenanted residential property.

David Mackmin is Professor of Property Studies at Sheffield Hallam University. He is the author (with Andrew Baum) of *The Income Approach to Property Valuation*, and is a regular contributor to professional property journals.

The Valuation and Sale of Residential Property

Second edition

David Mackmin

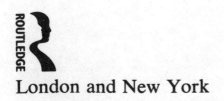

London and New York

Learning Resources
Centre

333. 3322
MAC

First published by Routledge 1989
Reprinted 1991

This edition published 1994
by Routledge
11 New Fetter Lane, London EC4P 4EE

Simultaneously published in the USA and Canada
by Routledge
29 West 35th Street, New York NY 10001

© 1994 David Mackmin

Typeset in Times by J&L Composition Ltd, Filey,
North Yorkshire

Printed and bound in Great Britain by
Mackays of Chatham PLC, Chatham, Kent

British Library Cataloguing in Publication Data

A catalogue record for this book is available from
the British Library

ISBN 0-415-09329-5

*Library of Congress Cataloging in Publication Data
has been applied for.*

2.3.95

To Sue, Sara and Thomas

Contents

Figures

Tables

Preface to first edition

The business of residential agency or brokerage has changed more radically in the past two years than in the whole of its preceding history. Gone, or going, are those familiar high street names of family firms, local partnerships and long-standing amalgamations. In their place the financial institutions – banks, building societies, insurance companies, travel agents and brokers are stamping new names and new images, leaving the historic origins in small print. All this change emphasizes that the growth in property ownership has turned a local service by local people for local people into a national industry with close linkages with the financial services sectors of banking, insurance, mortgages, and loans. Behind those doors growing numbers are employed to offer home-owners an agency service to bring sellers and buyers together. Ultimately the success of each operation will depend upon the quality of the staff employed.

In writing this book I have been conscious of these changes and of the general lack of material covering the work of the residential valuer and agent, available to the negotiator and to the general public. Hopefully the result is a book of interest to the residential valuer and negotiator and to the serious home-owner. The former is encouraged to move on to the further reading recommended in the text on each specialist area, for only by so doing can he or she gain the knowledge and possibly the qualifications to offer a proper service to the public.

I am grateful to the *Estates Gazette* for permission to include material previously appearing in their 'Mainly for Students' column, to Peter J. Byrne of Reading University for compiling the valuation tables in Appendix II, to the Alliance and Leicester Building Society for permission to reprint samples of standard forms used in their mortgage operations, to Anna Emmerton, former principal of Momentum training and former training officer of Reeds Rains Prudential Ltd, for permission to include extracts from Momentum training material and similarly to Derek Porter of *Property Forum*, to the Royal Institution of Chartered Surveyors, the Incorporated Society of Valuers and Auctioneers, Surveyors Publications and *Chartered Surveyors Weekly* for permission to include various material specified in the text. I am also grateful to HMSO for permission to reprint extracts from various statutes.

Errors and omissions are all my own and indeed I am only too aware of the hundred and one other matters that could have been included, but to have done so would have been to produce a practitioner's handbook, whereas my aim has always been to produce an introductory text.

My thanks are due to Sarah Colledge and Sue Dewar for interpreting my handwriting and to Eleanor Rivers, my editor at Routledge.

D.H. Mackmin
Silchester 1989

Preface to second edition

The first edition of this book was written during a period of unprecedented change in the housing market.

The house price boom peaked in 1988. Since then, unemployment has increased, interest rates remained relatively high until late 1992, the volume of house sales has fallen, house prices have fallen, estate agents have closed offices – Prudential Property Services sold their interests in residential agency – and mortgage repossessions and extended indebtedness have continued to increase. Market players talk in terms of negative equity and its medium-term effect on the ability of home-owners to trade up or down. However, the essentials of residential agency and valuations remain unchanged. This edition has been revised to reflect important changes in the law relating to the practice of estate agency and those relating to the landlord and tenant relationship in respect of tenanted residential property.

D.H. Mackmin
Bakewell 1994

Introduction

Every time a house, bungalow, flat or other unit of residential accommodation is bought or sold, someone will have prepared a valuation – even if it is only a personal opinion. No bargain can be struck between buyer and seller without both parties being satisfied that the price is right. Those wishing to buy seek out those wishing to sell; generally those selling will ask a price above the figure at which they are prepared to settle, in the hope that there might be a purchaser for whom the property has a special value, whilst rational buyers will pay no more than the price of a substitute property offered in the same market at the same point in time. This then is how the market for residential land and buildings operates.

However, unlike an open market for fruit and vegetables, buyers and sellers of property cannot be certain that their opinions on value are correct. The absence of a centralized market, the complex legal nature of property and the effect of construction and condition on value create a need for sound professional advice. Members of the Royal Institution of Chartered Surveyors, the Incorporated Society of Valuers and Auctioneers, and the Institute of Revenues Rating and Valuation are the professionals who by education, examinations and experience are best qualified to offer professional advice on the value of residential land and buildings. Their designatory letters, for Associates and Fellows respectively, are ARICS, FRICS; ASVA, FSVA; ARRV, FRRV. Members of the National Association of Estate Agents (NAEA) offer similar help to residential owner-occupiers seeking guidance on asking prices prior to sale. Members of all these societies and associations act as agents for the sale of residential property.

A valuation of residential property may be required for many different purposes, by a wide variety of different people. The most common requirement is for an open market valuation. This has been defined by the Royal Institution of Chartered Surveyors (RICS) as:

the best price at which the sale of an interest in the property might reasonably be expected to have been completed unconditionally for cash at the date of valuation assuming:

a) a willing seller;
b) that, prior to the date of valuation, there had been a reasonable period (having regard to the nature of the property and the state of the market) for the proper marketing of the interest, for the agreement of price and terms and for the completion of the sale;
c) that the state of the market, level of values and other circumstances were, on any earlier assumed date of exchange of contracts, the same as on the date of valuation; and
d) that no account is taken of any additional bid by a purchaser with a special interest.

The most frequent occasion on which a valuation is requested is when a property owner is thinking of selling their property. At this point an estate or house agent is contacted. Most will offer to provide a valuation provided they are subsequently instructed to find a purchaser for the property. Such an exercise may or may not be carried out by a professionally qualified valuer. The advice given on these occasions is that of the asking price that that firm of agents would suggest the vendor asks when offering the property to the market. In many cases it will be above the market value, not because the agent hopes to earn a higher fee, but because they wish to leave a margin for negotiation.

The assessment of an asking price may not be the same as a market valuation. At worst it will be inflated to encourage the owner to give a selling instruction – 'We can always lower the price if it does not sell' – or too low to achieve a quick sale – 'There are many similar properties on the market, so if you really want to sell . . .'. It may not be the same as market value, because the sales negotiator providing the advice has neither the time nor the knowledge to reflect fully upon the economic, legal, physical and other factors that might affect the value in a specific case. A sales negotiator may not have the same expertise as a qualified surveyor on matters of construction, so that in the case of a serious but not readily detectable fault asking price and market value may be very different. There is a need for sellers to be aware of the difference between an open market valuation and advice on asking price. The former, following the RICS definition, is an expression of value in realized terms as if a sale had been completed on the date of valuation. This is important in terms of a mortgage valuation. An asking price is by implication a figure suggested by a seller, with an agent's guidance, to stimulate market interest and to provide a basis for negotiations. On some occasions advice may be given by a qualified valuer and asking price and open market value may be one and the same. On many occasions a vendor will not be aware of any difference, and indeed the difference may have no effect on the outcome. On other occasions the difference becomes apparent once a prospective purchaser arrives on the scene with his or her surveyor.

There are other occasions when an open market valuation might be needed, for example:

1 When the property is to be offered as security for a loan, such as is the case where money is borrowed by way of mortgage for house purchase.
2 When property is to be offered for sale by auction and the vendor needs to fix a sensible reserve price, below which the property will not be sold at the auction.
3 When property is being compulsorily acquired for, say, the construction of a motorway.
4 When a value has to be returned for probate (inheritance tax) on the death of the owner and/or for the purpose of assessing other taxes.
5 When husband and wife are separating and one party wishes to remain in the matrimonial home.
6 When a second house or holiday cottage is sold and there is an assessment for capital gains tax.
7 When land is being bought or sold for the construction of one or more houses.
8 When plans are being prepared to carry out alterations to a property, when a 'before and after' valuation will be useful in deciding whether the cost will be recovered by an increase in value.

On other occasions a valuation on some alternative basis may be needed; indeed in some of the above cases the precise nature of value may be further defined by legislation.

A valuation may be required to assess reinstatement cost for insurance purposes, to assess value for the council tax, to determine the 'fair' rental value when a house or flat is to be let under the Rent Acts or market rental value where a property is to be let on an assured or an assured shorthold tenancy, to assess the price to be paid by a tenant purchasing the landlord's interest by agreement or as a right to buy under the Leasehold Reform Act 1967 or, in due course, to assess the price to be paid where a leaseholder exercises the right to buy a flat or maisonette. All of these require the specialist knowledge of the qualified independent valuer.

Valuations are required by buyers and sellers of residential property, but they may also be required by many other interested or involved parties. Solicitors may request valuations on behalf of clients when dealing with wills, when dealing with matrimonial claims, when dealing with partnerships; by accountants handling cases of bankruptcy and liquidations or for personal or business accountancy and taxation purposes; by insurance companies when settling claims for fire and accident loss; by property companies, developers, charities, housing associations, central and local government and the nationalized industries. Whenever a decision has to be made or a problem solved involving land or building, then a valuation will invariably be required as an aid to that decision-making process.

The various chapters that follow consider the nature of residential property; its value and its valuation for the majority of purposes that commonly give rise to the need for a professional opinion on value, and the nature of the agency process by which most property transactions are conducted.

Chapter 1

Residential property and the determinants of value

LEGAL TITLE

The first aspects of a property to be considered by the layman are usually the location, the appearance and the physical condition. Where it is, what it looks like, its accommodation, services and condition are all important factors when considering value, but for the valuer the most important initial considerations are legal. This is because it is the legal title to property with all its encumbrances that is bought and sold. 'Every man's home is his castle' summarizes most people's aspirations for home owner-ship, to own something which is theirs and which is defensible against all-comers. In practice, the main line of defence is title; if the title is in any way limited, then solid walls may not prove to be the best defence.

In England and Wales the titles to be valued will either be freehold or leasehold, but it is also possible to own no more than an interest for life in a particular parcel of land.

The fee simple absolute is the legal term for a freehold estate and this is the largest legal estate that one can hold in land. The owner of the freehold has the right to occupy and use the land, to transfer the title in whole or in part *inter vivos* or by will and to create lesser interests out of it such as periodic tenancies, other leaseholds and life interests. The legal rights are in perpetuity but held under the Crown, who is the absolute owner. Indeed, if a freeholder dies without having made a will and without any living relatives who could inherit under the rules of intestacy, then the title will revert to the Crown.

Although the freeholder has in theory absolute rights in perpetuity to the land, to everything above the land and to everything below the land, those rights are subject to a number of common law rights and statutory rights of one form or another.

Common law rights include the lawful rights of others. Thus others may enjoy rights of way over the property, or be entitled to rights of light if they hold adjoining property and to rights of physical support.

Civil and military aircraft may enter an owner's airspace, subject to certain limitations. All gold and silver found in mines belongs to the Crown. Coal is currently vested in British Coal, whilst other items found on or buried in the land or hidden in buildings may be termed treasure trove and may also belong to the Crown. Water in the form of ponds and lakes can be owned, but the ownership and use of other bodies of water is strictly controlled. Ownership of river frontages may or may not include fishing rights, and the riparian rights of others must be respected.

Two other title restrictions require special mention. First, on transfer of title it is possible for an owner to impose on a purchaser specific restrictions, known as restrictive covenants. From a valuation viewpoint the most important are those covenants that restrict the use; development may be restricted to a specific number of houses, occupation restricted to family occupation, use may be restricted to public open space, and there may be restrictions on parking of caravans. These restrictions may remain enforceable for many years, but the right to enforce may be lost if the person enjoying the benefit of that covenant has permitted breaches to occur. In other cases it may be necessary to apply to the Lands Tribunal under the Law of Property Act 1925 for the restrictions to be modified or discharged. Clearly such restrictions may hold values up where they help to maintain an environment, but they may also depress values where they prevent the land being used to its highest and best use in today's market. Thus land suitable for development at a density of ten houses to the acre may be restricted to one house per acre by a covenant inserted in 1890.

Second, it was possible for a freehold title to be made subject to a rent charge. This entitled a party with no legal interest in the land to receive an annual payment. The Rent Charges Act 1977 prohibits the creation of new rent charges and contains provisions for the gradual extinguishment or voluntary redemption of such charges as currently exist (see Appendix IA).

In addition, what a freeholder can do with land is restricted by the normal laws of the land. The most important of those relating to use and development of land are contained in the Town and Country Planning Acts, Public Health Acts, Housing Acts, Highways Acts and the Building Regulations, together with those that protect residential tenants such as the Rent Acts, Landlord and Tenant Acts, and the Leasehold Reform Act.

Overriding the freeholder's rights are those of the police, who may legally enter upon land for purposes of law enforcement, and those of central and local government and statutory undertakers who may have powers of compulsory acquisition which may be exercised in accordance with any vesting legislation and subject to compensation in accordance with the vesting legislation and/or the Land Compensation Act 1961 as amended.

Freehold property also includes improvements to the land such as buildings and those things so attached to the land that they are held to be fixtures. The distinction between personal property that is movable and personal property which has been so attached to the land as to become a fixture is often very fine, and has given rise to a branch of law known as the law of fixtures. In the residential market it has become the custom for questionable items to be listed as being included or excluded from the sale. The valuer will take the obvious fixtures into account in a valuation, as they may add to the value of the property. Clearly an item such as a central heating boiler is a fixture, but it is less certain whether a built-in hob and oven in a kitchen will be classed as a fixture. When in doubt the valuer should make it clear in a valuation report which items have been included in the valuation of the property.

Until the passing of the Leasehold Reform Act in 1967 it was quite common practice for residential property to be sold on a leasehold basis and in the case of blocks of flats, house conversions, sheltered housing or whenever property management may be a major issue it is still common practice to sell on a leasehold basis but possibly to include a share in a specifically created management company holding the freehold.

A leasehold estate in property will be for a definite term. This is an important value factor. Traditionally such leases in residential property have been for terms of 99 years or 999 years. But in addition the terms and conditions or convenants in the lease can have a significant effect on value. As a lease is a contract between the parties, so it is possible for it to contain any legally permissible contractual terms accepted or acceptable to both parties. Thus in addition to covenants to pay rent, there may be covenants to repair, insure, pay local taxes, to clean, to maintain grounds and gardens or to meet some or all such costs through a service charge levied by the landlord. In most instances these covenants impose a contractual requirement on the leaseholder to undertake everything that one would expect from a reasonable freehold owner of residential property. However, a freeholder has a choice of whether or not to paint the property, to clean the windows and to maintain the garden; the leaseholder will not necessarily have that choice. Further, the leaseholder may be specifically restricted in terms of the use and enjoyment of the property. There may be covenants about music after 11.30 p.m., about hanging out clothes to dry, about erecting TV and radio aerials and a requirement to obtain the freeholder's consent for all alterations and for any sale or further sub-leasing of the property. (See also Chapter 11.)

A valuer when instructed to prepare a valuation must satisfy himself by inspection and enquiry as to the nature of the title to be valued and any restrictions or other encumbrances that attach to the title. However, because of the time limits imposed upon the valuer by many clients, valuations are often prepared on the basis of an unencumbered freehold or on the basis of minimum information relating to a lease. A valuer is valuing on the basis of information supplied and will naturally reserve the right to review that valuation if that information is subsequently found to be incorrect. Nevertheless valuers are trained to observe and should therefore account for the obvious, such as signposted public footpaths, unmade and unadopted roads, shared driveways and shared areas in blocks of flats.

CHARACTERISTICS OF PROPERTY

When considering the determinants of value, most valuers will take account of or have regard to a number of important characteristics of property.

First, property has a fixed location – it can only be used at that geographical location and therefore its value will depend upon the market's attitude toward the benefits of owning a property at that specific location. Second, property in the sense of bricks and mortar has a long life so that any sum paid today to acquire property has to be a fair reflection in current value terms of future benefits over many years including, in the case of a freehold, the legal right of ownership in perpetuity. Third, property is purchased with relatively large amounts of capital. The availability of credit through a proper mortgage market and the costs of such credit are fundamental factors in the residential market. Fourth, total supply of certain types of residential property cannot be increased: at best it is only possible to build in a similar style, but similarity of appearance might not compensate for historic location and copies are rarely of the same value as originals. Additionally total supply can only change over a long time period. In the market-place, a number of behavioural observations can be noted:

1 The typical residential buyer responds in a fairly conventional and conservative manner to what he or she sees.
2 Conformity is important – the value of a superior property surrounded by inferior property will tend toward the value level of the inferior properties, whilst an inferior property surrounded by superior properties will tend toward the value tone of the superior properties.
3 The typical buyer will be well aware of the price of substitute properties and hence the maximum market value for any given property will be fixed by the price level of substitute properties offering the same utility.
4 Areas go through four stages of the urban cycle of growth, stability, decline and renewal. Value and rate of change in value will differ according to the stage which a particular area has reached. Similarly different areas, because of their point in the cycle, attract different purchasers. This in turn is a recognition that value is a reflection of future benefits of ownership and clearly depends upon, say, the state of decline of an area.
5 Value and cost are rarely the same. In part this is linked to the economic laws of increasing and decreasing returns, the effect being that the input

of capital into a particular property at a point in time may result in a more than proportionate increase in value – increasing returns. At a later point the returns will barely match the cost, and beyond that point the returns in the market value sense will be less than the cost. It is often thought that money invested in bricks and mortar must be safe, with the result that all too often residential owners alter, enlarge and improve property at enormous cost which is not reflected by changes in values. Again the principle of conformity means that the typical buyer will not acquire a superior non-conforming property at a price greatly in excess of the level for the area.

In summary, to have value, property must have utility and it must be scarce in relation to demand. For demand to be effective, it must be supported by credit facilities which in turn are dependent upon ability to repay loans, which depends upon general levels of income and other living costs. The property market must be seen as a dynamic place where the valuer tries to interpret the behaviour of typical buyers and sellers in order to give sound professional advice on values to clients.

Some of the more pertinent and typical factors are now considered in greater depth.

MARKET FORCES

The Americans when discussing market value talk in terms of the interplay of the four forces that affect human behaviour: social ideals and standards, economic activities and trends, government activity and intervention, and physical or environmental forces.

Each of these is made up of many influencing components, some of which at a point in time may have a major impact whilst at others they may appear to be dormant. The likely effect of each component upon value can be analysed in the classic economic model where everything is assumed to remain constant whilst one variable is altered. In this way it is possible to demonstrate how a factor might result in higher values by raising demand in a static supply situation. The world and the market for residential property are, however, dynamic and the residential valuer needs to be active in the market-place to sense and to measure the impact of the interplay of these forces. For this reason the residential valuer appears to be far more interested in prices in the market-place than in the underlying market forces; nevertheless an awareness of those forces is an essential part of the valuer's expertise.

THE MARKET

The residential market is imperfect. There is no central market place; as a result buyers and sellers are uninformed and even their professional advisors – valuers and agents – only have a limited knowledge of what is available for sale and of what is happening in the market. Every house, flat, bungalow or other unit of residential accommodation is unique in some respect. Even a pair of semi-detached houses differ as between right-hand and left-hand units. This makes the task of valuation much more difficult than in those markets where there are standard units or products such as stocks, shares, gold, apples and cars. It is further complicated by the fact that there is no acceptable unit of comparison. Residential property can occasionally be compared on the basis of a price per square foot (or metre) of floor space, but issues such as the number of bedrooms, reception rooms, car spaces, circulation space, views and the like can all vary between properties of precisely the same floor area, thus making the total unit of accommodation the only acceptable unit of comparison.

Traditionally the market has seasonal fluctuations, with greater activity and steadier, possibly rising prices in spring and early summer, a quiet period in August followed by a mini-spur in September. These seasonal movements are different in different parts of the country, and significantly different between London and popular holiday areas such as the Lake District. They can be affected by significant changes in market forces such as a change in mortgage interest rates. In addition to seasonal movements, there are cycles of under-supply and over-supply and other movements of a migratory nature such as the desire to balance proximity to work with proximity to the country, and leisure activities with travel time and cost.

In most markets, increases in effective demand against a fixed supply will lead to an upward movement in price. The upward movement in price encourages suppliers to produce more and for more suppliers to enter that market. In the residential market the response to such a shift in demand is slow. It is argued that planning controls impede the supply of land and hence the supply of new houses coming on to the market. Even without such controls there would be a delay caused by the inability of the housebuilding industry to raise productivity in the short run. It is difficult for the market to respond precisely to match an increase in demand in an area, because land becomes available in sizeable chunks and housebuilders tend to be market followers, not market creators. The result is that an increase in demand in an area may in time be followed by an over supply. The valuer's difficulty is interpreting the state of the market in an area at a point in time.

Over a number of years changes in consumer preferences occur which can be incorporated in new home design but are more difficult to incorporate in the existing housing stock. These style changes can shift the demand and hence value patterns of an area and must be monitored. The upper end of the market can be particularly vulnerable to these changes of fashion.

Residential property has a fixed location and can only be enjoyed at that

location. The enjoyment of a property will depend upon general environmental factors and specific local factors. In the case of owner-occupation,
the market reflects the relationship between employment opportunities,
communications, general facilities of an area and the environmental
factors. Growth in economic activity, more jobs and better pay, tends to
cause a rise in values because of the relatively fixed level of supply.
Analysis of the economic opportunities of an area is essential if house
buyers are to make sound house purchase decisions.

Total home demand has to be translated into effective demand. Effective demand is a function of the national economy and gross national
product. The valuer needs to know and to consider what is happening to
base indicators such as the level of unemployment, the way employment
is going, current wage levels, and the propensity of the population to save
and to invest in their own homes.

The reduction in employment during the early 1990s caused by cutbacks
and closures has led in some areas to reductions in value both in real terms
and in money terms. Money in bricks and mortar will not always be safe.

The housing market and levels of home ownership are closely connected
with the availability of credit. Effective desire can only be translated to
effective demand through the availability of credit, largely in the form of
funds for mortgage loans offered by the building societies, the banks and
the insurance companies. Availability and the cost of finance are socio-
economic elements in the market-place – as are the loan terms of such
organizations. In the period up to 1988 a multiplier of two and a half times
the husband's salary was replaced by a willingness by some to lend up to
three or four times the major salary plus the minor salary, thus joint
incomes of £15,000 per annum and £10,000 per annum could secure a
mortgage of £55,000–£70,000 and higher in the case of purchases by two
or more unrelated purchasers. Such changes in lending policy were seen
as a response to demand and rising prices or as a major influence in price
rises in areas where demand exceeded supply. A more conservative
approach has been adopted by most lenders in the 1990s.

Credit for house purchase offered by banks and building societies is
dependent upon two factors: the security of the property offered against
the loan, and the financial status of the borrower. Very simply, the more
one earns the more one can borrow. Thus in a housing market where
demand exceeds supply higher salaries and wages will provide purchasers
with greater purchasing power; this balanced against the fixed supply leads
to higher property prices through competition between buyers. The cost
of buying, the interest payable on house purchase loans (mortgages), is
outside the control of the banks and building societies in that to maintain
a flow of savings to sustain a flow of loans they have to compete in the
money market. As a result, mortgage interest rates can rise and fall with
the world's changing view of the British economy.

The government can influence the economy, finance and hence the market-place. Governments set minimum standards for new homes, through planning control, building and health regulations. These standards affect costs, which influence developers' attitudes as to feasibility and influence the volume of new houses in the market-place. EC regulations may also influence market forces as they certainly will if they impose VAT on new homes.

The government influences the market in other ways, such as by encouraging public sector tenants to purchase their homes, by imposing rent control and protection on the private rented sector, and by changes in taxation.

The general level of values depends upon the general and area-specific levels of economic activity – community income and wealth; the existing quality and quantity of residential property in an area; the rate of addition to that stock; the point at which a local market happens to be in a particular cycle, and the underlying confidence that people within and outside a particular area have in the economic future and prosperity of that area.

The fixed location of property means that the nature of the neighbourhood and the immediate surrounding properties are crucial factors in terms of buyers' attitudes and hence in determining a value for a property within the level of values for that area.

A number of factors affect the attitude of buyers. These factors in turn determine whether an area at a point in time is considered to be desirable with rising values, acceptable with stable values, or depressed with falling values. The same house in each such area would have very different values.

People need property, in this context people need somewhere to live. The size and composition of the population is an indication of the number and possible size of houses required by that population. But the residential market is a local market so it is important to consider the population within a definable area and to know its composition and the extent to which it is changing. Is it an ageing population, is it growing or declining naturally and/or by migration in or away from the area? Demand characteristics can change both across the country and within local areas. Over recent years developers have become niche operators, seeking to satisfy current demand. Market analysis identifies the need for, say, starter homes, single-person homes, family homes, luxury homes, retirement homes.

Market analysis will also identify preferences in terms of type of accommodation, design, materials, construction, internal layout and facilities.

All of these are aspects of society and social change which must be appreciated and interpreted by the valuer.

The socio-economic composition of a neighbourhood has a major impact on values. A socially deprived or underprivileged area will display that fact in the deterioration of the urban fabric, including the deterioration in physical condition of homes. Deprived means depressed, which signifies low incomes, multiple occupations and low values. In time, however, a combination of other factors – including the architectural and historic nature of an area – may draw in a wealthier class who will 'gentrify' or reinstate the properties to their original condition and turn such an area into a high value area. Such movements are observable but not always predictable.

In a similar way areas historically noted for housing the wealthier owner-occupier may go into decline as large units or large plots become a financial burden and are sold for conversion and multiple letting. In time the same area may revert back to single family ownership or be substantially redeveloped for low-cost housing or high-value housing, depending upon the level and nature of demand at a point in time when redevelopment is seen as the proper solution for a declining neighbourhood. The level of vandalism and crime are regretfully indicative of an area's desirability. Such changes are partly attitudinal and, like a disease, can spread very rapidly. If a community senses that no one cares about an area, in particular 'the authorities', then the residents cease to care. The result is decline, which is immediately reflected in falling property values. Active residents' associations and crime watch committees show concern by the community for their neighbourhood, which can stimulate pride in an area and lead to rising values.

The market and market values are obvious reflections of social desirability. The extremes of social deprivation and social well-being coincide with the extremes of values to be found within a defined geographic area. The residential valuer must be alert to the potential for change, and be aware that within broadly defined residential groupings there will be pockets of properties which appear to defy logic but nevertheless maintain high values in areas of low values or areas of low values in an area dominated by high values. Once a change in an area is signalled, the value movement tends to be fairly fast as the new socio-economic group moves in to replace the higher or lower socio-economic group.

These social features are closely related to the income profile of the population and the underlying economic activity of that section of the population that predominates in a given residential area. This is further reflected in market activity. Properties in desirable areas change hands quickly, with a minimum of properties remaining vacant. Properties in declining areas tend to remain on the market for longer periods, tend to become vacant and remain vacant, deteriorate, shift to multiple occupation, and may finally be condemned.

Local politics are a reflection of and a response to these changing social and economic forces. The future of a neighbourhood can be affected by the strength of the community in political terms. Strong representation can produce improvements to schools, health and community services and dictate the attitude of 'the authorities' to that area. Small changes on their own have little impact, but in combination can strengthen a neighbour-hood. Thus the attention of the authorities to street cleaning, refuse collection, repair and maintenance of roads and footpaths, street furniture, local schools etc. will all become part of the environmental picture which impacts upon buyers' attitudes and hence on their willingness to commit themselves to a purchase at a particular price.

Physical and environmental factors help to define neighbourhoods. Those which are, in physical terms, well maintained and environmentally most attractive are those which are likely to become socially most desirable and hence in time occupied by the economically stronger. That together tends to create community and political strength which becomes protective and perpetuates the status of the area. Natural and man-made features may provide the boundaries to identifiable residential areas. In some cases there may be a spill-over effect, with values declining gradually from high-value areas to low-value areas. In other cases, there may be pronounced changes in value either side of a building or road.

Roads, particularly motorways and main commuter routes, railways, rivers, lakes, village greens, sports fields, parks may all act as boundaries. Proximity to one or another may give rise to higher or lower relative values depending upon the desirability or otherwise of being close to such a feature. There are rarely any hard and fast rules about the behavioural attitude of the residential property market. This is because it is often the combination of many factors that creates good or bad in the eyes of the buyer. Some river locations are highly sought after, others far less so. Motorways and railways may act as boundaries but the combination of ease of access, visual intrusion and noise, together with other environ-mental factors, will determine whether they add to or take away from value.

Soil, subsoil, natural drainage, probability of flooding, micro-climate, topography, and aspect are all physical factors which historically may have determined the desirability of building in an area and may still today have an impact on values. Proximity to the right schools, shops, libraries, golf courses, country club, leisure facilities, may add to value. But on the other hand, proximity to anything likely to cause a nuisance such as factories, sewage-works, football grounds, bingo halls, discotheques or anything that might give rise to rowdyism and general misbehaviour will tend to depress values (see also Table 2.1).

Communications to the rest of the area, surrounding public open space, motorway linkages and places of employment are all very important locational factors. So too, is the existing quality of development, road patterns and standard of property maintenance in determining the good, the bad and the indifferent areas of a defined residential market.

Nor would it be a complete story without mentioning the importance of pressure groups in the form of conservationists, environmentalists, ecologists and politicians. All of these have an impact on the market for residential property. Thus at a given point in time these various forces will have combined together to create a particular level and pattern of values in an area. A change in one or more of any of the forces or components mentioned will alter the supply of or the demand for, all residential property, or for a sector of market or just for one specific property, the result being an increase in supply or a decrease in demand or a decrease in supply or an increase in demand and a corresponding change in prices and hence in values. It would be rare indeed for only one force to be moving, so interpretation of cause and effect can be very complex.

The general economic climate together with the quality of different residential areas creates a pattern of values for a defined market. Within that market the valuer must now consider the site-specific qualities of a house and its physical condition in order to assess its open market value.

Chapter 2

The effect of physical factors on value

SITE AND SITING QUALITIES

When considering the value of an existing residential property it is important to take note of specific site elements, including the manner in which the site has been developed. It is important to judge whether the specific combination of buildings and site together create a proper development of the site. For example, an extremely attractive site might have been developed in such a way that it has failed to maximize the potential of the site, in value terms, and so badly that it is impossible by further improvement to realize that potential without completely redeveloping the site. At a particular point in time it will have a low value by comparison with other properties, but possibly too high a value by such comparison for redevelopment to be considered. Alternatively, a relatively poor site might have been so carefully developed that the final product has overcome the disadvantages of the site and created an enhanced value.

The experienced professional residential valuer, because of that experience, is able to recognize inherently the features of good site development. For the layman it is often much more difficult, and for the agent much more embarrassing to point out that a property in market terms is 'a mess'.

First, it is important to correctly identify the site in legal terms – where are the boundaries and what do they actually enclose? In the majority of cases what can be seen on the ground is indeed that which can legally be sold and which therefore obviously is the site for valuation purposes. In other cases it is less obvious; owners, over time, may have encroached upon adjoining landowners' rights, and in such cases disputes may arise in the future. When in doubt, the valuer should try to establish the true boundaries for valuation purposes by checking with any description or plan or measurements included in the title documents. Even owners of houses on new estates have been known to have occupied them for some years totally oblivious of the fact that the developer erected the rear fence a number of feet away from the boundary line set out in the title deeds. For a residential valuation (as against asking price advice), the valuer will need to measure and note the length of boundaries. It is also important to check the responsibility for repair of boundary fences and walls, and their condition. Residential valuations are rarely undertaken other than on the assumption of an unencumbered interest; nevertheless, owners' rights over the site exercised or enjoyed by others must be allowed for in a residential valuation.

The nature of the soils and subsoils should be ascertained. These dictate the type of foundation that should be used and the natural drainage of the site. This might be important if the site as already improved has potential for future improvement, but it is also important in formulating a view about the existing improvements themselves. The knowledgeable valuer will be aware of the type and standard of foundation most typical to different periods of building in an area and should therefore be alerted to the possibility of ground movement, heave and subsidence, particularly in areas with clay soils. The extremely hot summer of 1976 revealed all manner of weaknesses; a current unknown is the affect that the loss of mature trees, close to existing houses, due to the 'mini-hurricane' of October 1987 may have on the moisture content of soils. Developments on made-up ground pose particular construction problems and can create unexpected difficulties many years later.

Natural drainage is important, as too is the proximity to rivers and their flood plains. Even areas where there is very little possibility of flooding may suffer from high water-tables, which may cause storm water to back up soak-aways, cellars to flood or water to penetrate in wet conditions to ground floor timbers. If the drainage system is to a septic tank rather than to the main drainage system, its function may be impaired in an area with high water-tables and poor natural drainage.

The shape and size of the site can be important. Each property must be treated on its merits, but buyers tend to prefer regularly shaped plots where the depth is between two and three times the width. Some buyers are attracted to properties with larger gardens, but for the valuer the question is whether the market places a higher value on the properties with gardens substantially different in length to the 'norm' in that area for that type of property. The answer is generally no; even in the case of underdeveloped plots the price is only marginally different. On new estates where plot sizes might be small a property with a slightly larger garden may sell at a small premium, and perhaps more significantly, may sell more readily. If the plot is much shorter than is normal for that type of property in that area then it may prove more difficult to sell and it may have to be offered at a discount.

Shape is also important, most buyers preferring regular shaped plots. There is some attraction to a plot which broadens out to the rear, but those that become narrower or reduce to a point may be considered less attractive. Properties with very poor frontages can be more difficult to sell.

Corner plots may be more valuable because they offer the opportunity for secondary access and in some instances the ability to sell off an area for development.

The next point to consider is the position of the dwelling on its plot in relation to the size and shape of the plot and the surrounding residential area. The building line or set-back of the property from its frontage and the road can affect its value. In many towns, very similar terraced houses will differ in value from street to street because in some streets they front onto the pavement, in others they have a very small forecourt and in others they are set back sufficiently to provide off-street parking. In other areas the set-back may mean the difference between having a short drive or a turning space in front of the house.

If the property is set too far back on its plot, such that the front garden is very much larger than the back garden, it may have an adverse affect on value compared to a plot with a similar property set in a position such that the front garden is half or a third of the size of the back garden.

There are cases where the garden is on the opposite side of the road, or runs to the side of the property or indeed runs behind a group of cottages, rather than from front to back. By comparison such properties will have a higher value than comparable properties with no gardens, but lower than comparables with traditional back gardens. Increases in value might be possible through rearrangement of ownership rights.

The type of road and position of the road are also relevant. Developers today are far more conscious of this factor than 50 or 100 years ago, when roads were built straight up hills and straight along the sides of hills. As a result, some houses are below street level; pedestrians can look straight in to bedroom windows, and storm water can run into the house or garage. Aspect and orientation may affect value when poor layout results in some properties enjoying sunshine all the day and others hardly ever.

The use of the road is an important factor; is it a quiet, safe road or a cul-de-sac giving quiet enjoyment, or a busy short-cut for rush-hour traffic, or a popular on-street parking area for local shoppers? Whichever it is, does it affect current values? To find the answer it is sometimes useful to pose the question 'if there was no through traffic, would this be a more popular residential road?'

In terms of value, the nature of the gardens can be important – gardens can sell properties. A beautiful, well-stocked garden can help to sell a property in the spring and early summer, and may achieve a sale at a higher price. The same property with an overgrown, uncared-for rubbish tip will suffer by comparison. As important is the nature of all the other gardens in the street and the street scene itself. The professional valuer must balance the visual attraction of trees and wall-climbing shrubs with the question of potential damage to roads, pavements, patios, concrete surrounds, drives, drains and foundations.

The availability of public utility services such as gas, water, electricity and drainage and telecom facilities are important factors for many buyers and must therefore be considered by the valuer. Electricity supply by overhead cables is more liable to damage and adds to the clutter of street furniture, with its posts and wires; the absence of gas limits heating choice for occupiers; the absence of mains drainage places an added responsibility upon owners, and in the case of system failures an added cost.

Finally, on the question of site factors there is the question of the immediate or near immediate land uses which may raise or lower values. It is important for the valuer to look beyond the adjoining properties, because noise and smell can carry considerable distances. Of increasing concern to buyers are questions of security and safety – particularly for children, and hence one is back with the problem of social considerations.

Table 2.1 at the end of this chapter is adapted from *Bean and Lockwood's Rating Valuation Practice*[1] and gives some idea of the many factors that can have an effect on value. The problem for the professional valuer is that in the comparative analysis of value it is not a question of one good or bad feature that has to be weighted and judged, but a complex combination of many factors including design, accommodation, construction and condition.

DESIGN AND ACCOMMODATION

Residential property through the centuries has been built by speculative builders and developers constrained by the cost/value equation and the need to make a profit; by local authorities, government bodies and housing associations restrained by cost limits; and by private individuals with or without cost limits. Until very recently the consumer has exercised very little influence on design, because of continuing under-supply of property in areas of high demand. However, in the last ten years more market research has been undertaken by developers as through it they hope to achieve faster sales of a more acceptable product at the highest possible price at the lowest level of commensurate cost, to achieve the greatest profit. The position today is that the residential market is dominated by the housing stock, much of which fails to satisfy consumers' real requirements. If supply in an area increases to a point where purchasers are able to choose, then those properties most closely matching purchasers' needs will sell more easily and possibly at higher prices.

External and internal design of residential property has an impact on buyers and their attitudes to certain types of property. Certain design solutions in turn influence levels of values, the more popular property rising in value at a faster rate than the less popular. In a freer market such as in America, it is far more important to create the right product at the right price, and far more important to monitor purchasers' reactions and requirements. From such research a few principles of domestic design emerge.

A home can be divided into three main areas – the sleeping area, the living area and the cooking-utility area. Such areas should be separate areas, with independent access off a common service core consisting of entrance, hall and staircase. Properties without a central core suffer in user terms because occupiers have to pass through rooms to gain access to other rooms. Where in the compact units this cannot be achieved, then division or separation must be achieved as far as is possible physically and otherwise visually by use, say, of different floor finishes.

The front door to many smaller houses and flats opens directly into the living room. This is as typical today as it was in the terraced housing or artisan dwellings of the eighteenth and nineteenth centuries. This arrangement means that all guests and visitors are seen by everyone in the living room, and all interruptions break up the social activities in the living room. Although some of this can be reduced by creating a small entrance hall, it cannot be cured, as access to all other parts of the home is through the living room, which thus functions as a hall/living room. It has the further disadvantage of bringing outside weather conditions directly into the living area.

Without a proper core, access to bedrooms may have to be through other bedrooms, access to bathrooms through bedrooms or, in the case of downstairs provision in older terraces, via the dining room and the kitchen.

Another design fault is the positioning of secondary areas such that occupiers must again pass through living areas to gain access to the garden to hang out clothes or to remove rubbish.

Access to garages and outside stores should be direct from the house or under cover. Kitchen and dining areas should be near to one another for convenience, and to keep food smells away from the rest of the property.

Building regulations control or controlled certain aspects of design such as daylight, ventilation, hygiene etc., but the design solution rests with the architect. Where cost permits, separate rooms should open off the core. If this is not possible, a compromise is needed and a decision has to be taken on which areas can best be combined – living/dining, dining/kitchen, living/bedroom. Here taste and preferences change from time to time, but the solution must provide sufficient space for that use or combination of uses. Adequate space in bedrooms must be provided having regard to cost, value and the expected market. It is useless to provide one small fitted cupboard in a bedroom in a two-room flat if the marketing is aimed at a high socio-economic group for whom two double wardrobes is barely sufficient for a married couple.

Kitchens need to be designed so that there is no direct route through the operation area. The operation area should be designed as a triangle between sink, cooker and preparation surfaces. If access goes through this zone then it raises the possibility of accidents to a high level.

Increasingly, buyers are looking for better quality kitchens and bathrooms and, above a certain price range, en suite master bedrooms as well.

Various government reports have recommended space standards for different size houses, but ultimately it has proved impossible to build to these standards even when interpreted as maxima rather than minima. The argument has been that it is too costly to provide homes to meet these standards, but an alternative view is that when effective demand is high the same price can be achieved from offering far less.

Within a higher price range further rooms and spaces will be expected, such as utility rooms, studies, ground floor cloakrooms, whilst outside garages, double garages and car standing spaces must all meet with the car-owning aspirations of the identified market sector.

Older properties will not meet modern design standards. In some cases the internal layout can be redesigned to meet current demand, in others little or nothing can be done to correct design faults.

External design may be more subjective; that regarded as good by some will be considered bad by others. Surveys that have been undertaken suggest that the design solutions of developers rarely satisfy the general public's aesthetic eye. The traditional Georgian and Victorian designs tend to have the greater appeal, but it is difficult to separate the aesthetic response of purchasers from their reaction to quality and quantity of space – the executive looking for 1500 square feet of housing with quality finish may have little choice other than the mock Tudor and Elizabethan styles. Such purchases under these conditions of limited choice may be interpreted as a popular vote for a particular house style, but more research is needed by developers to judge whether this is really the case.

The market's reaction to internal and external design solutions will be reflected over time in market prices. Those that fall short of buyers' expectations will be sold at a discount.

CONSTRUCTION AND CONDITION

The final factors to be considered are those of construction and condition. Most new homes will carry the 'Buildmark', the National House-Building Council's (NHBC) warranty against financial loss arising from a substantial structural defect. Other new homes may be sold with the benefit of insurance protection such as that offered by Municipal Mutual Insurance Foundation 15 or its successor. But even where this level of protection exists, value will be affected by condition.

For most purchasers, first impressions count particularly if they have a choice within their price range. The result is that properties in sound condition and decorative order sell more readily than those in poor condition, and the latter may have to be sold at a discount to attract a buyer ready, willing and able to take on the business of making good, five, ten, fifteen or fifty years of deterioration. Conditions will therefore affect the market's opinion of worth and should be reflected in residential valuations and asking price guidance.

Only when a valuer undertakes a full survey (see Chapter 9) or is provided with a full survey of a property, will it be possible to reflect fully upon the actual condition of the property. Without such surveys buyers may pay too much for their chosen homes. A residential valuation does not normally include a structural or full survey, and this point is firmly made in the RICS leaflet, *The Valuation of Residential Property*:

> The valuer will have regard to apparent defects and wants of repair in preparing the report on value and will take into account the age and nature of the property. The valuer will not, however, carry out the detailed search for defects which is undertaken as part of a structural survey, nor necessarily set out the various defects when making the report.

Certain defects can only be discovered by detailed investigations. For example, when valuing a dwelling house a valuer will not normally move the furniture or lift the carpets, which means that the most common indications of dry rot and woodworm in concealed places cannot be seen. A paragraph on the following lines may be included in the report:

> We have not carried out a structural survey nor have we inspected those parts of the structure which are covered, unexposed or inaccessible and such parts are assumed to be in good repair and condition.

Such a disclaimer is normally required by the valuer's professional indemnity insurance policy. Similar terms need to be incorporated when accepting instructions to carry out a residential valuation in order to comply with the Unfair Contracts Terms Act.

In the case of agent's guidance on asking price, the better agents make it clear that their advice is given following a limited inspection of the property and that their opinion may need to be reviewed if subsequent more detailed inspections reveal defects of which they were unaware.

Nevertheless, it is very important for residential valuers to have a sound knowledge of construction in order to give the best possible advice. Chartered Surveyors and members of the Incorporated Society bring that knowledge to their residential agency operations as they believe it is better to advise an owner to expect a certain price because the property needs re-roofing, than to subsequently explain why they are amending their views in line with the prospective buyer's offer.

Although we know quite a lot, from contemporary accounts, about life in British towns during the eighteenth century, our knowledge of the actual townscape, the size, design, numbers and materials used in residential dwellings is curiously muted. While paintings and sketches occasionally provide tantalizing glimpses of the residential areas, and commentators such as Daniel Defoe provide some anecdotal information about local building materials, we can say little with much certainty about residential buildings until the early nineteenth century, where we are on much firmer ground. This is because towns were then growing much larger, and were increasingly the centre of the attention of writers and public health reformers.

With the exception of architectural gems such as Bath, and many villages, in most towns it is mainly public buildings which have survived from the eighteenth century or earlier. Since public monies were contributed to pay for such buildings, they tended to be built of brick or stone, often imported from other areas. Although the use of brick for most buildings was becoming much more common after 1700 (to some extent a reaction to the ravages of the Great Fire of London in 1666, when many buildings were still built of wood), the supply of local bricks was highly variable, depending on the availability of locally obtained, suitable clay. In many areas of the country, other vernacular materials were still widely used. For example, where easily quarried local stone was available, this was widely, in some cases almost universally, used. Thus in the Cotswolds, much of Wales, and the Pennine areas, local stone was still the predominant building material. In parts of East Anglia, flint and wooden clapboard remained important in the building of both domestic and even public buildings such as churches.

This observation will seem strange to the late twentieth-century observer. Today, regardless of location, brick is by far the most common material used in most buildings, and nearly all domestic dwellings. So too is the legacy of the mid-to-late nineteenth-century housing, which still forms much of the housing in our inner city areas. Up until 1850 brick-making technology remained almost medieval, and was highly localized due to the limited availability of suitable clays. Brick-making firms were small, clay was dug out by pick and shovel, and bricks were individually made by hand. Only after 1850 did technological advances, e.g. the invention of a machine which pressed the clay into bricks, lead to both more rapid production and the possible use of harder clays and marls. Thus the later decades of the nineteenth century saw the replacement of local building materials by the increasingly ubiquitous brick, while local roofing materials (e.g. thatching, pantiles) were in turn replaced by Welsh or Westmorland slate; the monotonous bye-law terraces of 'Coronation Street'.

Another vital element in all buildings was of course windows, and glass to keep the elements out. In the seventeenth and eighteenth centuries, since only the wealthy owned houses, both building materials, and some of the finished elements of houses were a visible potential source for taxation. Thus there was an excise duty on bricks (only removed in 1851), while glass and windows were particularly attractive to the exchequer. In the eighteenth century there was an excise on glass (which was in any case expensive to produce), and a window tax. As the latter was a simple exercise for the tax collector it was successively raised as the century wore on, leading to the bricking up of many windows to reduce the tax bill. Again, during the nineteenth century, as working-class housing became increasingly common, these taxes were successively reduced and abolished.

If the technology of brick-making was slow to change, so too was the building industry itself. Indeed in many respects the industry remained unchanged from the medieval period. It was characterized by a myriad of small, local firms. The first of the large-scale builders was Thomas Cubitt, building in London in the early years of the nineteenth century. By 1828 he was said to have some 10,000 men in his employment. But he was the exception. Most builders still operated on a small scale, buying enough land to build a few houses at a time, and relying on finding a landlord to buy the completed houses to cover costs and make a small profit. It was a very risky business, and bankruptcies were all too common. In order to cut corners and increase profit margins many builders used substandard materials ('seconds' and even 'thirds'), and skimped on drainage, bricks etc. This was the origin of the 'jerry-builder'.

Although the profession of architecture was well established, there was no money to be made, and thus no interest in designing housing for the new urban proletariat of the early nineteenth century. Builders designed their own properties, using their experience, with an eye to costs and likely buyers. In the earlier part of the century each builder might build no more than four or five houses a year. The next tranche of dwellings in a street might be built by another builder, with a different 'design', while local topography also led to changes in design. Many surviving streets of older terracing show these subtle changes in visual character, which in turn disguise differing internal arrangements of rooms, stairwells, etc.

So what kinds of dwellings were actually erected during the late eighteenth and early nineteenth centuries? For the wealthy classes, who required large dwellings to accommodate living-in servants, urban dwellings were often four or five storeys high, with cellar-kitchens. At the other end of the scale were so-called 'back-to-backs' or 'court' housing. These at their worst had shutters instead of glass windows, and a ladder to the first-floor rooms in lieu of a proper staircase. They were normally four-roomed ('two up, two down'), with the rooms at the back having no light or windows as they backed directly onto similar dwellings – hence the name. They faced dingy, narrow courts which would contain a 'privy', ashpits and, occasionally, a water-pump. There was no interior sanitation or water supply. Virtually none of these dwellings survive, not surprisingly; they were so strongly associated with disease and morbidity that Manchester banned their erection as early as 1844. In many instances whole families would share a single room.

As the nineteenth century progressed, housing standards slowly rose, though so too did overcrowding since the rate of house-building never caught up with population growth throughout the nineteenth century. In 1875 a Public Health Act was passed in Parliament. This gave local authorities new powers to pass local (or 'bye') building laws and regulations. This meant much higher housing standards, larger rooms, and led to the regimental rows of monotonous bye-law housing. Hundreds of thousands of these small terraces were built between 1875 and 1914, and it is the surviving remnant of these which form the bottom of the home ownership ladder today.

Successive legislation covering building regulations and public health and planning gradually led to an improvement in space standards both within and outside dwellings. But it was the improvement in public transport, in the form of suburban railways lines, trams, trolley buses, and motor buses that made it possible for people to live at a distance from their place of work and led in turn to the suburban life and finally to the age of commuting. Most towns display the signs of urban growth and spread over time, and an appreciation of the historical evolution of many towns is a useful preliminary to understanding domestic construction.

Sufficient knowledge can only come from a detailed study of building construction and changes in building regulations over the centuries, backed by sound practical training and experience. The following are just some of the innumerable points that a residential valuer may need to take account of and reflect upon in formulating an opinion of value.

Construction

In every part of the country there are traditional regional styles of housing; the Cotswold stone cottage is possibly the best known example. The agent/valuer will need to come to terms with the architecture, construction and materials of his or her practice area. However, the majority of residential properties are constructed using a combination of the following elements (see also Figure 2.1):

Foundations: None
Timber or stone
Stepped stone or brickwork footings
Concrete strip
Concrete raft

Walls: Solid: brick, stone or other material
Cavity: with an outer skin faced in brick or stone and an inner skin of brick or breeze-block or insulation blocks

	Walls may be finished on the outside with render, pebble-dash, stucco, tile-hanging, weather-boarding or other surface finishes
Floors:	Solid or hollow timber ground floors, timber first floors, except in some blocks of flats where they may be solid
Roofs:	Flat, covered with lead, zinc, copper, bitumen or mineral felt Pitched, covered with thatch, slate, stoneslate, tile, interlocking tiles, pantiles
Services:	Water: normally mains, but may be private supply or from well or spring Gas: mains or from storage tank Electricity: normally mains supply but occasionally in rural areas from private generator Drainage: mains, or to septic tank, or to cesspools or to private sewage treatment works.

Foundations

It is impossible to determine the nature of the foundations in an existing building without excavation – and even then only a small area will be exposed. The older the property and the poorer the quality of the original construction, the less likely it is for there to be proper foundations. In some instances shallow trenches were dug and the walls built directly off the subsoil; alternatively stone, or even timber may have been laid at the bottom of the trench before constructing the walls. Old timber-frame properties tend to be built from timber foundations. On other occasions and in most modern developments, concrete will have been poured into the trench to provide strip foundations. In addition, in some earlier properties the walls below ground level would have been thickened to create stepped foundations or footings. No agent, valuer, or surveyor would comment upon the nature and condition of foundations without opening them up. But it is important to consider the age of the property, the probable type of foundation and to be able to relate the condition of walls to the probable nature of the foundations. Thus, if walls are found to be out of true in terms of the horizontal or vertical plane, or if they are cracked in any way, then there may be a weakness in the foundations, or the foundations may have been affected by excessive shrinkage of the subsoil; such movement may be accentuated by tree roots themselves, by lowering of the water-table due to the proximity of trees or following the gales of 1987/88 by an increase in the moisture content of the soil due to the loss of specimen trees.

Concrete raft or pile foundations may be found or used when, for example, houses are being constructed on weak subsoils or on made-up ground.

Walls

It is important to distinguish between solid walls and cavity walls. Unfortunately, it is not always possible to arrive at a positive diagnosis. The essential difference between the two is that in cavity construction there is a gap or cavity between the inner and outer skins or walls. The two skins become a structural whole through the incorporation, during the construction, of wall-ties. Traditionally built properties from 1950 are generally of cavity construction; brick-built properties up to 1950 may be cavity or solid. Surveyors tend to rely on the appearance or bonding of brickwork to distinguish between solid brickwork and cavity constructions; in cavity construction most of the bricks will be laid with the long face (stretcher) exposed, whilst a solid brick wall will consist of headers (short face) and stretchers laid in a pattern or bond. The problem is that the same bond can be created in an outer skin using whole and half bricks; for this reason it is important to note the thickness of the wall – solid walls will tend to be 9in. (230mm) thick, and cavity walls 11in. (255mm) thick, plus the internal plaster and/or external render or pebble-dash.

Old stone properties are invariably of solid stonework, but here care is needed as some are basically two skins filled with a mixture of broken stone and mortar. Modern properties may be constructed with an outer skin of stone or artificial stone.

The external faces of many properties have been altered during their life; tile-hanging or mathematical tiles looking just like bricks may be added, or slates fixed to an exposed wall to reduce penetrating dampness and currently the DIY enthusiast is being encouraged (ill-advisedly) to fix all manner of artificial finishes. The latter in a terrace of houses may take away from the value, rather than add to it.

The condition of the walls is important, as the walls are clearly there to keep the elements out. The agent/valuer must therefore observe the general condition, take note of any cracks and consider their significance, note the condition of the pointing, the presence of and adequacy of any damp-proof course to be found approximately 6in above ground level and to check that no water is being allowed to run down the walls due to cracked or blocked gutters and drainpipes. In the case of cavity walls there is the added problem of possible wall-tie failure. The internal inspection should indicate whether the construction and condition has allowed damp to penetrate the walls or to rise from ground level.

'Crosswall construction' is a term used to describe properties where the floor and roof loads are carried by flank (end) walls and a central or transverse wall and not as traditionally by front and rear walls. In this form of construction the front and rear walls may be finished with tiles or boarding on timber, with or without proper insulation between the outer surface and inner plasterboard finish.

Timber frame construction has been adopted by many of the leading residential developers, with a considerable number being built in the 1970s. Timber frame construction is faster than traditional systems. It is a dry system, so occupation can occur very shortly after completion, it is factory produced and tested so that faults are minimized, and as a home it provides a very high standard of heat and sound insulation, so it is energy efficient. The construction itself consists of an inner skin and partition walling of softwood timber studs usually 100mm × 40mm × 600mm centres. Internal surfaces are covered with plasterboard and external surfaces with either plywood or hardboard. The external skin is often of brick. The structural stability of timber frame housing is tried and tested, but materials on site must be stored correctly, the framing, damp-proof courses, vapour barriers etc. must all be installed precisely in accordance with the structural engineers' specification and hence sound on-site supervision during construction is essential. Subsequently it is important for the occupiers to be aware of the nature of the construction so that they do not destroy the stability.

Some concern was expressed in the 1980s about this form of construction. The National House Building Council undertook further researches and published a report in August 1983, also issuing Practice Notes for timber frame dwellings which set a standard for such construction in the UK which is not equalled anywhere else in the world. They have also published an advisory note for issue to new home-owners. If occupiers fail to abide by these guidance notes, then defects can develop. The agent/valuer should therefore be sufficiently familiar with these guidance notes to be able to detect abuse during even the most casual of inspections. It is particularly bad practice to fill the cavity in a timber frame with insulation, and if done in a property under ten years old, the NHBC guarantee will be withdrawn. Valuers are strictly advised by the Building Society Association (BSA) and the RICS to report on this point, to make appropriate recommendations and to fully advise builders or clients of the possible problems that may occur (see Appendix IB).

It is sometimes very difficult to tell the difference between timber frame and normal cavity construction; the clues are usually to be found around window openings. The residential agent/valuer must be quite certain of the correct identification before describing a property as timber frame. (The Timber Research and Development Association and Building Research Establishment information sheets are essential further reading on this subject for the residential valuer/surveyor.)

A number of experimental forms of construction were used in the immediate post-war era, particularly by local authorities, in an effort to create a large number of new homes as quickly as possible.

A short list of these concrete and concrete-type homes would include Airey, Cornish, Orbit, Parkinson, Hawksley SGS, Smith System, Unity, Woolaway, Gregory, Winget, Underdown, Wates, Blackburn, Howard steel-framed and British Iron and Steel. In total there are at least twenty-seven types, some of which have an external brick or rendered finish which at first sight is indistinguishable from a traditional property. Some of these began to show major defects in the 1980s, a major problem being the rusting of reinforcement in the concrete frame. These problems became significant in the market-place after many local authority tenants had exercised their right to buy and then subsequently found it impossible to resell their homes.

The Housing Defects Act 1984 (now Part XVI of the Housing Act 1985) was passed to provide (a) for compensation or repurchase and (b) for grants for certain classes of ex-public authority tenants to undertake the necessary essential repairs. As a result the NHBC will now issue a special ten-year guarantee in certain specified cases where proven schemes of repair are completed.

In most cases the purchase had to have been completed before 28 April 1984. Anyone buying such a property from a public authority after that date, or purchasing from an ex-tenant after April 1984, will be deemed to have bought with knowledge. The scheme does not extend to similar houses that have always been owned privately.

The residential agent/valuer must tread warily when confronted by any such properties and may feel he can only advise where a ten-year guarantee has been issued. In other cases to value without a thorough survey by an expert would be foolhardy.

Floors

The first-floor finish of most domestic properties is boarding on timber joists. In older properties the joist ends were built into external solid walls; if moisture penetrates the external wall, rot can occur in the joist ends and can rapidly spread to the rest of the floor. If rot has set in and is spreading it may be detected in skirting boards or in floorboards adjoining the external walls. Exposed timber should also be checked for attack by woodworm.

Ground floors may be of solid construction or of hollow timber construction. A hollow timber floor of boards or joists must be kept ventilated through air bricks in the external walls. Again, timber ground floors must be checked for rot and beetle infestation.

Roofs

Domestic roofs are generally pitched roofs but there are some flat roofs to be found, and many extensions have flat roofs. Pitched roofs tend to give rise to fewer problems if properly constructed and maintained than flat roofs, although the standard of construction of the latter improved in the 1980s. It is impossible to be certain about the condition of a pitched roof without a thorough inspection of the roof void, which would be an essential part of a full survey and valuation, but not for asking price advice, however much can be gleaned from an external inspection.

The most cursory of inspections will reveal missing slates or tiles, or slates held in position by tingles, tiles flaking from frost action, ridge and hip tiles in need of rebedding with fresh mortar, roofs that are sagging, and deteriorating cement fillets and cement flashings around chimneys. Experience and knowledge of an area alerts the agent/valuer to check lead valleys and to be particularly wary of the architecturally ornate roof where rain can collect and stand for long enough to penetrate the roof covering or cause damage if frozen in the winter.

Flat roofs have to be checked for signs of repair, for bubbling in the surface, and thought given to the possibility of condensation damaging the structure.

Thatch-covered roofs may look worse than they really are, but the true condition can only really be ascertained by a thatcher.

Services

The nature of the services needs to be noted: water, gas, electricity, drainage. Without full tests it is only possible to react to the adequacy of the services based on the probable age of wiring and pipework.

Decorations

The decorative condition will immediately be noted by prospective buyers. The value points to consider are whether the decorations are sound and whether they conform with the market. The agent/valuer is aware that decorations are a question of personal choice, but must also be prepared to down-value or down-price a property decorated in a very unusual or bizarre style, if such treatment is likely to deter buyers.

The good, qualified valuer/agent is naturally observant and will, when visiting properties, automatically note mentally or on file the conditions of downpipes, gutters, chimney stacks, chimney flashings, windows, doors, staircases, plumbing, electrics, central heating boilers, pipes, radiators, valves, chimney flues, painting, pointing, drives, footpaths and garden.

To the agent, the important issue is whether overall the property conforms to the 'market norm' for that type of property in that location. If the property is a better buying opportunity than one normally finds then a higher – but not excessive – asking price may be recommended. If it is poorer than one normally finds then a lower – but not excessively low – price will be suggested. In discussions with the vendor the agent may, perhaps should, forewarn the vendors of any significant issues that might require them to accept a lower price following a building society inspection or a full survey. Equally, the agent must be able to indicate that even though the property has been modernized and redecorated with no expense spared by the vendor, the asking price must conform to the patterns of value in that locality. Such discussions and advice are relatively easy when dealing with an estate property, but that much more difficult when advising on the larger, one-off, detached house. A factor to be borne in mind is that the larger the property, the more costly it will be to make good a major defect.

For the residential valuer the approach is very similar, but there is a much greater need to identify specific points and defects. Although a structural survey does not form part of a residential valuation there is a school of thought which suggests that the inspection needed to undertake a thorough residential valuation should be no less than that undertaken for a full survey. For example, if the valuation was required for probate purposes on the death of the owner, or if the valuer was acting for the Inland Revenue for compensation purposes on compulsory acquisition of the property, negotiations may well be necessary and in such cases the valuer needs to be able to support his or her opinion by reference to detailed file notes on condition. A valuer would look very foolish if a probate valuation of £150,000 were to be given and then subsequently the beneficiaries could only realize £120,000 for the property because the roof needed complete rebuilding due to dry rot.

If the valuation is for mortgage purposes the valuer must be able to assess the effect of the condition on open market value; to list the defects that need to be made good and to be able to advise on the amount, if any, that the mortgagees need to retain pending the completion of works of repair.

There may be a reluctance amongst some house agents to learn too much about domestic construction, arguing that their job is to sell the property at the best possible price, and not to be over-influenced in that object by a surfeit of knowledge that alerts them to every major and minor defect that might be picked up by a purchaser and the purchaser's professional advisors. The argument against this view is that without such knowledge the agent is unable to give sound advice to a vendor when a purchaser makes a low offer because of defects in condition. The professional agent and valuer will acquire such detailed knowledge because of the requirements of the professional societies to whom they belong and because such knowledge is essential if a professional opinion of value is to be offered.

The Royal Institution of Chartered Surveyors produced a booklet in conjunction with BBC television for the 1987 series, 'Bazaar', called *The*

Property Doctor. The booklet identifies a number of unhealthy symptoms in the home, their possible cause and the approved remedies, including dry rot, wet rot, woodworm, condensation, rising damp and penetrating damp. If one adds to this list structural instability in load-bearing walls due to inadequate foundations, subsidence or soil heave, and ground floor movement, then that might be regarded as the minimum list of important defects in construction likely to affect value. The booklet also provides a series of checklists for home-owners, which can just as easily be used by prospective purchasers when viewing property. An important point for the valuer/agent to note is that the general home-owning public is becoming better educated, more information is now available to all and as a result there is growing pressure on the agent/valuer to become even better informed on all aspects of domestic construction.

Table 2.1 Factors that may have an adverse effect on value

Proximity to:	Traffic/traffic fumes
Abattoir	Undertakers
Airport – civil or military	Warehouse – retail warehousing
Builder's yard, builder's merchants	
Bus depot	*Poor planning:*
Bus route	Site layout
Bus stop	Position of bathroom
Car park	Position of toilet
Caravan site	Awkward shape of bedrooms
Cemetery	Access through other rooms
Chapel of rest	Poorly designed kitchens
Church halls	Behind adjoining building lines
Cinemas/bingo halls	Back-to-front design
Clubhouses – general/jazz	Poor frontage
Council estate	Lack of storage
Derelict land and properties	Differences in floor levels
Discotheque	High heating costs due to poor and/or
Electricity pylons	insufficient insulation
Factory– noise, smell or other nuisance	Lack of drainage
Footpaths	Lack of electricity
Fried fish shop/takeaway	
Funfair	*Other:*
Garage and petrol station	Poor condition
Gasholders	Lack of adequate damp course,
Hen-houses	ventilation, daylight
Hospital emergency units	Lack of water supply
Loading depot	Lack of street lighting
Nursing home	Land liable to flooding
Piggeries	Land liable to subsidence/sea erosion
Refuse tip – household disposal	etc.
Rifle range – clay pigeon shoots	Isolated position or very poor or
Silage	restricted access
Telegraph poles	Environmental – radon gas etc.

Note: In some instances certain features which would normally be regarded as disadvantages may be viewed as advantages for discerning buyers.

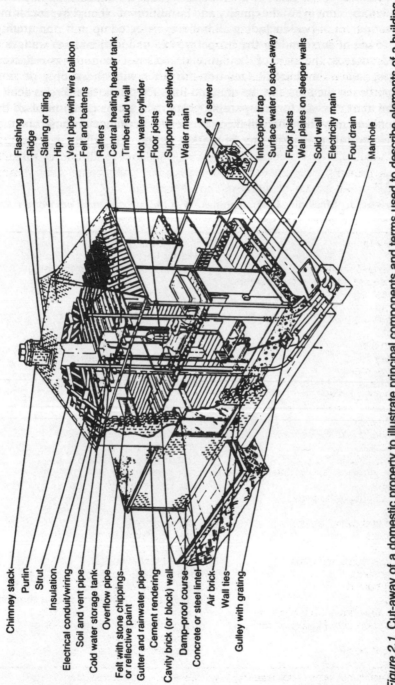

Figure 2.1 Cut-away of a domestic property to illustrate principal components and terms used to describe elements of a building.
Source: *The RICS Property Doctor Book*. RICS copyright reserved.

Flashing
Ridge
Slating or tiling
Hip
Vent pipe with wire balloon
Felt and battens
Rafters
Central heating header tank
Timber stud wall
Hot water cylinder
Floor joists
Supporting steelwork
Water main
To sewer
Inteceptor trap
Surface water to soak-away
Floor joists
Wall plates on sleeper walls
Solid wall
Electricity main
Foul drain
Manhole

Chimney stack
Purlin
Strut
Insulation
Electrical conduit/wiring
Soil and vent pipe
Cold water storage tank
Overflow pipe
Felt with stone chippings or reflective paint
Gutter and rainwater pipe
Cement rendering
Cavity brick (or block) wall
Damp-proof course
Concrete or steel lintel
Air brick
Wall ties
Gulley with grating

In summary, the value of a residential property depends upon the legal estate to be conveyed; the quality and condition of all improvements made to that parcel of land including all buildings erected upon it; the quality of environment surrounding the property, i.e. its locational advantages and disadvantages; the state of the national and local economy as reflected in wages, salaries and credit facilities, together with the supply of similar properties in the area and the demand for such properties. Prices achieved in the market-place for comparable properties are a reflection of all these factors and may therefore, in the absence of any change to those underlying forces, be taken as indicative of market value.

NOTE

1 Bassett, J., Mackmin, D.H., Thomas, W. (1987) *Bean and Lockwood's Rating Valuation Practice*, 7th edn., London: Sweet & Maxwell.

Chapter 3

The valuation of residential property and methods of valuation

The RICS *Manual of Valuation Guidance Notes* sets out general advice for valuers undertaking property valuations. These include specific notes on mortgage valuations (see Chapter 4). As with any service contract, it is essential for the valuer to set out the conditions of engagement in writing so that there can be no doubt in the mind of the client as to the nature of the valuation and the basis upon which the fee is to be calculated. Initially the valuer needs to discover the purpose for which the valuation is required, e.g. sale, purchase, loan, insurance, compensation, council tax, letting, etc. The value will differ for different purposes and the method of valuation may also differ according to the purpose.

At this stage of agreeing instructions the guidance notes recommend the use of the RICS publication *The Valuation of Residential Property*. This is a small leaflet which can readily be enclosed with the valuer's initial letters confirming instructions, fee basis etc. and can be made part of that contract.

The leaflet sets out the terms on which a valuation of residential property in England and Wales is normally undertaken and is reprinted here (RICS copyright reserved).

Where these conditions are inapplicable then the valuer must set out in writing the precise terms of the agreement, together with clear statements as to the valuer's liability and responsibility. All such agreements must include all the limitation clauses that the valuer intends to include in the valuation report and in most cases should include those listed in the leaflet above.

In preparing a valuation, the RICS guidance notes suggest that a valuer should consider the following matters, and that where appropriate other matters should be included.

THE
VALUATION OF
RESIDENTIAL
PROPERTY

**GUIDANCE
TO CLIENTS**

**& MODEL
CONDITIONS
OF ENGAGEMENT**
EFFECTIVE FROM 1 JUNE 1992

THE ROYAL INSTITUTION
OF CHARTERED SURVEYORS

THE VALUATION

This leaflet sets out general guidance and incorporates the terms on which a Chartered Surveyor will normally undertake the valuation of residential property in England and Wales. It does not cover every aspect of valuation nor does it deal with special problems.

1 WHAT IS A VALUATION?

A valuation is the individual opinion of a Valuer based on the relevant facts available.

In most cases an 'Open Market Value' will be given. This means the best price at which an interest in the property might reasonably be expected to be sold at the date of the valuation assuming:

(a) a willing seller;

(b) that, prior to the date of valuation, there had been a reasonable period (having regard to the nature of the property and the state of the market) for the proper marketing of the interest, for the agreement of price and terms and for the completion of the sale;

(c) that the state of the market, level of values and other circumstances were, on any earlier assumed date of exchange of contracts, the same as on the date of valuation; and

(d) that no account is taken of any additional bid by a purchaser with a special interest.

Valuations are, however, undertaken for a variety of purposes, including sale, purchase, letting, mortgage, compulsory purchase, probate and other tax purposes. Sometimes a basis of valuation other than 'Open Market Value' will be required, as, for example, when assessing a rent under the Rent Acts.

Valuations may also relate to different interests in property (e.g. freehold or leasehold) and may have to take account of other interests to which the property is subject, such as leases, rights of way, rights of light, etc.

2 WHO CAN UNDERTAKE A VALUATION?

In most cases there are no legal restrictions as to who can undertake a valuation of residential property, but obviously it is important to instruct someone with the necessary skill, knowledge and experience. Chartered Surveyors in general practice are qualified in these skills, both by training and experience, although some surveyors may specialise only in certain types of valuation.

3 CAN A VALUATION BE USED FOR PURPOSES OTHER THAN THOSE FOR WHICH IT IS PREPARED?

Generally no. A valuation is a confidential report for a particular Client and for the special purposes of that Client.

Usually a valuation report will contain a reminder of this point by including a paragraph on the following lines:

OF RESIDENTIAL

'This report is provided for (the stated purpose(s)) and for your sole use. It is confidential to you and your professional advisers. We accept no responsibility whatsoever to any other parties. Any such parties rely upon the report at their own risk.

Neither the whole nor any part of this report or any reference to it may be included in any published document, circular or statement nor published in any way without our written approval of the form and context in which it may appear.'

It may be misleading if such a valuation is relied upon by a person who knows neither the basis on which, nor the purpose for which, the valuation has been prepared. The extreme example is that a valuation for market purposes should never be confused with an assessment for fire insurance. The principles are entirely different. For fire insurance purposes the assessment is usually the cost of rebuilding; this may bear no relation to the 'Open Market Value' of the property.

4   VALUATION OR STRUCTURAL SURVEY?

It is important to appreciate that a valuation is not a structural survey. The Valuer will have regard to apparent defects and wants of repair in preparing the report on value and will take into account the age and nature of the property. The Valuer will not, however, carry out the detailed search for defects which is undertaken as part of a structural survey, nor necessarily set out the various defects when making the report.

Certain defects can only be discovered by detailed investigation. For example, when valuing a dwelling-house a Valuer will not normally inspect the roof space, under floor space, move furniture or lift carpets, which means that the most common indications of dry rot and woodworm in concealed places cannot be seen. A paragraph on the following lines may be included in the report:

'We have not carried out a structural survey nor have we inspected those parts of the property which are covered, unexposed or inaccessible and such parts are assumed to be in good repair and condition: This report does not purport to express an opinion about nor to advise upon the condition of uninspected parts and should not be taken as making any implied representation or statement about such parts.'

Similarly, it is extremely difficult without an investigation by a Chartered Building Surveyor or a structural engineer, possibly including chemical analysis, to check whether potentially deleterious or hazardous materials or techniques have been used in the construction of the building or have since been incorporated. Accordingly a paragraph on the following lines may be included in the report:

PROPERTY

'We have not arranged for any investigation to be carried out to determine whether or not any deleterious or hazardous materials or techniques have been used in the construction of this property or has since been incorporated and we are therefore unable to report that the property is free from risk in this respect. For the purpose of this valuation we have assumed that such investigation would not disclose the presence of any such material in any adverse conditions that will affect value.'

If the Client requires not just a valuation but also a structural survey, many Chartered Surveyors will be prepared to undertake such a survey and will be able to arrange for specialist investigations if the Client so wishes. Such additional work and responsibility will normally involve a higher fee.

5 WHAT SORT OF REPORT WILL BE PROVIDED?

This will depend on the instructions given, the extent to which the inspection was possible or permitted, the information provided or obtained, and in particular the time available in which to produce the valuation report.

Generally, in order to make a valuation, the Valuer will, subject to the qualifications in 4 above, make an inspection of the property and make appropriate enquiries or investigations. Detailed information on such matters as planning and title deeds is usually obtained by the Client's solicitors as part of their local search and replies to the usual enquiries.

When valuing leasehold property or freehold property subject to tenancies the Valuer will generally rely upon the information provided by the Client or the Client's solicitors.

The reliability of the Valuer's opinion will be affected by the time that the Client makes available in which to prepare the valuation, the extent of the examination of the property reasonably possible or permitted, and the accuracy of the information provided.

Sometimes an oral report is all that is requested, but it is preferable for a written report to be provided, which will include any assumptions which have been made and such relevant facts as have been ascertained.

6 INSTRUCTIONS

It will be apparent from the above that it is vital that the instructions to the Valuer are precisely expressed and contain as much information as possible.

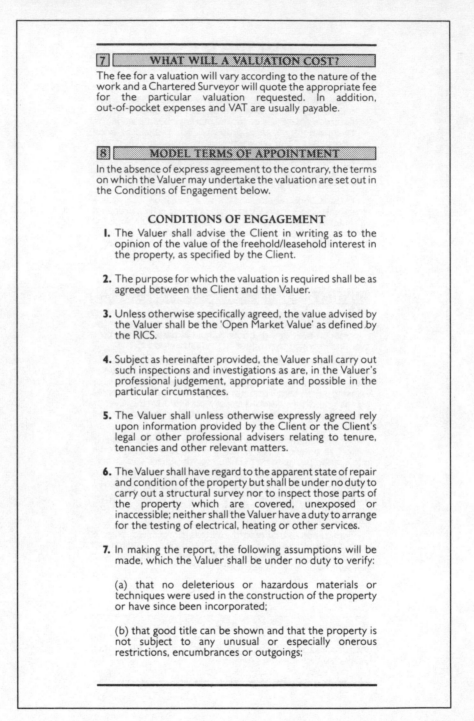

7   WHAT WILL A VALUATION COST?

The fee for a valuation will vary according to the nature of the work and a Chartered Surveyor will quote the appropriate fee for the particular valuation requested. In addition, out-of-pocket expenses and VAT are usually payable.

8   MODEL TERMS OF APPOINTMENT

In the absence of express agreement to the contrary, the terms on which the Valuer may undertake the valuation are set out in the Conditions of Engagement below.

CONDITIONS OF ENGAGEMENT

1. The Valuer shall advise the Client in writing as to the opinion of the value of the freehold/leasehold interest in the property, as specified by the Client.

2. The purpose for which the valuation is required shall be as agreed between the Client and the Valuer.

3. Unless otherwise specifically agreed, the value advised by the Valuer shall be the 'Open Market Value' as defined by the RICS.

4. Subject as hereinafter provided, the Valuer shall carry out such inspections and investigations as are, in the Valuer's professional judgement, appropriate and possible in the particular circumstances.

5. The Valuer shall unless otherwise expressly agreed rely upon information provided by the Client or the Client's legal or other professional advisers relating to tenure, tenancies and other relevant matters.

6. The Valuer shall have regard to the apparent state of repair and condition of the property but shall be under no duty to carry out a structural survey nor to inspect those parts of the property which are covered, unexposed or inaccessible; neither shall the Valuer have a duty to arrange for the testing of electrical, heating or other services.

7. In making the report, the following assumptions will be made, which the Valuer shall be under no duty to verify:

(a) that no deleterious or hazardous materials or techniques were used in the construction of the property or have since been incorporated;

(b) that good title can be shown and that the property is not subject to any unusual or especially onerous restrictions, encumbrances or outgoings;

(c) that the property and its value are unaffected by any matters which would be revealed by a local search and replies to the usual enquiries, or by any statutory notice, and that neither the property, nor its condition, nor its use, nor its intended use, is or will be unlawful; and

(d) that inspection of those parts which have not been inspected would neither reveal material defects nor cause the Valuer to alter the valuation materially.

8. The Valuer shall provide to the Client a report setting out the opinion of value of the relevant interest in the property. The report will be provided for the stated purposes and for the sole use of the named Client. It will be confidential to the Client and the Client's professional advisers. The Valuer accepts responsibility to the Client alone that the report will be prepared with the skill, care and diligence reasonably to be expected of a competent Chartered Surveyor, but accepts no responsibility whatsoever to any parties other than the Client. Any such parties rely upon the report at their own risk. Neither the whole or any part of the report nor any reference to it may be included in any published document, circular or statement nor published in any way without the Valuer's written approval of the form and context in which it may appear.

9. The Client will pay to the Valuer the fee agreed. In addition, the Client will reimburse the Valuer the cost of all reasonable out-of-pocket expenses which may be incurred and pay the amount of any Value Added Tax on the fee and expenses.

Published by RICS Books on behalf of
The Royal Institution of Chartered Surveyors
12 Great George Street, Parliament Square, London SW1P 3AD.

First published October 1984. Reprinted September 1986, June 1987 and April 1989. **Revised May 1992.**   © RICS May 1992.

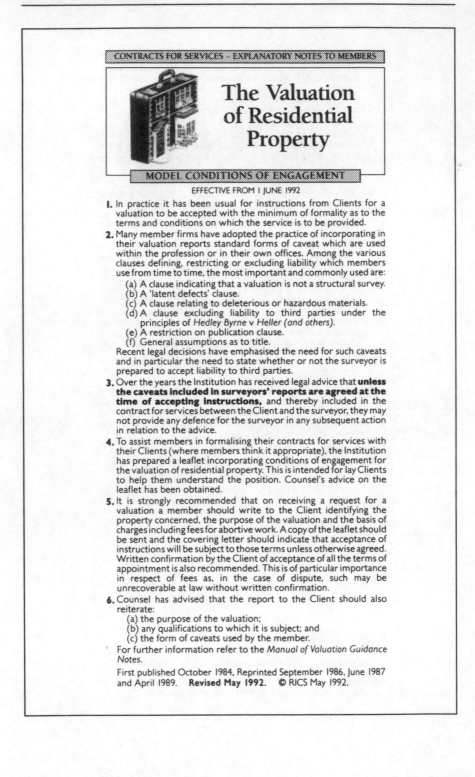

CONTRACTS FOR SERVICES – EXPLANATORY NOTES TO MEMBERS

The Valuation of Residential Property

MODEL CONDITIONS OF ENGAGEMENT

EFFECTIVE FROM 1 JUNE 1992

1. In practice it has been usual for instructions from Clients for a valuation to be accepted with the minimum of formality as to the terms and conditions on which the service is to be provided.

2. Many member firms have adopted the practice of incorporating in their valuation reports standard forms of caveat which are used within the profession or in their own offices. Among the various clauses defining, restricting or excluding liability which members use from time to time, the most important and commonly used are:
   (a) A clause indicating that a valuation is not a structural survey.
   (b) A 'latent defects' clause.
   (c) A clause relating to deleterious or hazardous materials.
   (d) A clause excluding liability to third parties under the principles of *Hedley Byrne* v *Heller (and others)*.
   (e) A restriction on publication clause.
   (f) General assumptions as to title.
   Recent legal decisions have emphasised the need for such caveats and in particular the need to state whether or not the surveyor is prepared to accept liability to third parties.

3. Over the years the Institution has received legal advice that **unless the caveats included in surveyors' reports are agreed at the time of accepting instructions,** and thereby included in the contract for services between the Client and the surveyor, they may not provide any defence for the surveyor in any subsequent action in relation to the advice.

4. To assist members in formalising their contracts for services with their Clients (where members think it appropriate), the Institution has prepared a leaflet incorporating conditions of engagement for the valuation of residential property. This is intended for lay Clients to help them understand the position. Counsel's advice on the leaflet has been obtained.

5. It is strongly recommended that on receiving a request for a valuation a member should write to the Client identifying the property concerned, the purpose of the valuation and the basis of charges including fees for abortive work. A copy of the leaflet should be sent and the covering letter should indicate that acceptance of instructions will be subject to those terms unless otherwise agreed. Written confirmation by the Client of acceptance of all the terms of appointment is also recommended. This is of particular importance in respect of fees as, in the case of dispute, such may be unrecoverable at law without written confirmation.

6. Counsel has advised that the report to the Client should also reiterate:
   (a) the purpose of the valuation;
   (b) any qualifications to which it is subject; and
   (c) the form of caveats used by the member.

For further information refer to the *Manual of Valuation Guidance Notes*.

First published October 1984, Reprinted September 1986, June 1987 and April 1989. **Revised May 1992.**   © RICS May 1992.

Referencing

1 Characteristics of locality and availability of communications and facilities affecting value.
2 Age, description, use, accommodation, construction of any buildings, installations, amenities and services.
3 Dimensions and areas of the land and buildings, confirming basis of calculation used.
4 Apparent state of repair and condition.
5 Site stability (including the effects of mining and quarrying).

Nature of interest

1 Tenure, with reference to relevant restrictions, terms of leases (if leasehold), easements, rights of way, etc.
2 Details of lettings and other occupations.

Planning and statutory requirements

1 Results of town planning, highway and other enquiries.
2 Apparent contraventions of any statutory requirements.
3 Outstanding statutory notices.

Other factors

1 Rating assessment (council tax band) and any outgoings.
2 Any plant and machinery which would normally form an integral part of the building and is therefore included in the valuation.
3 Fixtures, fittings and improvements.
4 Presence of potentially deleterious or hazardous materials or techniques; any non-standard methods of construction.
5 Allowances for disrepair.
6 Any development potential.
7 Any possible 'marriage' or 'break-up' value.

Marketing analysis

1 Details of comparable market transactions for either existing use or alternative use(s).
2 Market conditions and trends.
3 Consideration as to the period of validity.

Table 3.1 Content of the valuation report

	Paragraph VGN1	Ref BN
* 1 The source of the instructions and the identity of the client.	2	2
* 2 The purpose of the valuation	1	
* 3 The date of valuation		
* 4 The basis of valuation		
* 5 Any special instructions, unusual assumptions or omissions	3	2
* 6 The date and extent of inspection	6	3
7 Situation and amenities	6	3
8 Description, construction, accommodation, services, areas and a site plan	6	3
9 Plant and machinery – included/excluded	6	9
10 Apparent state of repair	6	4
11 Use	6	
*12 Comment on planning and environmental issues	6	6
13 Rating description and assessment	6	8
14 Any licences, permits, consents or certificates	6	7
15 Other statutory controls	6	7
*16 Tenure. If with vacant possession, whether whole or in part, with a list of all known tenancies		
17 Any taxation implications		11
18 Summary with any other relevant matters	6	9
*19 *Assumptions and caveats relating to limitations of responsibiiity:*	4 & 5	5 & 9
Assumptions as to good title and freedom from any borrowings and encumbrances.		
Matters that would be revealed by a local search, replies to usual enquiries or by any statutory notice.		
For examination of the structure and of inaccessible parts and of latent defects including rot and inherently dangerous or unsuitable materials and techniques (i.e. ensuring that the report cannot be construed as a structural survey).		
To the client and, where appropriate, the client's immediate professional advisors, but excluding responsibility to third parties and preserving confidentiality.		
Non-publication of the valuation and/or report in whole or in part without prior consent.		
Special clauses required for professional indemnity policy.		
For assumption of fact and law, e.g. present lawful user.		
Non-disclosure of material facts to the valuer.		
20 Consideration as to the period of validity		
*21 The opinion of value in words and figures		
*22 The valuer's/firm's name and address, qualifications and signature		
*23 The date of the report		

Source: VGN1 RICS *Manual of Valuation Guidance Notes*

THE VALUATION REPORT

The general form of the valuation report should have been agreed with the client when taking instructions. No standard form of report is suitable for all occasions, but generally it should cover the matters set out in Table 3.1 and any other specific requirements of the client.

The presentation of the valuation report will have regard to the need for any special format, but most reports should contain those items marked with an asterisk (*) in Table 3.1.

The importance of adhering to these guidance notes and to the advice offered by the RICS Insurance Services and the professional indemnity insurers cannot be over-emphasized. In particular the written report must be quite clear as to the limitation of liability and responsibility, it must contain the appropriate caveats (and even then, following the mortgage case of *Roberts* v. *Hampson & Co* (1988) the courts may hold that the valuer should move furniture, even though a caveat might state it would not be moved); it should not go beyond statements of fact other than to express a final opinion of value; if the valuer relies upon information provided by others such as local authorities, planning departments, solicitors, etc., the source of and responsibility for such information must be stated in the report.

When undertaking a valuation the valuer must open a file and keep careful file notes of the inspection, enquiries made and the names of any individuals spoken to, whose verbal information may have influenced the valuation. This is essential, as frequently it is impossible to obtain written confirmation in the time given for the valuer to complete the valuation.

METHODS OF VALUATION

The four principal methods of valuation used by the residential valuer are:

1 The comparative or market sales approach.
2 The income or investment approach.
3 The contractors or cost approach.
4 The residual or developer's approach.

The comparative or market sales approach

This is the most important method for the residential valuer, as it is a true market valuation. It can be broken down into four steps:

1 Select comparables.
2 Extract, confirm and analyse comparable sale prices.
3 Adjust sale prices for noted differences.
4 Formulate an opinion of open market value for the subject property.

Residential valuers are usually employed by firms of surveyors and estate agents involved in sales of residential property in a defined market area. Such firms over many years of operation have built up a substantial data bank of knowledge of that market area and in a good practice will have recorded the salient details of all residential sales handled by that firm. In addition, most firms also undertake valuations for loan (mortgage) purposes and residential surveys for house buyers, and again the salient details will have been recorded. As agents they will also be carrying lists of the sales they are currently handling. All of this together provides the valuer with the comparables necessary for most residential valuations.

The valuer is able to search this data bank for those comparables which in terms of shape, size, accommodation and location best match the subject property. In the older established practices this data search may well reveal previous involvement with the subject property, as well as comparable data. The aim of the search is to find, as far as is possible, matching pairs. The ideal match would be to find a very recent sale of an identical property in the same road or on the same estate. In most cases the match will be less than perfect, and adjustments will have to be made to bring the comparable evidence into line with the subject property. The main adjustments that have to be made are for time, location, physical characteristics and conditions of sale. When the market is very active this data search and adjustment exercise may well be made subjectively by the valuer whilst inspecting the subject property because he or she is conscious of all the relevant current sales data. Examining the various steps is, however, indicative of the objectivity of this method of appraisal.

Adjusting for time differences

Where a comparable property has been sold on an earlier date then it is possible with a sound knowledge of the movement in market prices between sale date and valuation date to adjust the known sale price by an appropriate and supportable percentage to reflect the market movement. Such percentage adjustments can often be supported by reference to published indices of house price movements. However, it is always sensible to discard historic figures in favour of current prices, i.e. those achieved on sales within the preceding month or so of a valuation.

Adjusting for differences in location

Adjustments for differences in location may also need to be made. In some areas exactly the same house styles can be found in two or more distinct locations. The valuer will be aware of buyers' preferences for each location and therefore an adjustment to prices in area A might be possible to support an opinion of value in area B in the absence of sales in area B. This might be a percentage adjustment or a lump sum adjustment. However, as location is such an important factor in the market it is preferable to use comparables from the immediate surrounding area. In practice it is not unknown for values for similar properties to differ over a very short distance not by 5–10 per cent, but by 50 per cent or more.

Adjusting for condition and accommodation

Comparables may need to be adjusted for differences in condition or accommodation. It may be necessary to adjust for differences in plot size, for the number of bedrooms and/or living rooms, for poor decoration etc. Precisely how much more a typical buyer is prepared to pay for additional features or precisely how much less for poor decorative order is very difficult to ascertain. In most cases the adjustment will not equate with the current cost, but it may approach at the lower end of the market a do-it-yourself cost figure. At the top end of the market, poor condition can render some properties unsaleable at realistic prices; on the other hand a river view in Central London may compensate for poor condition.

If there is a serious physical defect then in theory the valuer must determine by comparison the value of the property as if sound and then deduct the cost of making good the defect. For example, a property suffering from subsidence will only sell after the cause has been rectified and the property made good, or at the equivalent discount on the normal market value.

It is clearly essential for the valuer to have full details of all comparables; if not, then there is the danger of adjusting twice for a feature or a defect by taking an already adjusted price and then adding or subtracting a similar sum.

Where very good regular data is available for an area it is sometimes possible to analyse the data against those variables or features known to most influence purchasers' decisions, to discover more precisely the amounts being added on or deducted. Statistical techniques such as regression analysis have been used for this purpose. However, for most valuers active in the residential market this approach would be seen to be too academic and too removed from the market-place. It is argued that the buyers make the market, and their personal attitudes cannot be readily subjected to statistical analysis. The valuer in the market has the advantage of being close both to the known facts of a sale and to the parties involved.

Adjustment for sale conditions

Finally it may be necessary to adjust the comparables for differences in sale conditions. This is to take account of or preferably exclude any sales data arising from sales not conducted at 'arm's-length' – when the sale conditions were not normal market conditions. It could have been a sale between members of the same family, a quick sale to a cash buyer, a forced sale by a building society to recover mortgage debts, or a sale forming part of a larger business deal. All such sales can be misleading.

The home-owner is apt to point out to the residential valuer that his or her property is worth X because Mr and Mrs A obtained that for theirs, or because they have seen a similar property advertised at that price in the paper. It should be obvious from the above that only if a valuer has full knowledge of a property and the circumstances of the sale will it be possible to use a known comparable sale price correctly. Misinformation can very quickly lead to false valuations.

A number of house agents are beginning to see the wisdom of using comparables to support their advice on recommended asking prices. In some cases a good agent will meet prospective vendors armed with details of recent sales in order to support their advices and to ensure that a sensible asking price can be agreed, rather than one so high that it effectively drives away prospective buyers.

Where an open market valuation has to, or may have to, be supported or proven in court or argued before a valuation officer of the Inland Revenue, it is sensible for the residential valuer to formalize the comparative exercise on a sales comparison sheet as shown in Table 3.2.

When using the sales comparison approach it is better to have one good

Table 3.2 Sales comparison sheet

	Subject property	Comparable 1	Comparable 2	Comparable 3
Address:				
Description:				
Sale price:	£	£	£	
Adjustments for:				
1 Time of sale	£	£	£	
2 Sale conditions	£	£	£	
3 Physical condition	£	£	£	
4 Accommodation	£	£	£	
5 Services etc.	£	£	£	
Net adjustment:	+/−£	+/−£	+/−£	
Adjusted value:	£	£	£	

genuine comparable than half a dozen sales that require so much price adjustment that clearly they are in no way similar, let alone matching pairs.

Direct sales comparison is the best and only recognized method of valuing frequently sold freehold vacant possession residential property. It can also be used to value frequently sold long leasehold vacant possession residential property such as might be found in blocks of flats or where an estate of properties was developed on a leasehold basis, but see Chapter 11 for further consideration of vacant possession leasehold valuations.

It is important when using this method for the valuer to be able to value on the assumption of vacant possession and that the property to be valued is of a type that is frequently bought and sold.

The more unusual the property, the more difficult it is to find comparables. In some instances greater attention has to be given to the comparison of location and environmental benefits than the purely physical attributes of the property. Thus very dissimilar properties adjoining a golf course may have similar values. Dissimilar properties in terms of geographic locations may also have similar values because of similar attributes such as ease of access to airports, privacy, security, access to leisure pursuits such as yachting and similar adequate accommodation for guests and entertaining. Country houses fall typically into this category, where comparison is made over a wide geographic area and where the residential valuer is using his experience of a very specialist market to arrive at valid supportable opinions of value.

If a property has to be valued subject to the rights of an occupying tenant, then the income or investment approach must be used.

The income or investment approach

In a number of cases, residential property will have to be valued by the income approach. Before the introduction of protective legislation for tenants, residential property was a very popular form of investment for residential builders, families and individuals. Until the Second World War the developers of large residential estates frequently sold some properties freehold and let some on weekly unfurnished tenancies. If the government continues to amend the current protective legislation and to encourage the residential lettings market, then one may again see the emergence of residential property as a popular form of investment. As it is, this sector has dwindled and it is only at the luxury end of the market and in the form of furnished accommodation that one finds continuing support for owning and letting residential property. The discussion here of this method of valuation is restricted, as the added complications of legislation mean that the valuation of such properties should be left to the experts. Particular applications of the method will be found in Chapters 11 and 14.

This method recognizes that property can be purchased not for occupation by the purchaser but in order to let the property and to receive income from that property in the form of rent. As such, property is comparable to other forms of investment where capital is exchanged for income or interest or money.

In an active investment market there will be a relationship between investment income and investment value or price. This relationship is known as the yield on the investment. Thus an investment producing an income of £100 a year and selling for £1,000 is producing a return for the investor of 10 per cent.

$$\frac{Income}{Price} \times 100 = \text{Yield}$$

$$\frac{100}{1,000} \times 100 = 10\%$$

If a similar investment with similar risks is producing an income of £200, it is possible by a form of indirect comparison to put a price or value on that investment. If it is offering the investor a similar investment in terms of risk to his or her capital and in terms of the probability of receiving the income, then it too should produce a 10 per cent yield. Thus:

$$\frac{200 \times 100}{x} = 10\%$$

$$\text{and so } x = 200 \times \frac{100}{10}$$

$$x = 200 \times 10$$

$$x = £2,000.$$

Valuers refer to this process of converting income into an expression of investment worth as capitalization. This simple investment approach to valuing property can only be followed in respect of freehold properties currently let at or available to let at their full or market rental value and where there are no outgoings or expenses to be met out of the rent for such items as repairs, insurance, rates, heating, lighting etc., i.e. where the income can be assumed to be receivable in perpetuity, that is, for ever. All that is then necessary is to ascertain the right level of yield for that type of property investment by comparison with sales of similar property investments in the market.

In other cases the approach, although broadly similar, is more complex and requires an appreciation of investment arithmetic.

All surplus money can be saved to earn interest in post offices, banks and building societies. Money so deposited will, if left alone, gain over time as a result of interest being added to interest.

For example, £100 saved today for three years at 10 per cent would (ignoring tax) grow as follows:

£100 + interest* after 1 year at 10%   =£110
£110 + interest after 1 year at 10%   =£121
£121 + interest after 1 year at 10%   =£133.1.

* The amount of interest is calculated as follows:

$$100 \times \frac{10}{100} = 100 \times 0.1 = 10$$

In a savings book, interest would be added and subtotals made. Underlying this is simple mathematics which can be expressed and derived in the form of a formula. The formula in this case is that for compound interest, which is frequently expressed as:

$$(1 + i)^N$$

where i = rate of interest earned per period of time per £1 invested and N = number of interest-earning periods

Here i is 10 per cent and N is 3, so the formula becomes:

$$(1 + 0.1)^3 = (1.1) \times (1.1) \times (1.1)$$
$$= 1.331$$

So £100 saved for three years at 10 per cent will compound to £100 × 1.331 = £133.10.

Investors recognize that by purchasing investments they are giving up the ability to earn interest on their money. They also recognize that most investments are more risky than saving money and that questions of risk influence the return (yield) that they will expect from different types of investment.

So if instead of saving money they were offered an investment producing an income of £100 a year for three years, they would have to decide upon a sensible price to offer. To do this they discount the future benefits of ownership such that the price paid today for those benefits will produce for them an acceptable return (yield) on their money. This is done by reversing the compound interest process. This again can be re-expressed mathematically by taking what is known as the reciprocal of the compound interest formula, thus:

$$\frac{1}{(1 + i)^N} = \text{the present value (PV) of £1 after } N \text{ years at } i \text{ per cent.}$$

Many calculators will perform these investment calculations, or alternatively tables of such factors can be purchased similar to those shown in Appendix II.

So using a yield of 10 per cent the investment opportunity becomes:

			PV factor	
Time	Income		at 10%	PV sum
1	£100	×	0.9090	90.9
2	£100	×	0.8264	82.64
3	£100	×	0.7513	75.13
				£248.67

The investor can afford to pay £248.67 for an investment producing £100 each year for three years, provided all that is required is a 10 per cent return.

The correctness of this can be proved as follows:

	1	2	3	4
Time	Capital (1–4)	Income	Interest at 10% on 1	Return of capital (2–3)
0	£248.67			
1		£100	£24.867	£75.133
2	£173.537	£100	£17.357	£82.646
3	£ 90.89	£100	£ 9.089	£90.91*

* rounding error

Thus the investor receives a 10 per cent return on the invested capital, which is repaid over the three years.

When the benefits to be discounted are constant over N periods it is simpler to perform the calculation in one step rather than N steps. Thus 0.9090 + 0.8264 + 0.7513 can be added to produce 2.4867, and £100 multiplied by 2.4867 produces £248.67. The summation of the PV factors produces the present value of £1 per annum (see Appendix IIB). These two tables, PV of £1 and PV of £1 per annum, provide the valuer with the investment tools to carry out an investment valuation.

The formula for calculating the present value of 1 per annum (or per period) is:

$$\frac{1 - \dfrac{1}{(1+i)^N}}{i}$$

An important point to note is that where N is infinite, as is the case with a constant income in perpetuity, the formula simplifies to:

$$\frac{1}{i}$$

Valuers have traditionally called the PV of £1 per annum a figure of years purchase, but in this text the expression PV £1 p.a. is used.

To use the investment method the valuer needs to be able to assess some or if necessary all of the following factors:

1 The terms and conditions under which the tenant occupies the property, in particular:
   (a) the rent currently payable;
   (b) the length of the lease;
   (c) the length of time to the next rent review or to the lease termination, whichever is the sooner;
   (d) the maximum rent in today's terms that might be expected at the review – this will either be the market rental value or the maximum recoverable rent permitted by legislation;
   (e) the responsibility of the landlord and tenant for repairs and insurance and other outgoings for the property.
2 The current market capitalization rates (market rates of return) for that type of property.

For example, assess the value of the freehold interest in a house currently let at £5,000 per annum, assuming that the property is not protected by the Rent Acts, the lease was for seven years and has two years of the term to run, the freeholder is responsible for external and structural repairs but the insurance premium is recoverable from the tenant and the current rental value on similar terms is £10,000 per annum.

Income for the next two years			
Rent		£5,000	
Less for			
Repairs	£500		
Management	£500	£1,000	
Net income		£4,000	
PV £1 p.a. for two years at 10%		1.7355	£6,942
Income in two years' time			
Rent		£10,000	
Repairs	£600		
Management	£750	£ 1,350	
		£ 8,650	
PV £1 p.a. in perp. at 10% =	10		
× PV £1 in 2 years at 10%	.826	8.26	£71,449
			£78,391

The main problems for the valuer are the assessment of rent, the assessment of outgoings and the assessment of the correct capitalization rate.

Where there is a lease or tenancy in existence, the rent payable can be found by inspection of the lease or rent book. This must be checked against the most likely level of legally recoverable rent if the property is subject to Rent Act protection (see Chapter 11) or against market rental values. Inspection of the lease will also indicate the nature of the outgoings to be borne by the freeholder. In the case of most residential lettings of seven years or less, the landlord is responsible for external repairs and all repairs to the structure under the provisions of the Housing Act 1985 (Sections 11–14). This also includes the electrical, plumbing and other services to the building and the external decorations. Residential property requires intensive mangement, and an allowance of 10–20 per cent of the rent plus VAT is normally deducted. The valuer will base his allowance for the average annual cost of repairs on the actual costs involved and/or on the level of repair costs generally associated with properties of a comparable age, size and condition.

If the freeholder is responsible for the insurance of the building then it is first necessary to assess the building's reinstatement cost before calculating the annual premium based on current tariffs (see Chapter 15).

In the case of properties such as flats and maisonettes (see Chapters 11 and 14) there may be services provided by the freeholder in the form of cleaning, lighting, lifts etc. In most cases the cost of these is fully recoverable by means of a service charge. If not, then a deduction will have to be made for the annual cost of those items paid for by the landlord.

In every case there is a specific relationship between the income pattern (the frequency with which rent may be reviewed and the probable rate of rent increase over time) and the percentage rate used in the capitalization exercise, the income pattern being one of the risks to be gauged by the valuer. The others relate to the quality of the property as an investment and the quality of the tenant in occupation. Thus the method effectively reduces the value of the under-let property compared to its counterpart let at full rental value for the loss of income up until the rent review or lease renewal date.

Alternative approaches to this investment valuation exercise are to be found in Appendix II and further discussion in applied cases in later chapters.

The residual or developer's method

In order to build a house one needs land, materials, labour, capital and entrepreneurial skills. The residual method of valuation is used to assess the value of land in an undeveloped state but with development potential. It is a totally logical method, which recognizes that the combination of the previous factors in the right way will result in a specific site being developed to its highest and best use within the legal, physical and economic constraints that exist at that point in time for that site.

The entrepreneur exercises skill in determining the highest and best use and in bringing the other factors together; for that, his reward will be profit. Capital will be needed to buy the land, to buy materials and to pay for the labour; the cost of this capital is the interest forgone or interest payable. Once built, the house will have a market value, and thus the market value less the cost of labour, materials and profit will leave a residual sum which must represent the reward to the landowner for bringing the land to the market.

This can be summarized as:

> Gross developmental value (value of the finished house) less the costs of development other than the land = residual value of the land

The application of this method and the more complicated cash flow approach for larger sites is considered in detail in Chapter 12.

The contractor's or cost approach

The cost approach is the method of last resort. A valuer will rarely have to use this for assessing the open market value of residential property, but in rare cases the valuer might conclude that there is no other more suitable method. The valuer must not lose sight of the fact that cost and value are rarely the same, and that the final opinion, however arrived at, must be an opinion of open market value.

There are five steps to the method:

1 Estimate the value of the land as if vacant.
2 Estimate the cost of building the subject property as a simple substitute.
3 Estimate accrued depreciation.
4 Deduct depreciation from cost.
5 Add site value to the depreciated cost of the building.

Even if the subject property is so unique that there can be no comparables, there will usually be sufficient market evidence of land values in order to value the land by direct sales comparison. It is then necessary to calculate the cost of building the subject property or a modern simple substitute property which would provide an owner with the same satisfaction of ownership and utility.

Cost can be calculated by the quantity survey method. Bills of quantities are prepared for most construction work other than the simplest of buildings. If the original 'bill' can be found, then a quantity surveyor should be able to revise the cost estimate with current figures. If not, then it may be simpler to use the unit cost method. Very simply, the total gross external floor area of the house is calculated and this is multiplied by an overall building cost per square metre or per square foot. Great care needs to be exercised in selecting a cost per square foot, as building costs can vary considerably depending upon location and the design, services and quality of materials and finishes.

Once the cost of building the subject property has been found, it must be written down for age, condition and obsolescence. The allowance for this will depend upon the extent to which the valuer considers the property to be obsolete. Obsolescence in this sense may be physical, economic or functional. Because this method is used so rarely for residential property, few guidelines exist in the UK. One method is to depreciate the building over its life. Thus a building with an estimated original life of eighty years which is now forty years old would be written down by 50 per cent.

$$\frac{40}{80} \times 100 = 50\%$$

A more accurate approach is to base the depreciation factors on observable market events. The conundrum here is that if there were a market, one would not need to be resorting to the cost approach! The experienced valuer will inevitably use his or her knowledge to deduct a simple straight percentage to reflect what he or she believes a prudent buyer would reduce the equivalent new cost figure to, before being induced to buy.

Adhering to the principle of substitution, the cost approach can provide a useful check when market evidence is thin. Working on the assumption that no prudent buyer would pay more for an existing property than they would be prepared to pay for an equivalent property to be constructed on a site of their own, then the cost approach may under certain circumstances approximate to market value. However, it would never normally be used by valuers in the UK to arrive at open market value, because in the end the valuer would still have to answer the question 'But what is it worth?'.

Chapter 4

Residential agency

Approximately 65 per cent of residential homes are now owner-occupied. The remaining 35 per cent are expected by market analysts to remain tenanted and in the ownership of housing associations, local authorities and private landlords. Proposals to return the rented sector to a more open market with financial support going to tenants by way of housing benefits may marginally redress this trend.

This movement toward a 'home-owning democracy' has increased the demand for the services of the residential or house agent, a demand which has been accentuated by increases in population and increases in the frequency of moves; in some areas in the 1980s, people were moving on average once every three or four years.

Residential agency has changed rapidly in the last twenty years. In the 1970s most firms were owned and run by sole principals and partnerships from a single town centre location. There was a rapid growth in multi-office practices in the late 1970s, with many firms becoming regionally based. In the 1980s, major financial institutions moved into house agency. At one time they were reported to be operating over 30 per cent of all offices, and included Prudential Property Services, Royal, Hambro Countrywide, Nationwide Anglia, General Accident, Black Horse, Halifax, Fox Holdings and William H Brown. However, the collapse of the market after peaking in 1988 has severely reduced the activity level of all agents in the residential market. The Prudential eventually decided to sell off all their agency operations, whilst others have rationalized their operations.

Anyone who sets out to provide a service to the community can expect to receive some complaints sometimes from someone. On some occasions the criticism will be justified. Frequently the problem can be traced to a breakdown in communications between the parties. Even with the strong institutional involvement and with the statutory established controls under the Estate Agents Act 1979, complaints against house agents persist. The agency fee on the sale of a property can vary between 1 per cent and 3 per cent inclusive or exclusive of related expenses, plus VAT, and can run into thousands of pounds. If people complain about a plumber's bill, then it is not surprising that they complain when they receive an account for thousands of pounds for a service they may not have fully understood and where the quality is in doubt. Good communication between the agent and his or her client is crucial.

The residential agent must communicate and explain in greater detail than required by the Estate Agents Act 1979 precisely what service is offered, how the fee and other expenses will be calculated and what duty the agent owes the seller. These and other points can be considered by examining the house sales process from instruction to completion.

SALES INSTRUCTIONS

In most cases a home-owner will have to choose between a number of competing agents. This means that each and every member of an agent's staff must be able to explain accurately and in full detail the services that their agency is able to offer. To do this well they must believe that their firm is the best.

In some cases an agent may be confronted by a property that that firm is not competent to handle; in such cases the position should be explained and recommendations offered. If such instructions were accepted, that firm would be offering poor advice, and client dissatisfaction and complaint would be inevitable.

Securing instructions is an ongoing process. A seller may select an agent from the yellow pages; from the local newspaper; because they like the firm's image as reflected by advertising, for sale boards etc.; because of personal recommendation or convenience of location; because of a major advertising campaign, or for many other reasons. Once contact is made it is essential for the sales staff to turn that contact into an instruction. Clients can be lost for the silliest of reasons, but once lost they rarely return and so it is essential in residential agency practice, as it is within any service industry, for all staff to be properly trained and to put the client and prospective client first. The larger group practices recognize this and encourage their staff to seek qualifications and couple that with in-house training programmes, a strong corporate image, good public relations, good publicity literature and office manuals covering everything from office hours and appearance, to procedures and statutory compliance.

The first point of client contact is usually over the telephone or face to face in the agent's office. If the contact is on a social level at, say, a party, then it must be handled with great care. A good agent will maintain a high and respected profile in the community if he or she hopes to gain instructions from personal contacts, but the business of selling residential agency services is best handled at the prospective client's home or in the office, where extraneous matters can be kept out of the discussion. Enthusiasm, a phone number and a promise to contact as soon as the agent gets back to his or her office is preferable to the loss of a client through misunderstanding.

Telephone enquiries

The telephone is as dangerous as it is convenient. Like any piece of equipment, the user needs to be instructed on how to use it properly. Different firms have different systems for handling incoming calls, but the rule is if it rings it must be answered. In the absence of a switchboard or telephonist then all staff must co-operate to see that no telephone caller is kept waiting, and this must be achieved whenever possible without negotiators having to interrupt office discussions with vendors or applicants.

The response is important for the caller. The American response of 'Hi, this is Wendy of Johnstone Realtors here, how can I help you?' has never been adopted in the UK; nevertheless, it does convey four important messages to the caller:

1 it states that their call is welcome;
2 it states precisely with whom they have made contact; and
3 which member of staff has answered the call; and
4 that that individual is ready to attend to the call.

The English response is usually more formal and may convey quite minimal enthusiasm to the caller. Telephone technique should be part of any in-house training programme. All incoming (and outgoing) calls should be logged, and each office and each negotiator needs to note calls in such a way that at intervals during the day the record can be checked to see that all pending matters have been dealt with. On a daily or weekly basis, all relevant calls should be noted on a client's file.

Once it has been established that the caller is considering selling a property, then established office procedures must be followed. Each practice or firm operates in a different way; thus there is the unsatisfactory free-for-all approach where negotiators are competing with one another for instructions, or the opposite extreme of all instructions being handled by one member of staff. The danger of the former is that someone with too little experience may try and handle an instruction which is beyond their personal competence. The danger with the latter approach is that clients may go elsewhere, rather than holding on or waiting for a return call. In either case only the minimum of matters should be discussed over the phone, as it is essential to establish face-to-face contact and to view the property at the earliest possible time.

Vendors react to first impressions, so the right response to telephone enquiries is important. A prospective vendor should not be asked to hold on. If no one can take the call, their name and number should be taken and a return call made within five minutes.

Face-to-face enquiries

The reception given to vendors and applicants when they walk into an agent's office is vital to the success of that relationship. Clients and applicants will wait for service, if they can see why they are waiting, if they are told why they may have to wait, and if there is something to occupy them whilst they are waiting.

The shape, size and design of the office will dictate how the visitor will be received. In a busy office a good receptionist can help establish a good relationship by showing interest and asking sensible questions: 'Have you been in before? Did you wish to see anyone in particular? Is your enquiry about buying or selling?'

If a member of the sales staff is free, there should be no waiting and the enquiry should be dealt with promptly. If the rest of the office can be seen from the reception area or entrance, then the onus is on staff who are free to come forward and welcome the visitor. Discussions between staff in front of clients and applicants is wrong, as too is the practice of gesticulating across the office indicating clearly to the visitor, 'Oh, no not me again, I am far too busy!'

If all staff are engaged and can be seen to be engaged, then the receptionist should be trained to provide prospective vendors with the firm's literature on 'Selling your Home' and to provide buyers with literature on 'Buying your Home'. If the delay is going to be long, then the offer of coffee may be one way of stopping a prospective vendor from going to a competitor.

In the open plan office, the 'GOYA' principle must apply; translated it means 'get off your backside'. In practice it means that anyone not on the phone or talking to a vendor or applicant goes forward to see if help can be given.

This initial phase in the process is important to both parties as it establishes the vendor's confidence in the agent. The capital investment made by many agents helps to support this relationship by creating a warm, attractive, welcoming and interesting office to encourage the passerby to enter and to convey by image to all prospective vendors visiting the office that they have chosen the right firm to sell their home. A vendor should be encouraged to feel that they want a photograph of their home to be on display in that office with a set of attractive details and that the staff are there to help and that they will help.

Until the agent has seen the property it is only possible to discuss the agency relationship and other matters in outline. The prospective vendor may, however, be phoning around or comparing services, so the sales staff must be able to discuss the agency agreement, to be able to comment generally on the advantages of sole agency, to comment sensibly on the benefits of private treaty and auction sales and to be able to explain fully and correctly the basis of fees and/or other charges that the vendor can expect to pay, and what services will be covered by such fees.

AGENCY AGREEMENT

The appointment of an agent used to be undertaken on a relatively informal basis. Certainly in the past a home-owner would no more think of entering into a formal contract with their agent than they would when instructing a solicitor or accountant. Such informality has frequently led to all manner of dispute between vendors and agents.

The position currently is that anyone acting as an 'estate agent' as defined in Section 1 of the Estate Agents Act 1979 must comply with the requirements of the Act and the various orders and regulations made under the Act (see pp. 63–5 and p. 94).

The agent needs to check whether the vendor has approached or instructed other agents, and if so, whether the vendor intends the appointment to be on a sole agency basis or multiple agency basis. The idea of instructing more than one agent to act at one and the same time, but not jointly, to sell the same property seems to predominate in London and the Home Counties. Elsewhere it is normal practice for a vendor to appoint one agent to act as sole agent.

From a vendor's and agent's point of view, sole agency is preferable. Sole agency creates the best professional relationship between a good agent and the vendor. It reduces potential confusion in the market place, because only one agent is acting, the sole agent handles all enquiries and negotiations and so is in a better position to judge the reaction of the market to the property and the price. Sole agency avoids confusion in the mind of the vendor as to which agent sent which prospective buyer. It gives the agent the necessary breathing space to draft details for the vendor's approval, to take photographs in good light at the best time of day. It provides the agent with the maximum incentive to find a buyer. It eliminates abortive work and as a result, a reduced rate of remuneration will generally be offered. It does not preclude the vendor from selling the property privately. All offers have to be made through the sole agent, thereby allowing that agent to judge and advise professionally on each offer.

It has been suggested that some sole agents adopt too relaxed an attitude, because they know they have no competition from other agents; such a situation can be avoided by restricting the length of the sole agency agreement. It is also felt that sole agency may not achieve maximum market exposure for the property. This is a point of debate and is in part linked with the nature of the agency contract and remuneration. Naturally sole agency given to the wrong agent will result in poor marketing and limited prospects of sale. Given to the right agent it will receive maximum attention and the best possibility of an early sale.

Vendors have a tendency to believe that if two or more agents are instructed, greater market penetration will be achieved through two photographs in two windows, two advertisements in the local papers, two sets of details being circulated. In practice, where an inclusive of advertising fee is charged, each agent will only meet advertising up to a predetermined maximum amount. The amount will depend upon whether the agent has been given a sole agency or not – thus a sole agent may be prepared to spend as much on advertising as the combined amounts of two agents acting in competition. Thus the total exposure of the property to the market does not necessarily increase in proportion to the number of agents instructed. In addition, the quality of details, photographs, advertising and accompanied viewing may be poorer in the case of multiple instructions than that which can be offered by a sole agent. In those areas where advertising costs are charged in addition to a base fee, and will be charged to a vendor whether or not a property is sold, a vendor could be faced with legitimate accounts from a number of agents and may well lose control of the advertising budget.

There are advantages to purchasers in a multiple agency area, in that from any one agent they may receive details of more properties than in a sole agency area. Recent changes in the market-place may alter this pattern, however, as two major institutions may be less willing to enter into competitive property selling in quite the same way as two local firms. What may alter the picture is the limit of one 'for sale' board per property.

The vendor's doubts as to market exposure may be real in some instances. In such cases the agent should suggest a joint sole agency, a common practice for country properties, where a good local agent works with a London agent. In other circumstances greater coverage might be possible through the use of sub-agents; if an agent considers that sub-agency may be desirable then the right to appoint sub-agents must be agreed when drawing up the agency terms.

Whilst outlining the alternatives to the vendor, the agent must indicate the difference in fee structure. A common practice is no sale no fee, an arrangement which seems clear to most vendors, but the precise details must be set out in accordance with s.18 of the Estate Agents Act, together with appropriate 'warning notices'. It is also normal to quote a lower fee for sole agency instructions. Joint sole agency is often at one and a half times the sole agency fee to be shared between the two agents, whereas in the case of sub-agents the arrangement is usually that the instructed agent's fee will be shared between the agent and the sub-agent 50/50, or 60/40 in favour of the agent introducing the buyer. The remuneration is negotiable and must be agreed in each case in writing prior to confirming instructions.

Most reputable agents would never seek to elicit sole selling rights, as such an arrangement means that even if the vendor arranges a sale privately the agent's fee will still be payable. The Provision of Information Regulations requires appropriate 'warning notices' to be issued.

The amount of the remuneration must be discussed and the conditions under which it will become payable must also be explained. No sale no fee is the only fair system and the only basis readily understood by vendors.

In addition, the vendor must be advised of any additional charges that will be payable. Again practice varies between one part of the country and another. In the South of England it is common practice to charge a fee of, say, 1.5–2 per cent plus VAT and for the agent to meet all expenses out of the fee. Elsewhere the customary practice has been to agree a fee and for the vendor to agree to pay for other expenses in addition to the fee to cover advertising, sale boards, photographs, accompanied viewing and similar expenses. The legal requirements are those set out in s.18 of the Estate Agents Act 1979, namely:

18 – (1) Subject to subsection (2) below, before any person (in this section referred to as 'the client') enters into a contract with another (in this section referred to as 'the agent') under which the agent will engage in estate agency work on behalf of the client, the agent shall give the client –
(a) the information specified in subsection (2) below; and
(b) any additional information which may be prescribed under subsection (4) below.

(2) The following is the information to be given under subsection (1)(a) above –
(a) particulars of the circumstances in which the client will become liable to pay remuneration to the agent for carrying out estate agency work;
(b) particulars of the amount of the agent's remuneration for carrying out estate agency work or, if that amount is not ascertainable at the time the information is given, particulars of the manner in which the remuneration will be calculated;
(c) particulars of any payments which do not form part of the agent's remuneration for carrying out estate agency work or a contract or pre-contract deposit but which, under the contract referred to in subsection (1) above, will or may in certain circumstances be payable by the client to the agent or any other person and particulars of the circumstances in which any such payments will become payable; and
(d) particulars of the amount of any payment falling within paragraph (c) above or, if that amount is not ascertainable at the time the information is given, an estimate of that amount together with particulars of the manner in which it will be calculated.

18 – (3) If, at any time after the client and the agent have entered into such a contract as is referred to in subsection (1) above, the parties are agreed that the terms of the contract should be varied so far as they relate to the carrying out of estate agency work or any payment falling within subsection (2)(c) above, the agent shall give the client details of any changes which, at the time the statement is given, fall to be made in the information which was given to the client under subsection (1) above before the contract was entered into.

(4) The Secretary of State may by regulations –
(a) prescribe for the purposes of subsection (1)(b) above additional information relating to any estate agency work to be performed under the contract; and
(b) make provision with respect to the time and the manner in which the obligation of the agent under subsection (1) or subsection (3) above is to be performed; and the power to make regulations under this subsection shall be exercisable by statutory instrument which shall be subject to annulment in pursuance of a resolution of either House of Parliament.

(5) If any person –
(a) fails to comply with the obligation under subsection (1) above with respect to a contract or with any provision of regulations under subsection (4) above relating to that obligation, or
(b) fails to comply with the obligation under subsection (3) above with respect to any variation of a contract or with any provision of regulations under subsection (4) above relating to that obligation, the contract or, as the case may be, the variation of it shall not be enforceable by him except pursuant to an order of the court under subsection (6) below.

(6) If, in a case where subsection (5) above applies in relation to a contract or a variation of a contract, the agent concerned makes an application to the court for the enforcement of the contract or, as the case may be, of a contract as varied by the variation –
(a) the court shall dismiss the application if, but only if, it considers it just to do so having regard to prejudice caused to the client by the agent's failure to comply with his obligation and the degree of culpability for the failure and
(b) where the court does not dismiss the application, it may nevertheless order that any sum payable by the client under the contract or, as the case may be, under the contract as varied shall be reduced or discharged so as to compensate the client for prejudice suffered as a result of the agent's failure to comply with his obligation.

18 – (7) In this section –

(a) references to the enforcement of a contract or variation include the withholding of money in pursuance of a lien for money alleged to be due under the contract or as a result of the variation and

(b) 'the court' means any court having jurisdiction to hear and determine matters arising out of the contract.

In addition, a number of new orders and regulations have been made by the Secretary of State, including:

The Estate Agents (Specified Offences) (No. 2) order 1991 (S.1.1991 No. 10910) and (Amendment) order 1992;

The Estate Agents (Undesirable Practices) (No. 2) order 1991 (S.1.1991 No. 1032); and

The Estate Agents (Provision of Information) Regulations 1991 (S.1.1991 No. 859).

The position now is that prior to entering into an agency contract, the seller must be provided with the following information:

1 particulars of the circumstances in which the client will become liable to pay remuneration to the agent (s.18(2)(a));
2 particulars of the amount of the agent's remuneration, or if that amount is not ascertainable at the time the information is given, particulars of the manner in which the remuneration will be calculated (s.18(2)(b));
3 particulars of any payment other than the agent's remuneration (s.18(2)(c));
4 particulars of the circumstances in which amounts other than remuneration are payable (s.18(2)(d));
5 where the amount of any payment other than remuneration is not ascertainable at the time the information is given, the estate agent must give:
(a) an estimate of the amount of the payment (s.18(2)(d)),
(b) particulars of the manner in which the estimated amount will be calculated (s.18(2)(c) and (d)).

(Points listed in a letter to the RICS from the Office of Fair Trading dated 8 September 1988.)

The above information must be given in writing, and it is customary for the agent to request confirmation of acceptance from the client.

If the phrases 'sole selling rights', 'sole agency' or 'ready, willing and able buyer' are used, then under the Provision of Information Regulations the seller must be served with a 'warning notice'. The warning notices should be drafted using the following words, which must not be materially amended:

Sole Selling Rights

You will be liable to pay remuneration to us, in addition to any other costs or charges agreed, in each of the following circumstances:

if unconditional contracts for the sale of the property are exchanged in the period during which we have sole selling rights, even if the purchaser was not found by us but by another agent or by any other means, including yourself;

if unconditional contracts for the sale of the property are exchanged after the expiry of the period during which we have sole selling rights but to a purchaser who was introduced to you during that period.

Sole Agency

You will be liable to pay remuneration to us, in addition to any other costs or charges agreed, if at any time unconditional contracts for the sale of the property are exchanged:

with a purchaser introduced by us during the period of our sole agency or with whom we had negotiations about the property during that period; or

with a purchaser introduced by another agent during that period.

Ready, Willing and Able Purchaser

A purchaser is a 'ready, willing and able' purchaser if he is prepared and is able to exchange unconditional contracts for the purchase of your property. You will be liable to pay remuneration to us, in addition to any other costs or charges agreed, if such a purchaser is introduced by us in accordance with your instructions and this must be paid even if you subsequently withdraw and unconditional contracts for sale are not exchanged, irrespective of your reasons.

In addition the agent must advise the vendor/seller if the agent is offering or intends to offer other services to any prospective purchaser. This would be the case if an agent intended to offer mortgage advice. These requirements extend to 'connected persons' as well as the agent *per se*.

The RICS in their publication *Putting the Estate Agents Act 1979 and its Orders and Regulations into Practice* suggest by way of illustration that the agency agreement should contain the following information, or information on the following points:

1　Agent's name and address.
2　Client's name and address.
3　Address of the property to be sold/let etc.
4　The client's title to the property – freehold/leasehold.
5　Outstanding loans to be redeemed on sale.
6　Sale conditions – vacant possession/subject to tenancies.
7　Asking price – details of fixtures and fittings.

8 Offer arrangements (under the Undesirable Practices Order an agent must supply the client with details of all offers, unless the client has agreed that they do not wish to receive offers below a specified figure).
9 Contract period.
10 Solicitor's name and address.
11 Viewing arrangements.
12 Warning notices (as appropriate).
13 Remuneration.
14 Other charges – itemized.
15 Other services that may be offered.
16 Termination charges.
17 Recovery of other charges if property remains unsold.
18 Responsibility in the event of the property being vacant.
19 Client's agreement and consents to 'for sale' boards, accuracy of sale particulars, keys, deposits, payment of remuneration by solicitor, interest on unpaid remuneration or other charges, disclosure of personal relationship to the agent or person associated with the agent.

The need for this degree of detail will be examined in appropriate sections of this and the following chapter.

During the discussion stage, the agent may be asked to advise on the most sensible method of sale.

SALE METHODS

The majority of residential sales are by private treaty, but under certain circumstances auction or tender may be recommended. Two factors mainly influence the choice; the first is the property itself and the second the requirements of the vendor.

Sale by private treaty is generally cheaper than other methods, it allows the property to be offered to the market as soon as the agency terms have been agreed, and all negotiations are private, so no one need ever know the precise details of the sale price other than vendor, agent and purchaser. The agent needs to be confident of his opinion of market value, as the custom is to advertise the property at a price, or to invite offers in excess of a price or at least to give a clear indication during negotiations of the sort of price the vendor is seeking. Thus the method is ideal for that type of property for which there is a ready market.

In some cases private treaty sales stimulate such interest that the agent will be dealing with several negotiations at the same time for the property. Gazumping is a phrase used to describe the position where an offer from A is accepted subject to contract, but before exchange of contracts a higher offer is accepted from B. This in turn may lead to a contract race, where the vendor agrees to sell to the purchaser first able to sign the contracts.

In other cases the interest is so strong that the agent will advise the vendor to seek highest sealed offers by a given date. In the latter case this may or may not be on the understanding of a sale to the highest offerer. Where private treaty sales explode in this way there will inevitably be a degree of ill will all round, most of which will be aimed at the agent. This is unfortunate, as the agent is simply acting on behalf of the vendor to secure the most acceptable deal and must refer all offers to the vendor – see the Undesirable Practices Order, s.1.1991, 1032.

Such a situation is most likely to occur (a) in a multiple agency operation and (b) in respect of a property which was better suited to sale by auction. In (a) it arises where purchasers are negotiating through different agents, and each agent is therefore very keen that their applicant should succeed. A very grey area then develops as to whether the agent is acting for the vendor or the applicant. Certainly there is very little that the vendor can do, other than set one party against the other to see who withdraws first. In the second case the problem may arise because the vendor wishes to maintain control over the date of the sale and to have some choice in the selection of buyer. Family attachment to a home may be such that the owners want to be sure that the 'right sort of people' buy it. This control cannot be exercised where property is sold by auction, nor can any selective process be exercised by the agent.

The Estate Agents (Undesirable Practices) Order states that all agents must:

1 forward all offers 'promptly' in writing, other than those that the client has indicated in writing he/she does not wish to receive;
2 not misrepresent orally or in writing, knowingly or recklessly, any offer; this would apply to the 'existence of, or details relating to any offer' and/ or to the 'existence or status of any prospective purchaser'; the provision applies to representations made to any party including the client, applicants, prospective purchasers, valuers, solicitors etc.;
3 notify the client whenever any interrelated services are to be offered or are to be provided in respect of each offer made. This last point is in addition to the general requirement for notification made at the time of agreeing instructions.

These provisions were felt to be necessary following reports in *Which?* and by other journalists of a number of 'undesirable practices'. These provisions mean that agents are no longer permitted to indicate that offers have been made when none exist, or to suggest that higher offers exist when this is not the case, or that a cash offer has been made when in fact the offer depends upon completion of another sale; in addition the client must be advised in writing if a prospective purchaser is to receive financial services such as mortgage assistance: clearly it is an offence for an agent to discriminate on grounds of race, sex, etc.; it is also an offence to discriminate on the grounds that a prospective purchaser will not be accepting interrelated services from the agent.

If the vendor is only interested in obtaining the best price then the agent may invite the various parties to attend a private auction in his offices. This may be of a formal nature, such that the successful bidder will be required to sign a contract before leaving the agent's offices.

Private treaty sales are usually conducted subject to contract, survey and finance, so there is always the possibility of the sale falling through before contracts are signed.

Sale by auction should be recommended whenever there is a legal need to satisfy beneficiaries, executors, mortgagees, liquidators, stockholders and trustees. A sale by auction is regarded as proof that every effort was made to obtain the best price for the property. An auction should also be recommended where one can expect excitement, interest and open competition amongst prospective purchasers. If successful, an auction has a final result; on the fall of the hammer the successful bidder is under contract to purchase in accordance with the terms and conditions set out in the auction details, a 10 per cent deposit has to be handed over and completion will occur on the date specified in the auction documents. The auctioneer has the authority to sign the memorandum of agreement (the contract) on behalf of the bidder.

Auction sales are usually subject to an undisclosed reserve price and the auctioneer will usually reserve the right to bid on behalf of the vendor. Without such protection the vendor would have to accept whatever bid was made, even if that bid were ridiculous. The disadvantages of auction sales are that they are public sales, they can put off some purchasers, e.g. those who need to sell in order to buy and who do not wish to use bridging finance, or because they have not been able to complete their surveys, legal enquiries and financial arrangements in time for the auction.

Tender is rarely used for the sale of private residential property, but may be recommended for the sale of residential land or estates of houses. The agent needs to be confident that the sale will generate interest. The advantage of tender is that all offers have to be submitted by a specified date but the vendor is free to select the offer he or she prefers. It need not be the highest bid and the price accepted need not be disclosed to the public.

Auction sales and sale by tender are more expensive than by private treaty as the documentation is more complex and becomes a legal document, and all the costs are borne by the vendor including, in the case of an auction, the hire of the auction room.

It is unusual to discuss the method of sale in anything other than outline until the property has been inspected.

RECORDS AND SYSTEMS

Before viewing the property the agent may or may not complete any one or more of the following tasks. The action taken will depend upon established office procedures and the nature and efficiency of the office systems.

1 Open a file and cross-reference the file or folio number with the vendor's name and address.
2 Enter preliminary details, as provided by the vendor, in the properties for sale register. This alerts other members of staff to the possibility of a new instruction; if suitable enquiries are received at this stage they must be handled with care until the agency agreement has been established.
3 Check the clients register to see if the firm has previously acted for the client in any capacity, and enter the client's name for future reference.
4 Check the property register to see if the firm has previously sold the subject property and to check for comparables. In the case of estate properties, extract copies of original sale details.
5 Check street maps or OS sheets for location and to be certain of the best route of approach to the property from the agent's office. The agent should arrive by car on the correct side of the road.
6 Leave full details in the office of time left, property to be visited, vendor's name, telephone number, and expected return time.
7 Check equipment: tape measure or measuring rod, clipboard, inspection pro formas, dictaphone if used, pens, pencil, compass, camera(s), torch.
8 Check visiting cards, presentation folder, vendor's folder which may contain samples of sales literature, information on the firm and its services, details of the sales process, method of sale and type of agency instruction, specimen agency agreement including typical fee structure, notepad for the vendor to record details of applicants viewing the property and check lists.
9 Check or arrange to check with the prospective client and within the practice whether any 'personal interest' needs to be disclosed and whether the client needs to be advised (in writing) of any 'services' that may be offered to any prospective purchaser.

A good agent operates from an efficient office. The growth in institutional ownership of agencies is likely to lead to more organization and more standardization. The growth in computer facilities means that much more data should be available for the agent at the tip of a finger.

The efficient agency practice is likely to operate some or all of the following systems:

Clients register

A simple register that records alphabetically the names and addresses of everyone the practice has acted for, coded to identify the nature of the service provided.

Property records

These contain brief details of every property the practice has been involved with, coded to identify the service provided. In the case of sales and valuations, brief details of the property, price etc. will be recorded.

Property register

This is the active record of all properties currently being handled by that agency, coded to identify the office or staff member handling the instructions. It must be readily accessible for the whole staff and it must be kept right up to date in terms of progress, e.g. under offer. If computerized, this register can also be used to make a property search. Individual negotiators may prefer to back the main register with their own price, type or area-based register.

Particulars store

Property details should be readily accessible for all negotiators. Many agents now display the majority of the properties on their register on special self-selection display stands. Each property is illustrated with a colour photograph, the asking price is printed clearly and sets of details are stored above or below the photograph. Where such systems operate negotiators should keep their own master sets at their desks so that they do not have to borrow applicants' sets.

If computer systems are not in use, then a daily bulletin needs to be issued to the whole sales team detailing any changes over the previous 24 hours.

Applicants register

The requirements of all prospective purchasers must be entered on the applicants register. In theory, as each new instruction is received this should be checked against the applicants register. If the two match or come close to matching, the applicant(s) should be contacted and details of the property forwarded. The problem is that no system has yet been devised to handle this process expertly. Nevertheless, it is an essential requirement for mailing and marketing and must be made to work as well as possible.

Each negotiator should also keep a list of those applicants they have personally seen, in order to maintain their purchase requirements. This is particularly important in the case of those applicants who must buy – because they have sold their house or are being moved to the area by their employer. In most areas there will also be some 'triple A' properties and roads; keeping a separate list of people interested in those very specific properties and locations may produce instant sales in the future.

Files

Files must be kept for each instruction and should contain the fullest possible details of the sale as it progresses. This includes any correspondence, sales details, circulation or mailing information, enquiries received, phone calls etc. Some files are overprinted with sales progress information or have a sales progress pro forma inserted in the front cover. These systems allow the negotiator to monitor each sale accurately and to be able to check easily that all action needed has taken place.

Advertising records

It is very important for the agent to be able to show precisely where and in what form a client's property has been advertised. The record system will contain copies of all advertisements placed and printed, and there should be a regular transfer from the master record to the property files.

Board records

Some local authorities are tightening up on the control of 'for sale' boards in specific areas. In some they are not permitted at all where the authority creates board-free zones. In addition the government may bring in tighter controls over the size of boards and over the length of time they can be displayed and the number that can be displayed at any one time on a single property. (See Town and Country Planning (Control of Advertisements) (Amendment No. 2) regulations 1987, operative from 28 October 1988.) Regulation of boards means that each agent must exercise proper control over the placement of boards. Even without regulating controls an agent needs to keep accurate records of boards, needs to inspect them regularly for safety and to see that they are providing a good advertisement for the property and the agency. Similarly, details need to be recorded in the property file. In particular the agent needs to ensure that:

1 Specific instructions are given as to the placement of boards on site.
2 No damaged or defaced boards are ever used or left on site.
3 No 'sold' boards are used, only the words 'Sold Subject to Contract'

to be displayed at the appropriate time on previously erected 'for sale' boards.

4 All boards are recovered in accordance with any statutory requirements and in any event on completion of the sale or within 14 days of completion.

Key records

To facilitate the sale process and when accompanied viewing is essential or requested, the agent will hold keys to the property. These keys must be kept safely, out of sight and with a system that prevents the immediate identification of key and property. Keys should never be passed to a third party; it should be a golden rule that all access must be accompanied. An exception might be that of a known surveyor undertaking a survey on behalf of a purchaser with the client's approval, in which case proper identification is essential and proper records must be kept.

The agent, having completed the office investigations, can now set off to inspect the property, confident that all the information needed to fully advise the vendor has been collected.

The agent will be seen by the vendor or the vendor's children arriving from the most obvious direction. The agent will not be flustered and will arrive on time.

The confidence of the vendor collapses if he/she witnesses the antics of the agent looking for somewhere to turn round, having driven past the house on the wrong side of the road.

The agent will identify himself or herself, and hopefully the efficient office will allow the agent to talk with confidence about the property, the locality and all recent local sales in the immediate area.

The agent continues to operate fluently, handing over a neat folder containing useful information about the firm, how they work, what services they provide, a check list on what to do when moving home, and explaining how their fees might be calculated – 'Just so you and your husband can talk it all over quietly tonight'.

From this moment the agent should be certain that s/he has become the vendor's agent. A polite check to see that his or her shoes are clean and dry, and the agent is away upstairs with the six-year-old carrying the torch and tape measure. The vendor, confident that the right agent has been found, is busy preparing tea and biscuits.

No, this does not happen every time, but good interpersonal skills are a clear requirement for a good residential sales negotiator.

Chapter 5

Taking on residential property for sale

TAKING DETAILS

Some agents believe strongly in pro formas. Others believe that it is essential to treat each property individually. The truth probably lies half-way.

Pro formas are very useful as check lists and simplify the taking of details when dealing with a standard property such as an estate-built semi-detached house. They serve very little purpose when taking details of a country mansion in five acres of land.

A pro forma is, in effect, a draft of the sales details. As the agent inspects the property he merely fills in the blanks. M.J. Vivian FSVA in his book, *The Art of House Agency*, includes an excellent example of a typical pro forma instruction sheet.

A check list may prove of greater value than a pro forma, particularly as the latter tends to dictate both the content and layout of the sales details. The object of a check list is merely to remind the agent not to leave the house until all the information necessary to complete the sales particulars and to complete the sale in due course has been collected.

A check list should include at least the following points:

Full names of vendors
Address of property and post code
Title, freehold, leasehold
Description of property
Construction of property
Age and condition of property
Accommodation
Services/facilities and suppliers
Local authority – council tax
Local amenities
Grounds/gardens
Garages
Outbuildings

Agent's valuation. Agreed asking price
Fixtures and fittings
Viewing arrangements – keys
For sale boards
Photographs
Agency terms
Vendor's solicitors
Moving date and new address, if known.

In some practices, sales details are prepared in a standard style to maintain a corporate image; pro formas can simplify this exercise.

There are good agents and bad agents. A good agent will complete his inspection in the shortest possible time and in a logical way. Nothing will be missed and nothing will have to be rechecked.

As well as taking the basic descriptive details, the agent is also considering those factors likely to affect value and saleability, in particular looking for features and benefits that will help to sell the property.

Before arriving at the property the agent will have checked the immediate area and the position of the property on its plot in the street. As every purchaser knows, the property for sale always seems to be the wrong one in the road – if only it was nearer the top end or on the other side. The agent knows from experience when first viewing the property whether it will sell readily. The agent looks at the property from the outside and looks at the outside from the inside. Does it overlook open country, playing fields, a graveyard, river, undertaker's premises, or sewage works? Also, are the house and its garden in a saleable condition?

The agent considers the principal selling points, the best way of presenting the property on paper and the best way to view the property. In marketing terms, people buy benefits. Most benefits can be listed under the headings of safety, performance, appearance, comfort, economy, and durability. In terms of a home the benefits may be: convenience in terms of work, motorways etc., quiet and peaceful location, no through traffic, open views, good design, attractive material, traditionally built, a good investment for the future, energy efficient, sheltered position, modernized, enlarged, improved, quality guaranteed. Identifying the benefits helps the agent to assess the right benefits to highlight in respect of a specific property provided they can be stated within the provisions of the Property Misdescriptions Act.

The agent must also listen to the vendor for clues which may help to identify the benefits enjoyed by the vendor, such as local schools. The benefits may relate to the property, to the location or to local facilities.

The agent must also consider the best way to direct applicants to the property. The shortest route from the agent's office may not be the quickest, nor the simplest, nor the most attractive.

Inside the property the agent must balance the logical tour with the selling features and benefits. In most cases the logical tour from the front door is preferred, but a beautiful view and garden may be a better starting point, leading next to the completely redesigned kitchen.

The agent may spot minor 'irritants' when inspecting the property, and professional advice might include recommendations to rectify some before placing the property on the market. This is especially important if the 'irritant' would appear dangerous or unhealthy to an applicant – broken windows, loose steps to the front door, badly stained and/or cracked sanitary goods. The agent's experienced eye immediately notes age, condition, essential repairs, decoration, services, and an unkept and uncared-for garden and property.

Individuals may perhaps be involved in only two or three sales in a lifetime, whereas the agent may be handling that many a day. Thus the agent knows instinctively what are good and bad selling points. Part of the agent's fee is for this expertise, which the agent must convey to the vendor in the advices offered.

The notes taken by the agent must be sufficient to prepare sales particulars and sufficient to answer questions and conduct negotiations.

Having fully inspected the property, the agent is free to discuss all the details with the vendor(s). In the case of joint vendors it may be better for the agent to call back in the evening when all owners are at home.

THE MARKETING PROGRAMME

The owner will first need to be advised on the marketability of the property, its probable selling price and the agent's recommendations on asking price. A number of agents try to avoid this question by asking the owners, 'How much do you need to complete your next purchase?' The professional, well-prepared agent will open the discussion by giving some information on the market for that type of property, and on sales recently completed on comparable properties, before detailing his or her views on a sensible asking price. If the agent is unable to satisfy the vendors at this stage as to the rightness of his/her opinion, then instructions are unlikely to follow. In some cases the vendors will have fixed their minds on a price, in which case the agent may have to explain why that figure is too high or too low. If the vendors insist on marketing the property at too high a figure, then the agent has the choice of accepting or declining their instructions. It is the brave agent who declines, but if the property does not sell the market will conclude that the agent gave wrong advice.

Perhaps the most difficult issue is explaining to a vendor that just because they spent £15,000 on a kitchen does not mean that they can expect to get £15,000 more than for comparable properties. If the vendor is unhappy with the agent's view, then the agent should explain precisely why they are of that opinion. A 5 per cent error in judgement by an agent may make or break a move or a chain of sales.

The agent should also indicate approximately what proceeds net of fees and expenses the vendors can expect from a sale at that asking price. On some occasions the agent may feel that the mortgage valuation or private survey might down-value the property – if this is a possibility, the vendors should be forewarned at this stage of the process.

The agent must advise on the recommended method of sale – private treaty, auction or tender. The agent must then outline the normal marketing procedure adopted by that agency practice and the agency terms under which they prefer to operate. Many agents now provide a short booklet setting everything out, with examples of fee calculations and specimen agency agreements. All of this helps the agent to explain the process and the cost to the prospective client.

An important part of the discussion is the question of fees and expenses. The details required under the Estate Agents Act were referred to previously. At one time, almost every agent charged a fee based on a nationally agreed scale of 5 per cent on the first £500, 2.5 per cent on the next £4,000 and 1.5 per cent on the residue of the sale price. This kind of scale may reflect the fact that whatever the price of the property, the agent will incur similar set-up costs but that the total cost does not rise proportionately with the sale price. However, since the Restrictions on Agreements (Estate Agents) Order 1970, all manner of different fee bases have been adopted by different agents throughout England and Wales. Many now adopt a fee of between 1 per cent and 2 per cent. Some firms argue that the better-quality property requires a higher level of service and hence a higher fee. What is significant is that the fee in almost every case is a percentage of the final sale price, irrespective of the actual work done by the agent. It is probably this aspect of agents' fees that causes most aggravation to vendors.

Agents are, however, becoming increasingly flexible regarding the basis upon which the fee is to be calculated. Some will give a reduction on their basic fee in the event of a quick sale; most will give a reduction when granted sole agency; some charge a minimum fee plus their expenses. The point is that when entering into an agency agreement it is open to the parties to agree the basis of the fee and so whilst some argue for the equitable treatment of all vendors, others maintain that in a free society bargaining is expected. Disputes will occur if the final basis is not clearly documented in accordance with s.18 of the Estate Agents Act.

The agent's fee is always exclusive of VAT and vendors need to be told that VAT at the current rate for professional services will be added to the agent's account.

A further point that needs to be clarified between owner and agent is precisely what the fee covers. Here again practice differs around the country. In some areas the fee as quoted is seen as a charge for the agent's expertise, and the owner is charged in addition for advertising and other incidental expenses. In other areas the fee is accepted as covering the agent's normal expenses of sale. In the latter case the owner would not expect to pay additionally for the cost of advertising in the local paper, nor for the placing of a 'for sale' board on the property, but they might have to pay extra if they required a full-page advertisement in *Country Life*. Again, it is essential that the agent makes it absolutely clear what the fee covers, how it is to be calculated and the circumstances under which it will become payable; hence the increasing practice of providing this information in a leaflet containing an example of how a fee is assessed.

It must be made clear under what circumstances the fee becomes payable. The professional agent should make this as clear as possible – for instance, the advertising slogan, 'No Sale No Fee'. Here the agent is endeavouring to reassure vendors that a fee will only be charged if the person who eventually legally completes the purchase of the property is introduced by that agent. Even in this case, disputes can occur if there is some doubt as to who introduced the purchaser, particularly if the purchaser (a) receives sale details from an agent, and (b) sees the owner's personal advertisement in a newspaper. It is said that honesty is the best policy, but when several hundreds of pounds are involved, vendors are tempted to argue that the purchaser was introduced through their own efforts. Where doubt does exist it will rarely pay to litigate and under such circumstances one trusts that most vendors and most agents would reach an agreement whereby the agent is at least compensated for his costs.

In order for the agent to be able to demonstrate that s.18 of the Estate Agents Act has been complied with, there will need to be a letter or contract setting out all the terms and conditions, which should be countersigned by the vendor.

At this stage if the vendor indicates that the agent is to proceed on the agreed terms, then the agent will need the following further information:

1 Arrangements for viewing the property.
2 Arrangements for accompanied viewing – an agent should be able to sell a property better than a vendor.
3 Vendor's home and business numbers.
4 Vendor's solicitors.
5 Details of restrictive covenants, easements, etc.
6 Details including a copy of the lease in the case of leasehold properties plus the name of any appointed managing agents and secretary of any residents' association or management company.
7 Why the vendors are selling, and how quickly they want to sell.
8 Whether the vendor wishes to approve the details before circulation.
9 Whether a 'for sale' board can be put on the property. This is an

important marketing tool as it identifies the property and the agent. Objections to boards may be overcome by discussing the style and position of the board on site with the vendors.

If a vendor has to sell, and wants a quick sale, then the vendor's solicitors should be asked to prepare a draft contract for sale and to obtain the deeds from the building society or bank. One argument for the so-called one-stop property service is that contracts can be pre-prepared by conveyancers in the same office or building as the vendor's agents, and can be in the hands of the purchaser's solicitor the day after an offer has been accepted by a vendor. This can save between four and eight weeks in the tedious process following subject to contract agreement.

SALES PARTICULARS

Having received verbal instructions to act in the sale of a property, the agent can return to the office to prepare the sales particulars. The following guidelines are based on material previously used by Momentum Training:

1 Particulars of sale are in fact a detailed advertisement; as such, the aim is to get the facts across to applicants. The details should read like a well-presented and interesting news-sheet. It is better that the applicant is pleasantly surprised, than feels the agent has over-exaggerated. Information should be correct, otherwise legal proceedings may be brought by a purchaser against the vendor and vendor's agent. Be factually correct if describing construction – never comment on condition, other than where the property is 'in need of modernization or improvement'.

2 Details should be kept as simple as possible, but descriptive words may be used to create pictures in the reader's mind, i.e. note the difference between 'Bedroom 4 – 10′ × 8′, 3 power points', and 'Bedroom 4 – 10′ × 8′, south-facing, sloping ceiling, 3 power points'.

3 Photographs of the house should show the house at its prettiest; be careful when using interior photographs, as these may alert criminals.

4 The height of principal rooms and the direction the rooms face may be relevant for some properties.

5 Lay out and particulars floor by floor – or the way most people walk about the property – upper floors should begin at the top of the stairs and proceed clockwise.

6 Location maps should always be given out or attached to the details. The location must be clearly described with directions as to how to find the property.

7 Check the details very carefully. Copy should be checked for accuracy by the vendors before any are mailed out.

8 Make sure there are *no* spelling mistakes.

9 Check that all copies are legible and printed straight and within the printed guidelines.
10 Keep track of the number of particulars sent out, in order to prove to vendors how many were circulated.
11 Leave some copies of the particulars for the vendors to hand out at the property.
12 Include floor plans (not to scale) for complex properties.

The details should be simple and concise and should contain enough information for the prospective purchasers to decide whether or not they wish to inspect the property. A description of the property together with details of accommodation, location, viewing arrangements and price are crucial. The order in which this information is presented is a matter for debate, and every agent will have his or her own views, but it would seem sensible to follow the logical path of a prospective purchaser. All buyers want to know what it is, where it is and how much. If the answers to their questions are favourable, then an appointment to view will be requested. The details should begin with a clear photograph – preferably in colour – followed by a brief summary of the property, and the asking price. This can then be followed by a comment on the location and the viewing arrangements.

How much detail to include is again a matter for careful deliberation. An expensive, quality property will be described in more depth than a simple estate property. The details must be fair and not misleading. The Misrepresentation Act 1967, Trade Description Act 1968, Unfair Contract Terms Act, the Estate Agents Act 1979 and Property Misdescriptions Act 1991 all exist to protect the general public, and in the preparation of sales details and advertisements the agent must see that the codes expected in such legislation are followed. With today's technology, there is no excuse for poorly produced, badly written and misspelled details. The draft particulars should be sent to the vendors for approval, together with the agency agreement for signature.

At this stage the agent is in a position to market the property by advertising, by mailing details to applicants, insertions in property papers, by telephoning the 'five star' or 'hot' applicants, i.e. those who must buy, by display of photographs, and by placement of 'for sale' boards. On all these points office procedure needs to be followed, especially in multi-office practices and firms where details need to be held by all branches in a regional area.

There are two forms of advertising: free advertising in editorials, and paid advertising. A good agent will make maximum use of property editorials run in local newspapers by providing the editor with good copy for unusual or exciting properties. In such cases the news item may simply (with the permission of the owner) be confirmation that a well-known local person is moving. Normal advertisements in local newspapers are an advertisement for the property and for that agency. Each insert needs to be simple to understand, make sense when read out, and be eye-catching (if possible) and convey the facts. If not carefully handled, a page of property adverts can become a blur of repetitious statements under poor quality photographs badly printed. Vendors like to see that their property has been individually advertised. This can be achieved, even if it is one of twenty on a page, with the right choice of words to describe the property.

The Property Misdescriptions Act 1991 makes it a criminal offence to make a representation which is misleading or false. The Act applies to oral and written statements and to photographs and will also apply to plans, videos and any other method of signifying meaning. This places a more onerous burden on the agent to produce factually correct details. It should be noted that the current practice of asking the vendor to agree that the details are correct will not be sufficient in itself as a defence. To avoid committing an offence the agent will have to be able to demonstrate that in preparing the details all reasonable steps were taken and all due diligence was exercised. It is probable that a new form of wording will be developed to replace the standard misrepresentation statement included by most agents at the end of their sales details, but such statements will not remove the responsibility for compliance under the Act.

In future it will be an offence to apply a false or misleading description, whether orally or in writing to the following prescribed matters set out in the Property Misdescriptions (Specified Matters) Order 1992 No. 2834 (footnotes amended to provide consecutive referencing):

1 Location or address.

2 Aspect, view, outlook or environment.

3 Availability and nature of services, facilities or amenities.

4 Proximity to any services, places, facilities or amenities.

5 Accommodation, measurements or sizes.

6 Fixtures and fittings.

7 Physical or structural characteristics, form of construction or condition.

8 Fitness for any purpose or strength of any buildings or other structures on land or of land itself.

9 Treatments, processes, repairs or improvements or the effects thereof.

10 Conformity or compliance with any scheme, standard, test or regulations or the existence of any guarantee.

11 Survey, inspection, investigation, valuation or appraisal by any person or the results thereof.

12 The grant or giving of any award or prize for design or construction.

13 History, including the age, ownership or use of land or any building or fixture and the date of any alterations thereto.

14 Person by whom any building, (or part of any building), fixture or component was designed, constructed, built, produced, treated, processed, repaired, reconditioned or tested.

15 The length of time during which land has been available for sale either generally or by or through a particular person.

16 Price (other than the price at which accommodation or facilities are available and are to be provided by means of the creation or disposal of an interest in land in the circumstances specified in section 23(1)(a) and (b) of the Consumer Protection Act 1987(**a**) or Article 16(1)(a) and (b) of the Consumer Protection (NI) Order 1987(**b**) (which relate to the creation or disposal of certain interests in new dwellings)) and previous price.

17 Tenure or estate.

18 Length of any lease or of the unexpired term of any lease and the terms and conditions of a lease (and, in relation to land in Northern Ireland, any fee farm grant creating the relation of landlord and tenant shall be treated as a lease).

19 Amount of any ground-rent, rent or premium and frequency of any review.

20 Amount of any rent-charge.

21 Where all or any part of any land is let to a tenant or is subject to a licence, particulars of the tenancy or licence, including any rent, premium or other payment due and frequency of any review.

22 Amount of any service or maintenance charge or liability for common repairs.

23 Council tax payable in respect of a dwelling within the meaning of section 3, or in Scotland section 72, of the Local Government Finance Act 1992(**c**) or the basis or any part of the basis on which that tax is calculated.

24 Rates payable in respect of a non-domestic hereditament within the meaning of section 64 of the Local Government Finance Act 1988(**d**) or, in Scotland, in respect of lands and heritages shown on a valuation roll or the basis or any part of the basis on which those rates are calculated.

25 Rates payable in respect of a hereditament within the meaning of the Rates (Northern Ireland) Order 1977(e) or the basis or any part of the basis on which those rates are calculated.

26 Existence or nature of any planning permission or proposals for development, construction or change of use.

27 In relation to land in England and Wales, the passing or rejection of any plans of proposed building work in accordance with section 16 of the Building Act 1984(f) and the giving of any completion certificate in accordance with regulation 15 of the Building Regulations 1991(g).

28 In relation to land in Scotland, the granting of a warrant under section 6 of the Building (Scotland) Act 1959(h) or the granting of a certificate of completion under section 9 of that Act.

29 In relation to land in Northern Ireland, the passing or rejection of any plans of proposed building work in accordance with Article 13 of the Building Regulations (Northern Ireland) Order 1979(i) and the giving of any completion certificate in accordance with building regulations made under that Order.

30 Application of any statutory provision which restricts the use of land or which requires it to be preserved or maintained in a specified manner.

31 Existence or nature of any restrictive covenants, or of any restrictions on resale, restrictions on use, or pre-emption rights and, in relation to land in Scotland, (in addition to the matters mentioned previously in this paragraph) the existence or nature of any reservations or real conditions.

32 Easements, servitudes or wayleaves.

33 Existence and extent of any public or private right of way.

Notes:
(a) 1987 c.43.
(b) 1987 No. 2049 (N.I. 20).
(c) 1992 c.14.
(d) 1988 c.41.
(e) 1977 No. 2157 (N.I. 28).
(f) 1984 c.55.
(g) S.I. 1991/2768.
(h) 1959 c.24.
(i) 1979 No. 1709 (N.I. 16).

There is a feeling that these provisions will remove some of the 'colour' associated with sales particulars. This need not be the case, provided the details do not mislead or misrepresent. Nevertheless, there are still grey areas, in particular in respect of omissions; for example, could it be held to be misleading to include photographs of the rear of the property whilst omitting to show the front abutting a main road? The only guide is that a statement needs to be made before there can be an omission by silence. The agent's problem is that the seller will not be very happy if the particulars end up dissuading all potential buyers from visiting the property.

In other instances agents will have to be more careful in checking information provided by sellers and in drafting representations made in details.

'A new damp-proof course has been installed at the property' might be factually correct as far as it goes and as far as the seller and agent are concerned, but it could be held as misrepresenting the truth if only part of the property had been treated. To say that 'company X carried out damp-proof work to the property in 1990 and their inspector's report, receipt and guarantee can be inspected at the agent's office' should be a statement of fact.

Similarly, 'the property has been rewired' could be held to be misleading if in fact some wiring had not been renewed.

It is agreed that greater care will be needed where measurements or site areas are provided and these should be based on the RICS/ISVA Code of Measuring Practice.

Further information can be obtained from the National Association of Estate Agents, the RICS and the ISVA.

HANDLING THE SALE – NEGOTIATIONS

Having secured the agency instruction, some agents seem to spend the next few weeks waiting for a buyer to turn up. As there are so many agents it might seem reasonable to assume that this is all that is necessary, but a good agent will always be trying to increase the volume of sales handled and the rate of sales. Few agents have any factual evidence of how long it takes to sell a property, yet they will argue they are the experts. It seems so obvious for any salesman to keep a record of the product being sold and the rate of sale. Every door-to-door salesman and shopkeeper knows from observation and from ledger records which items sell easily and which have limited demand. An estate agent should be able to provide clients with the same service in relation to the different types of homes sold. If records are kept the agent can more readily monitor the market movement, which is an important factor for the correct pricing of the product. Getting the price right in the first place is the key to successful selling. The price must not be so high that it turns every buyer away, nor so low that it attracts everyone. An agent is more likely to get it right the more active he or she is in the market and the more care that is taken in maintaining records.

As soon as an agent takes on a property the 'hot' list and the applicants register must be checked to see if anyone is currently looking for a home of the type just inspected. This problem of matching applicants to properties is one that should concern agents, as it seems to vex applicants. Most of the systems evolved and used by agents are only capable of handling a restricted number of variables. Thus people seeking properties are asked to indicate the price range, the type of house, the number of bedrooms and the area. Unfortunately for most applicants these details are either forgotten and they receive details of every property on the market, or they are treated as absolutes, so that Mr X looking for a detached house up to £Y,000 never receives details of his ideal home because it is on the market at the lower figure of £X,000.

A number of firms of agents and computer companies have developed computer programs for improving this aspect of the agent's service. This means that instead of the agent having to work through a card index or whatever, the details of applicants seeking a house of the type described can be displayed on screen for perusal.

Occasionally, there will appear to be a perfect match, in which case the agent should contact that applicant immediately. This very rarely happens in practice because of the inefficient systems in most estate agents' offices, and a frivolous truism is that the last person to hear about a property is the person who ends up buying it.

Details should be circulated to all relevant registered applicants. There may be variations from an applicant's ideal in price, size, location, as few people end up in the home they want; most, regrettably, have to be satisfied with second or third best. Perfect matching in an imperfect market is rare; most purchases are a compromise but this fact should not be used as a reason for not trying.

A record needs to be kept of all telephone calls and enquiries for the property. Follow-up calls should be made to check the reaction of applicants to the property. This allows the agent to monitor response to the property and to its price in order to better advise the vendor; it also assists the agent in the search for the right property for that applicant. The vendor must also be encouraged to keep a record of visitors and their comments, if any, on the property.

After about two weeks and thereafter weekly, the agent must contact the vendor to compare notes and to review the position. There may be evidence to suggest that the price is too high or that the vendors are making it too difficult for applicants to view.

Although the agent is the agent for the vendor, it is essential to make every effort to encourage applicants to view and to make offers – for unless offers are made, there can be no sales or negotiations.

More attention is now being given by agents to the training of negotiators. To begin with, a negotiator needs motivation – the will to succeed in business; that motivation must be nurtured by the employer through education, encouragement and correct financial inducements. Negotiators must themselves undergo self-analysis to discover their good points and to correct their bad points. Amongst the attributes of a good negotiator are:

1 A sound business sense.
2 A good understanding of human nature.
3 A good personality.
4 Absolute loyalty to the client and the employer.
5 Punctuality and courtesy.
6 Good conventional dress sense.
7 The ability to gain the confidence of the vendor and applicants.
8 The ability to listen without being critical.
9 Patience.
10 Ability to solve problems.
11 Persistence and determination.
12 A willingness to plan carefully.
13 The courage to probe and check information – is the buyer really a cash buyer?
14 Tact and discretion.
15 Honesty and integrity.
16 The ability to see the hidden needs and reactions of purchaser and vendor.
17 High standards of business and professional ethics.
18 Decisiveness.
19 The ability to work clearly and rapidly under pressure.
20 Self-control.
21 Imagination – the art of always being able to answer questions. This comes from a sound knowledge of the property business, knowledge that enables the negotiator to overcome any objections or problems; for this the negotiator needs to acquire a knowledge of the Estate Agents Act, The Property Misdescriptions Act and other relevant consumer and property law, a knowledge of building construction, a detailed knowledge of the area and the local residential market, a knowledge of the legal and financial sides of buying and selling residential property, a knowledge of property insurance and good business contacts in the practice area.

Once the property has been taken on by the agent, attention must turn to the applicants, who are not clients, but customers for the client's property. A good negotiator is one who communicates well, listens attentively, asks the right questions and is able to help the applicant take the decision to buy, is totally knowledgeable about the property business and his/her client's products – the homes being offered for sale; and is capable of recognizing buying signals and knows when to stop talking and close the sale.

The first lesson for the negotiator is to learn how to ask applicants the right questions and how to listen to the answers. Anna Emmerton, former training officer for Reed Rains, lists the following questions as being some of those that an agent may need to ask an applicant, which can be extended with those from point 18 onwards:

1 Names of applicants (use their names whenever possible).
2 How soon do you need to move?
3 Would you mind telling me why you are thinking of moving?
4 Do you live in this area?
5 Is this your first visit to this area?
6 Where do you live now?
7 How long have you lived there?
8 How long have you been looking for a house?
9 Have you seen any properties you really like?
10 What stopped you from buying that property?
11 Mrs . . ., so that I can get a better picture of you and your family, would you mind taking a moment to describe your present home to me, and what you like and what you dislike about it.
12 Are there any features in your home that you would particularly like to see in your next home?
13 And anything you particularly don't want to see?
14 Are there any special requirements that you must have in your next home?
15 How much do you feel you will get from the sale of your present home?
16 Is it already on the market, or do you need some advice on selling it?
17 What price range had you been considering?
18 How much money do you want to put down (not the percentage – the actual figure)?
19 Why are you looking for another property?
20 Do you want a property that is ready to move into?
21 Are you looking for a family home – somewhere to live for the next ten to twenty years?
22 Are you looking for investment property?
23 Are you looking for a short-term stay – husband's job may mean another move?
24 Do you have children?
25 How many children do you have?
26 What are the ages of your children and their sex? (Separate bedrooms.)
27 Do you need extra accommodation for anyone else? (Granny flat.)
28 What is the minimum number of bedrooms you must have?
29 Exactly what accommodation do you need? (Need, not want.)
30 Do you want a new house?
31 Would you mind living in a house in a new development?

32 How many bathrooms do you need?
33 Is a dining room necessary?
34 Are you looking for a property that needs work done on it?
35 Do you want a garden? Do you enjoy gardening? (Small garden or large garden.)
36 Do you need outbuildings for your hobbies? (Stables, barns to work on old cars, boats, aircraft).
37 How many cars do you have? How many garages do you need?
38 Do you have animals?
39 Elderly people – are stairs important?
40 Do you need transport – bus routes for easy access to shops, hospitals, schools?
41 Where do you work? (Rush-hour problems.)
42 Will your children attend local schools or private schools? How will you transport them there?
43 What is the amount of mortgage you are capable of paying, i.e. monthly payments?
44 Have you been saving with a building society?
45 What is the name of your building society?
46 How long have you been saving with them?
47 How much have you saved?
48 Does your building society have any restrictions when making loans? (Some societies will not lend money on older properties, thatched etc.)

Many agents have developed their own applicants' questionnaires along similar lines. The questions are useful and if asked in an interested way encourage the applicants to talk about themselves and the kinds of property they are looking for; it is the answers that provide the negotiator with the clues to a possible successful sale. Negotiators must learn to listen carefully for clues to discover what are really the important features an applicant is seeking. Negotiators need a good memory for faces, as applicants do like to be addressed by their correct names.

A new applicant, particularly a 'hot' applicant, should be accompanied on his or her first tour of the area. An approach adopted by some agents is to draw up a shortlist of similar properties that might satisfy the applicant's requirements and to view them in ascending order of desirability, or to keep until last the property that seems to be so much better value for money. As a selling technique it can be successful, but would be regarded with suspicion by some professional agents. Pre-planning for accompanied viewing is necessary in order to point out the locational benefits, in order to approach from the best direction, preferably on the correct side of the road to suggest easy, simple direct access to the places considered important by the applicant, to go past the best private schools if the applicants are going to move young children to local private schools and to arrange the visits in an orderly manner to fix the benefits of each in the applicant's mind. Planned sensibly, the personal comparisons made by the applicants will become a self-fulfilling successful sale.

Accompanied viewing also helps the agent to monitor the applicant's reaction to areas, to properties and to prices.

There are further skills for the negotiator to acquire when accompanying applicants. On arrival at the property the negotiator must take control; it is wrong to let the vendor show applicants around the property; if the vendor is out the negotiator must remain within view of the applicants at all times for security reasons and to listen for buying signals. If the property is empty, it will be necessary to overcome negative feelings: 'Try to imagine the property redecorated with new carpets and your own furniture', 'Imagine this room in the winter with a big fire burning in that inglenook'. If a negotiator knows that a property is going to be empty before it is marketed, then a folio of photographs can be taken to show the property as it looked fully furnished.

Since the disappearance of the young negotiator Suzy Lamplugh, it has become a prerequisite to ask applicants if they can identify themselves and for the negotiator to leave precise details with his/her secretary, receptionist or colleagues, and to check back to the office after viewing. Female negotiators and juniors should carry personal alarms.

Applicants moving to an area may have to adjust their views of their 'ideal home' once they have come to terms with the area and local values. The good negotiator must be a witness to this adjustment in 'hot' cases, to help the applicant make that adjustment. The negotiator must learn how to overcome objections without misrepresenting the client or the property. Most properties have good and bad features, and when viewed by a couple will be seen differently by each. Asking the right question may identify the negative factors preventing one or other of the applicants from saying 'Yes'. Buyers who offer objections are not implying that they won't buy, merely that they have not yet been convinced that they should buy – questions such as 'If that problem could be overcome, would you be interested?' may give the opening for negotiation.

If applicants cannot be accompanied then they should be persuaded to call back at the office to discuss the properties visited; if that is not possible the negotiator must follow up by telephone. A 'hot' applicant should not be lost to another agent.

The young negotiator should pre-prepare the questions to ask when telephoning an applicant. There are at least two scenarios. The first is where the applicant has found a property through another agent – this is not a no/no situation. The response is not, 'Oh right, I will take your name off our books', but 'Oh I am pleased, do you mind telling me what you have decided to buy . . . and was that within your price range . . . well that is good news, I hope all proceeds satisfactorily and if I or my firm can help in any other way you have only to ring.' The second is where they are still looking; here it is important to back-check on properties they have seen to try and identify what was wrong in order to try and fulfil their requirements.

In due course an applicant will make an offer. If it is for the full asking price and it is the only offer, then the agent has little choice other than to recommend to the vendor that the offer be accepted. If there are several interested parties at the asking price it may be necessary to assess who is most likely to complete within a reasonable period, or to go back and explain the position and take higher offers and/or final offers by a specified date. Several offers at the asking price means that the property may have been offered at too low a price. If an offer below the asking price is made within a few days of the property going on the market then the agent may feel that the vendor should wait to see if any other offers are made during the following two to three weeks. The danger here is that if none are made and the agent has to go back to the original offeror, they may submit a lower offer. In any event it is essential and a matter of law that all offers are put to the client in writing. The circumstances in each case will differ, and rarely can an agent be expected to have estimated the price to the nearest pound. A marginal reduction is acceptable and might be considered as part of the bargaining processes within the property market. The Undesirable Practices Order has provided agents with a code of practice in relation to offers. This means that agents can no longer legally use some of the so-called negotiating tactics such as: 'I am afraid there is a higher offer in on the property' when in reality there are no offers; 'We have received a cash offer', when the cash depends upon the successful sale of another property.

Agents are agents for the sellers and should use their best (legally permissible) endeavours to secure the best offer. They should not indicate to applicants the level of offer that might be acceptable unless the client has indicated their consent to this. Nor can an agent withhold or otherwise refuse to submit an offer unless they have clear written instructions not to submit offers below a certain price.

The following are just a few suggestions for residential negotiators made by Anna Emmerton and Derek Porter (former proprietor of *Property Forum*) in their sales negotiator programmes.

> Vendors must leave all negotiations to the agent – the agent's potential to negotiate will be undermined if the vendor gives any indication that an offer might be accepted.
>
> The agent's loyalty is to the vendor.
>
> The agent's responsibility is to obtain the best possible price.
>
> Never submit an offer to the vendor in front of the purchaser.
>
> If the offer may not be acceptable to the vendor discuss it in person, not over the telephone.

Prepare a list of points before submitting an offer.

Never begin a negotiation if the discussion is likely to be interrupted.

Telephone negotiations save time and produce quick answers, but they can go wrong because too much information is exchanged too quickly; the phone demands a decision before the discussion is completed and so it tends to force the vendor to say 'no' without considering all aspects of the offer; omissions are common; be careful that all points of the offer are included, such as fixtures and fittings. Negotiators often blurt out an offer before establishing whether the vendor is ready to discuss the matter.

The agent should try to gauge the vendor's reaction by assessing their own reactions to such an offer.

An agent should not apologize if the offer is too low, nor should the agent try to justify a low offer by criticizing the property.

There is no such thing as a 'final offer'; it is usually negotiable. If a vendor accepts an offer the agent should not proceed until all details are confirmed in writing.

If an offer is turned down, is the vendor prepared to make a counter-proposal?

The agent must discuss the difference, the purchaser's reasons, the possibility of persuading the purchaser to raise an offer, the possibility of waiting for another offer, and the problem of meeting any sale deadlines.

When analysing an offer, the agent should consider deadlines from both parties' points of view; does either party need to move by a certain date, are there essential repairs to be done, is the house empty, are there any ongoing outgoings to be met, will bridging finance be necessary if the vendor defers acceptance, can a better agreement be reached on fixtures and fittings, is it a cash offer, has the purchaser a property to sell?

The agent must not encourage a purchaser to make a silly offer.

The agent must not disclose the vendor's lowest price to the purchaser.

The agent should always be looking to improve upon a purchaser's offer – 'I cannot say what the vendor's reaction will be but if it is not acceptable can you go a little higher?' On a face-to-face basis most purchasers will reveal that a higher offer is possible.

The agent could indicate to the purchaser that another £1,000 is only another 30p a day on the mortgage.

The agent should check the purchaser's position before submitting an offer, e.g. is there a property to be sold, is a mortgage necessary, is it subject to survey, does it include fixtures and fittings, when could the purchaser complete, are they being moved by their firm?

Prepare the purchaser for a refusal by the vendor.

The agent must know the property well enough and the market well enough to judge whether the purchaser will seek to renegotiate at a later date once the property has been surveyed and/or inspected by the mortgage valuer. It is poor advice to recommend an under offer on the grounds of repairs and conditions if five weeks later the purchaser comes back with a further reduction in the offer because of further defects in the property.

When an offer is made subject to survey the agent should encourage the purchaser to have the survey undertaken as quickly as possible. Some purchasers will delay this until a few days before exchange of contracts to use the then urgency to secure a price reduction. Such tactics again leave the agent in the difficult position of advising the vendor as to whether they should call the purchaser's bluff at the risk of losing the sale. For this reason the agent should continue to market the property even after the offer is accepted, in order to maintain some pressure on the purchaser.

DEPOSITS

As a further token of goodwill it was customary for agents to ask buyers for a pre-contract deposit. An agent who has a personal interest in a sale cannot seek or receive a pre-contract or contract deposit (s.21(4) Estate Agents Act). All pre-contract deposits or deposits paid on exchange of contracts must be held in a Client Account (Estate Agents (Accounts) Regulations 1981), and such accounts must be with the Bank of England, the Post Office, Trustee Savings Bank, banks or building societies. Pre-contract deposits are held on behalf of the buyer and not as stakeholder, and are returnable to the buyer on demand. Contract deposits are generally held by solicitors but when the agent is to hold contract deposits this should be provided for in the contract terms and should be held as stakeholder or as agent for the vendor.

Under the account regulations, agents holding deposit monies other than as stakeholder must account for interest to any person entitled to the money. But interest is not payable on sums of less than £500 or when interest earned is less than £10. The general rules on interest are that on pre-contract deposits the interest is payable to the buyer, on deposits held as part of the contract interest is payable to the vendor if held as agent for the vendor, or to the agent if held as stakeholder and so provided for in the contract.

The administrative difficulties and the accounts regulations relating to deposits deter most agents from accepting deposits.

The proper time for a deposit and when indeed one must generally be paid, is when contracts are exchanged, for at that point the purchaser's solicitor has confirmed the vendor's title to the property. If a vendor is handling the legal side of the sale personally, purchasers and or their solicitors may be reluctant to hand over the traditional 10 per cent, today more customarily 5 per cent, to the vendor on exchange of contract. In such cases the agent may be asked to hold the contract deposit as stakeholder.

INSTRUCTING SOLICITORS

As soon as an offer has been accepted subject to contract, the agent should instruct the vendor's solicitors. Some agents will leave it at that, but a common practice is to send similar details to the purchaser's solicitor, with copies to the vendor and purchaser. Again, most agents have a standard form or letter of instruction which details the address of the property, the vendor's name and address, the vendor's solicitors, the purchaser's name and address, the purchaser's solicitors, the agreed price subject to contract, the amount of any deposit paid by the purchaser, whether sold with vacant possession, if not then brief details of any tenancies are included; and whether completion is to be by a certain date. It is also sensible for an agent to arrange with the vendor for the agent's fees to be settled directly by the vendor's solicitors on completion of the sale.

SALE TO COMPLETION

The agent's work is not completed merely because instructions have been given to solicitors. The agent should continue to monitor the sale and to maintain contact with all parties. The agent may help the process by referring the applicant to financial advisors to arrange a mortgage (specific advice can only be given if the agent is registered under the Financial Services Act). In addition the agent should be available to help with access to the property for surveys and with any other matters such as identification plans.

The agent may be called upon to sell the purchaser's own property. If financial or other related services such as this are to be offered to prospective purchasers then the agent must have made provision for this possibility in the agency agreement. Specific services for a buyer must have been detailed at the time the offer was submitted in writing to the vendor.

The subject of conflict of interest has been debated at length by the RICS and other professional bodies. Technically, having introduced a buyer, an agent has fulfilled the contractual obligation to the seller, but many professionally qualified agents would hold that to offer any other form of services to the buyer could only give rise to conflicts of interest. In practice, subject to compliance with the Estate Agents Act, there is nothing to prevent other services being provided.

The most complex situation can arise with some of the agencies owned by financial institutions. Here a purchaser could arrange a mortgage, obtain a mortgage valuation and home buyer's report all through subsidiaries of the same holding company through whom the house is to be purchased.

When the agent is advised or learns that contracts are about to be exchanged he/she will normally prepare the fee account and forward it to the vendor's solicitors together with the balance of any deposit monies held. From the agent's point of view it is better to submit the account to the vendor's solicitors than to the vendor – the solicitors being able to settle the account out of the sale proceeds.

Many agents can also help the vendor find a new home either locally, nationally or internationally through one or other of the national and international agency links. The agent's firm may also be assisting the vendor by carrying out surveys of the new home being purchased.

COMPLETION

On completion of the sale the agent is once more free to think of his/her own business future which will, in the long run, depend upon maintaining good business relations with everyone who has had dealings with that practice. A letter should be sent wishing vendors well in their new home or new venture and some attention can now be given to the purchaser.

The extent to which, within his professional code of conduct, an agent is able or willing to participate in after-sales services depends upon a number of factors too complex to consider in this book. Suffice it to say that nothing in life is free, so that if an agent gives something to a purchaser it has probably been paid for out of the vendor's fee, a fact which raises moral issues. If the agent sends a 'welcome to your new home' gift to the vendor, he has almost certainly paid for it out of his fee commission. Nevertheless, such gifts are given, and if done tastefully can be acceptable.

Agents may certainly hand over house keys in a nice leather key case with the agent's name on the inside and the purchaser's initials on the outside. Nor should purchasers have to discover for themselves when the refuse is collected, where the stopcock is on the rising main, where the late-night grocer's is, or where the local doctors and dentists have their surgeries. The agent can easily visit the vendor shortly before they move and obtain answers to all these day-to-day questions, including the names of the next-door neighbours. A suitable 'welcome to your new home' card can be left enclosing all this essential local information for the purchasers.

THE AGENT'S POSITION IN LAW

A number of references have so far been made to the Estate Agents Act 1979, to other Acts of Parliament and to the legal responsibility of an agent, so it would seem sensible to end this section on residential agency with a brief summary of the most important aspects of the law that affect the work of the residential agent.

From the point of view of the day-to-day work of the agent, the most important sections of the Estate Agents Act 1979 are those dealing with clients' money (Sections 12–16), Section 18 dealing with the information an agent must give a client before the client enters into an agency contract, and Section 21 dealing with the disclosure of personal interest. In brief, any money paid over to an agent as stakeholder or to hold as a pre-contract deposit must without undue delay be paid into an account separate from the firm's account, called a clients' account. For safety this will often be with a different bank, but under the Act it must be held with a bank or other specified body. Only agents who have entered into a 'bonding' or other insurance protection arrangement may hold deposit moneys – this is to protect the parties concerned should the holder fail to account properly for the money. The RICS and ISVA have established special schemes to provide such protection. Finally on deposits the Act requires an agent to account properly and, when required, to account for interest earned on deposit sums.

Section 18 has already been considered. This section has given rise to much debate and has been subject to action by the Office of Fair Trading where they felt an agent had not complied with the letter of the law. It is strongly recommended that for simplicity an agent, except when selling by auction, should operate on an overall inclusive fee basis; when the agreement is on the basis of fee plus expenses, extreme care must be taken to comply with Section 18 in setting out the nature of the expenses and precisely how they will be incurred and charged. Further, that the vendor be asked to enter into a formally drafted agency contract.

Section 21 deals with the question of disclosure of personal interest. Agents are bound by their professional codes of conduct to disclose any interest they may have in a property but this section makes it a legal requirement to disclose under certain conditions:

S.21(1) A person who is engaged in estate agency work (in this section referred to as an 'estate agent') and has a personal interest in any land shall not enter into negotiations with any person with respect to the acquisition or disposal by that person of any interest in that land until the estate agent has disclosed to that person the nature and extent of his 'personal interest in it'.

The section also covers the case where the agent could have an interest after the transaction and makes it clear that it applies equally to the case where an agent is negotiating on his own behalf. Nor can an estate agent seek or receive a contract or pre-contract deposit in respect of a property in which he has or will have a personal interest. The expression 'personal interest' extends this responsibility to disclose situations involving employees, employers, associates, and relations. Breach of this section will not lead to criminal proceedings, but may be used by the Office of Fair Trading in other actions against an agent or firm.

Two situations are likely to arise. The first, under Section 21, is when an agent wishes to sell his or her own property or that of a relative or 'connected person'. In such cases, either the instruction should be referred elsewhere with an explanation, or the particulars must carry a suitable disclosure under the Estate Agents Act 1979. This declaration of a personal interest must also be made to any party making an offer and to a prospective purchaser's solicitor.

The second occasion is when an agent, associate, relative or other connected person wishes to purchase a property in respect of which the firm or practice has been instructed to act as selling agent. In these cases the interest must be declared and the vendor advised to contact another agent.

A duly appointed agent will have a contractual responsibility to the client. Normally an agent is instructed to sell a property and therefore in most cases the client (principal) will be the vendor. Occasionally an agent may be appointed to find a property, in which case the agent is acting for a specific purchaser. As agent for the vendor an agent must act in accordance with the agency contract, hence the advisability of setting this out in a simple written form. The agent must act honestly in the best interests of the vendor and must not accept bribes, secret discounts or commissions without the consent of the vendor.

The agent must comply at all times with the provisions of the Estate Agents Act 1979, particularly s.18 and s.21. The agent needs to exercise reasonable care and skill in carrying out the agency instruction. The agent must not use information gained for his or her or another client's benefit without the client's consent, nor must any information be disclosed to third parties.

Over a number of years a large number of cases have been heard in the courts concerning the rights and duties of principals and their agents, the relationship between them and third parties. The details are fully written up in *The Law of Estate Agency and Auctions* by J.R. Murdoch. Anyone intending to practise as an agent in his/her own name or in partnership is strongly advised to read Murdoch's text. For negotiators, the important points to adhere to are compliance with the Estate Agents Act and the Property Misdescriptions Act, compliance with all office procedures, compliance with the professional codes of conduct of the RICS, ISVA or NAEA, and at all times to remember that the client is the person paying the fee, i.e. the vendor, and that no reward of any kind should be accepted from any other party, to treat all information in strictest confidence between the client and the firm and to declare any interest.

The Unfair Contract Terms Act 1977 applies to all contracts such as the contract to carry out a valuation or to sell a house.

The Misrepresentation Act 1967 deals comprehensively with the subject of misrepresentation, and since 1967 almost every agent has included a disclaimer clause, often in small print, at the bottom of their sales details. A typical clause might read:

> While these particulars are believed to be correct, they are not guaranteed by the vendor or the vendor's agents and neither does any person have authority to make or give any representation or warranty on their behalf. Prospective purchasers must satisfy themselves by inspection or otherwise as to the correctness of each statement contained in their particulars. The particulars do not constitute, or form any part of, an offer or a contract.

The RICS have advised their members to use the full caveat approved by counsel in 1985 and to see that it is displayed and printed in the same size print as used for the sales details. These are set out in full under Sales By Auction, p. 103.

If any purchasers feel that they have suffered a loss due to misrepresentation by an agent, they have to prove that 'they had entered into a contract; that they had done so after a misrepresentation had been made, as a result of which they have suffered loss; and that the misrepresentation albeit incorrect, would have given rise to damages if made fraudulently'.

This legislation is primarily to allow a purchaser to rescind a contract which that purchaser was induced to enter into by a false statement made by the vendor. However, it will not always be clear without going to court whether or not statements were made falsely and further, if not made falsely, whether or not they nevertheless amount to a sufficient misstatement or misrepresentation for the contract to be rescinded. In other cases, a court may award damages for innocent misrepresentation. In a recent case, damages of £3,000 were awarded following the sale of a flat. The dispute arose over representations made by the vendor in respect of the service charges which amounted to £800 a year and not the indicated £250.

The agent is not party to the contract but may be liable in negligence to the vendor if a successful claim for misrepresentation succeeded against a vendor arising out of statements made by the vendor's agent. The position is complicated by the fact that some solicitors now ask for an assurance from a vendor that the agent's details are correct in every detail. For this and other reasons, agents are advised to avoid all representation in the details and to provide prospective purchasers with factual information only, to check that that information is correct and to have on file a record from the vendor to the effect that the details as prepared were acceptable to and approved by the vendor.

The provisions of the Property Misdescriptions Act 1991 make it an offence to make a false or misleading statement about a prescribed matter (see p. 81), and in this context an 'omission' may be a misleading statement. This new legislation alters the position relating to misrepresentation from the viewpoint of the agent. If the Trading Standards Officer believes an agent to be in breach of the Act they may investigate the position and bring an action against the agent. On summary conviction a fine not exceeding £5,000 can be levied by a magistrates court. There is no limit on the level of fine that can be levied in a crown court.

The Estate Agents (Specified Offences) (No. 2) Amendment order makes an offence under the 1991 Act a specified offence under the 1979 Act and hence a proven (mis)representation could lead to a banning order under the 1979 Act. But none of this will help, or compensate, a buyer who believes they have suffered a loss due to a false or misleading statement, other than to strengthen any possible action they may have under the Misrepresentation Act 1967. For this reason the author believes that it will remain common practice for agents to include a disclaimer clause, reworded in the light of the 1991 Act, as a warning to buyers.

The 1991 Act should improve agency practice and by so doing reduce the number of complaints about sales details and generally lead to an improvement in the factual quality of such details. The following points should be noted:

1 False representations will have to be false to a material degree – trivial matters are unlikely to lead to prosecution
2 Representations may be in writing or conveyed in any other form
3 An omission may be held to be a misleading statement
4 Information provided by the vendor or any other party must be verified by the agent – the agent must take reasonable steps and exercise due diligence
5 Caveats or disclaimer clauses will not exempt an agent from his liability under the Act
6 All misleading or false statements made inadvertently must be corrected as soon as the agent becomes aware of or is notified of the error.

Agents will need to operate tighter procedures if they are to comply with this legislation. In many cases new quality control procedures will need to be developed for checking printed details but it will be difficult to establish training and practice procedures to avoid offences being made orally by employees.

Finally an agent must always act within the law. In particular they must never discriminate in their dealings with actual or prospective employees, buyers or sellers on the grounds of sex, race, nationality, colour, ethnic origin or any other grounds (see Code of Practice in non-rented (owner-occupied) housing published by the Commission for Racial Equality).

The Office of Fair Trading in their July 1991 *Estate Agency Guide* provide a summary of 'all the things which are required of you (the agent) by law'; these are reprinted in the following table:

'You should:	Section	Regulation or Order
check that you know who your connected persons are	ss.21, 31, 32	1991 no.859 reg 1(2) 1991 no.1032 art 1(2)
check that you know if you or a connected person will receive a benefit from another person offering services	s.18(4) 2.3(1)(d)	1991 no.859 reg 2 1991 no.1032 art 2(b) and sch 2 para 2(a)
provide advance written information about fees and charges	s.18(1),(2) and (4)	1991 no.859 reg 3 and 4
make written statements of when fees become payable	s.18(2)	1991 no.859 reg 3 and 4
provide written information about changes to fees and charges	s.18(3)	1991 no.859 reg 4
give written definitions of terms in contracts or agreements	s.18(4)	1991 no.859 reg 5 and 6
tell clients in writing if you or a connected person or another person will offer services to a potential buyer	s.18(4)	1991 no.859 reg 2
set up procedures so you know whether there is a personal interest to disclose including that of connected persons	s.21	1991 no.1032 art 2(a) and sch 1
tell all potential buyers in writing about any existing personal interest (including that of connected persons)	s.21(1)	1991 no.1032 art 2(a) and sch 1

You should:	Section	Regulation or Order
tell clients in writing about possible future personal interests (including those of connected persons)	s.21(2)	1991 no.1032 art 2(a) and sch 1
check, as far as possible, that first time and cash buyers are as they say	s.3(1)(d)	1991 no.1032 art 2(c) and sch 3 para 1
promptly send written information to the client when you receive offers	s.3(1)(d)	1991 no. 1032 art 2(c) and sch 3 para 2
tell the client whenever the buyer asks you or a connected person to provide services	s.3(1)(d)	1991 no.1032 art 2(b) and sch 2 para 2
make sure all buyers are treated the same, regardless of their value to your business	s.3(1)(d)	1991 no. 1032 art 2(b) and sch 2 para 1
open client account(s) to hold deposits	s.14	1981 no.1520 reg 6
provide receipts for deposits with all the necessary details	s.14	1981 no.1520 reg 6
pay interest on deposits if appropriate	s.15	1981 no.1520 reg 7
keep records of money paid into and out of client accounts	s.14	1981 no.1520 reg 6
arrange for an annual audit of client accounts	s.14	1981 no.1520 reg 8
be able to produce the latest auditor's report for Trading Standards Officers on demand'	s.14	1981 no.1520 reg 8

Source: Estate Agency Guide (1991)

Chapter 6

Sales by auction

In addition to the need to comply with the Estate Agents Act and other legislation, auctioneers need to note that sales by auction are covered by the Auctioneers Acts of 1845, Sale of Land by Auction Act 1867, Auctions (Bidding Agreements) Act 1927 and Auctions (Bidding Agreements) Act 1969.

Once the decision to sell a property by auction has been made, the agent must draw up a timetable or programme, which must be adhered to if the sale is to be a success. A time and place for the auction must first be agreed with the vendors. The date selected must be checked to ensure that there is no clash with major national or important local events, both of which could prevent prospective purchasers from attending the auction or arriving on time. The time for the auction should be determined having regard to the distance and type of transport most likely to be used by purchasers. The auction itself can take place at the property or at a local hotel or indeed at some prestigious location, which in itself will attract interest. This decision is important as the room must be large enough to accommodate everyone attending, but not so large that people feel exposed and inhibited. The auctioneer must therefore exercise skill and experience at this planning stage having regard to the property and its suitability for sale by auction. If the property is being sold by auction to satisfy beneficiaries, trustees and the like but in itself would not normally be sold by auction, then it may be better to arrange for its sale at a collective auction either locally or through one of the top London residential auctioneers.

The agent must ensure that the vendor fully understands the nature and implications of a sale by auction – in particular that, subject to a reserve price, the property will be knocked down/sold to the highest bidder at the auction, that a memorandum of sale will be signed at the auction and copies exchanged creating a binding contract, and that completion will occur on the date specified in the sale conditions contained in the auction details or book. If the sale is with vacant possession then vacant possession must be given on that date.

Having agreed the date of the auction, which should be some eight to twelve weeks after agreeing the terms and conditions of the auction (agency) agreement, the auctioneer can prepare the timetable for the marketing campaign. This planning is essential if maximum use is to be made of the time to advertise and market the property adequately, to allow purchasers to view and to allow time for interested parties to complete all their surveys, legal enquiries and financial arrangements. The first step is to prepare preliminary details of the property and preliminary advertising to alert the market and interested parties to the fact that the property is to be offered for sale by auction on the given date. For quality properties it is usually possible to obtain editorial commentary in one or other of the national papers. In special cases the auctioneer may feel that it is better to do nothing until the final auction particulars are prepared, in order to make a single significant launch of the marketing campaign.

Preparation of sales details is more complex than for sale by private treaty, as the details include the conditions of the sale and the contractual memorandum of sale, which can be signed by the auctioneer to create a binding contract on behalf of the highest bidder.

Auction particulars are a joint exercise between the auctioneer and the vendor's solicitors. The details or particulars of the property are referred to in the conditions of sale and become part of the contract, so need to be prepared with great care.

Auction particulars may be produced in a similar format to normal sales details and for preliminary details they will look very similar; however for a quality property, that is a property which for one reason or another is going to attract interest and is going to produce an exciting occasion, it is customary to produce a more expensive brochure or booklet.

An auction book should contain colour photographs and plans which should be prepared by professional photographers and qualified technicians in order to maintain the image of a quality property throughout the book.

The auctioneers have the choice of a plain cover with a simple statement of facts or of displaying on the front a full-colour photograph. This is a matter of choice given the nature of the property; however, a full colour photograph with the name of the company or firm and the name of the property is very effective and can also be used for display purposes. The book itself should contain:

1 A location plan based upon the Ordnance Survey showing clearly the principal access routes to the property.
2 On a facing page the address of the property, a brief description with summary of the accommodation, land, other buildings etc. and a clear statement that it is for sale by auction with the day, place and time for the auction. This should also specify viewing by appointment only, and give the name and address of the auctioneers.

3 The main content of the book consists of the preliminary and descriptive information. It can include a brief history of the property but essentially and simply stating what it is, where it is and how to get to it.

4 The next section is the property itself; this must be factually correct and if the description is to include authoritative statements as to the architect, interior designer, landscape architect, then the facts must be checked. (See also Property Misdescriptions Act 1991.)

5 The third section lists under general remarks and stipulations all matters that the auctioneer and vendor feel potential buyers should be made aware of; this would include details on services, rights and easements, boundaries, fixtures and fittings, names and addresses of local authorities, water authority etc., details of outgoings such as council tax, planning, arbitration in the event of disputes. The remarks and stipulations will be deemed to form part of the contract. A standard misrepresentation clause will be included at this point along the lines of:

> Messrs X, Y and Z for themselves and for vendors or lessors of this property whose agents they are give notice that:
> (i) the particulars are set out as a general outline only for the guidance of intended purchasers or lessees, and do not constitute, nor constitute part of, an offer or contract;
> (ii) all descriptions, dimensions, reference to condition and necessary permissions for use and occupation, and other details are given without responsibility and any intending purchasers or tenants should not rely on them as statements or representations of fact but must satisfy themselves by inspection or otherwise as to the correctness of each of them;
> (iii) no person in the employment of Messrs X, Y and Z has any authority to make or give any representation or warranty whatever in relation to this property.

Although such statements are always made, such provisos are unlikely to be of any value in the case of statements made knowingly and fraudulently to induce a purchaser to make a bid. Nor do they exempt the agent in any way from the need to comply at all times with the Estate Agents Act and the Property Misdescriptions Act.

6 The fourth section contains the general conditions of sale prepared by the vendor's solicitors together with any special conditions of sale. These include information on title, deposit, interest.

7 The final section is the memorandum of sale. This will be completed after the auction by the successful bidder and/or auctioneer.

A detailed site plan is generally included at the end of the book and most importantly under the stipulations the vendor and or agent must reserve the right to bid and must indicate that the property will be sold subject to an undisclosed reserve price. It is generally held that an auctioneer bidding on behalf of the vendor up to the reserve cannot make two successive bids on behalf of the vendor. The skill of the auctioneer is in persuading interested purchasers to start the bidding at sensible figures, preferably above the reserve price.

As well as circulating the auction details the auctioneer must use his/her experience in recommending and placing advertisements in the right paper and journals to expose the property to that segment of the market most likely to be interested.

The costs of selling by auction are greater than when selling by private treaty, and all these costs as well as the commission (fee) basis must be clearly set out in the agreement between agent and vendor to sell the property by auction.

The auctioneer needs to monitor the process throughout the period up until the auction itself. The auctioneer needs to know who has asked for details, who has viewed the property, who has had the property surveyed, who has consulted the vendor's solicitors, who has made an offer before the auction. All this helps the auctioneer to gauge the market interest in the property and helps the auctioneer in the difficult task of advising on the reserve price.

Before the auction itself the auctioneer must make sure that the room is booked, that there will be adequate seating, that the vendor's solicitor has noted it in his diary and will be there, that there will be sufficient members of staff available on the day to act as clerks and to help on the day, that if permissible and necessary, 'To the Auction' notices have been posted, that reminders have gone out to everyone who viewed the property, that an appointment has been made to reinspect the property before the auction and to speak to the vendors to obtain their written agreement as to the reserve price.

Shortly before the day of the auction the auctioneer should contact those applicants who have shown the greatest interest to confirm that they will be coming to the auction and to remind them gently that if successful they will need a bankers draft for 10 per cent of the price, and that they will need subsequently to insure the property. With this information the auctioneer is armed with enough 'hope' to advise on a reserve.

The auctioneer's responsibility for the security of an empty property is the same when selling by auction as when selling by private treaty, particularly if it is a period property and furnished. In these cases all viewings must be accompanied and the keys must never be handed over to anyone. A period property stripped of the period features 24 hours before the auction can destroy all the auctioneer's careful planning.

On the day of the auction, if held at the property or near to the property, the auctioneer will reinspect to check on precisely what is being sold. It is also important to check with other staff and with the vendor and vendor's solicitor to see whether there are any matters that need to be brought to the attention of the prospective purchasers that are not covered in the auction details. The reserve must now be agreed with the vendors in writing.

The auctioneer will be accompanied by his clerk, by the vendor's solicitor and clerk. The auctioneer opens the auction by welcoming everyone, introducing himself (herself), the vendor's solicitor and the clerks, and explaining their role. The participants are reminded of the purpose of the auction, the nature of the auction and that whoever the property is knocked down to after the third offering will be expected to sign the memorandum and to hand over the 10 per cent deposit. The auctioneer then proceeds to describe the property being offered, to restate that it is offered subject to an undisclosed reserve, to bring to their attention any changes to the details or conditions of sale and to ask if there are any questions. The auctioneer must control the latter, as some participants endeavour to create an upset by emphasizing or asking questions on difficult legal points – where possible the auctioneer must indicate that such matters are quite clearly stated and will have been checked by prospective purchasers' solicitors before that day.

It is then for the auctioneer to offer the property and to try and obtain a realistic bid. Normally a suggestion is made with the hope that someone will offer at or around that figure. If the auctioneer is aware that there are several people in the room who have shown interest at around £X,000 then it is worth starting below that level to try and induce an offer. When there are no willing bidders the auctioneer (provided the right to bid on behalf of the vendor has been reserved) may make a bid on behalf of the vendor, but only where there is a reserve price. This practice is perfectly permissible, but there does appear to be a conflict of opinion as to whether the auctioneer could, for example, make consecutive bids up to the point where a genuine bid is made; one view is that to do so could amount to an offence under the Theft Act 1968. It is, however, clear that it is illegal for the vendor or the auctioneer to use a number of 'puffers' to raise the bids to the reserve level. It is submitted that the auctioneer may bid on behalf of the vendor against a purchaser up to the reserve. Great care is needed in case by accident the last bid by the auctioneer proves to be the final bid and by accident is the reserve figure or above! The auctioneer must also try and set a sensible pace, reducing only as the need arises from £5,000 bids to £1,000 bids to £500 bids. If the participants slow the process down too soon the excitement is lost and the auctioneer can find the bidding falling away.

Once the reserve has been passed and in order to encourage further bids the auctioneer will state that the 'property is in the market' or 'I am here to sell'; this indicates that the reserve price has been exceeded, but no one knows by how much. A number of issues arise under the Estate Agents

Act, the most difficult to resolve being that of 'personal interest'. The extreme would be the case where the auctioneer was personally interested in the property as owner or as potential buyer. The obvious solution is to decline the instructions and/or arrange for another auctioneer to conduct the sale. In these circumstances, disclosure must be made in compliance with s.21.

Similarly if the property belongs to an employee or connected person, or if an employee or connected person is interested in purchasing the property, then the auctioneer must take great care to comply with the letter of the law. The position of an auctioneer confronted in the auction room by the unexpected bid of an employee could pose problems of compliance. However, the public nature of the auction, coupled with proper notice in the conditions of sale and notification of the possibility to the vendor, should cover most eventualities.

When it looks as if a final offer has been made the auctioneer will offer it for the first time, the second time, and then knock it down to the highest bidder. Care is essential at this point, as some bidders use this psychological point to enter the market for the first time; it comes as a shock to the party who previously felt confident. So during this phase the auctioneer and clerk must watch every gesture in the room. When knocked down the successful bidder is asked to come forward to sign the memorandum and to hand over the deposit. The auctioneer thanks all participants.

Agents who act as auctioneers on a regular basis will work to an *aide-mémoire* so that at each stage of the process they can readily check that everything that should have been done has been done.

Chapter 7

Selling new homes

The new homes market is different to that for existing homes. In particular the sale of new homes on the larger residential developments is a very different form of marketing to the sale of an existing nineteenth-century terraced house.

Many new homes are sold by sales teams employed directly by the developer or on behalf of the developer by one of the major residential agencies.

The new homes market begins with market research to identify unsatisfied demand and developable sites. The two are continuing processes working in parallel to assist the developers in their aim to provide the right home in the right place at the right time at the right price. Success in this aim is measured by the speed with which units are reserved and by the response of the new home-owner to post-purchase market research. It is through such ongoing research that developers have identified the need for sheltered housing, executive housing, and flats for young professionals.

Marketing and market research are interlinked so that as research identifies demand and as designers create an acceptable design solution to satisfy that demand at the best possible market price, so the marketing team need to aim their marketing campaign at that segment to achieve success. The less alert developer follows the trend set by the market leaders, so that unsatisfied demand becomes an over-supply situation. For successful residential development the research and sales team must become part of the development team.

The new homes motto is 'sell to build' not 'build to sell'. The developer, having identified the market segment, expects initial sales to be agreed on the basis of plans and presentations. Not only does this reduce the developer's risk, it also stimulates interest in the scheme and encourages local and national press reporting which then assists in the sale of subsequent phases or similar schemes elsewhere.

The marketing of new homes depends upon the size of the scheme. In the case of a one-off infill site it may be best to defer marketing until the structure is complete so that buyers can see what that individually designed home looks like and so that the agent can assess its market price more accurately. At that stage the sale can be conducted along the lines of a normal private treaty sale.

In the case of developments of fifty or more, however, a full marketing campaign is necessary. If the researchers and designers have completed their work properly then the homes will sell so long as they and their benefits are brought to the attention of that market segment. This marketing campaign will include the naming of the development, the placement of attractive site boards, the production of attractive brochures, good advertising and a show property. In some cases, such as flat developments, a show flat may be created in site huts in order to convey the quality of finishes and fixtures during the construction.

Selling from plans, artists impressions, and specifications will need careful review by developers and agents acting for developers in the light of the Property Misdescription Act. Only when a specific unit is complete will it be possible to check the actual property against all the information previously provided to a purchaser when reserving a plot or unit.

Only at this point will the agent be aware of any discrepancies and only at this stage will the agent be able to correct any false or misleading representations. But there would appear to be a need for such a check to be made in respect of every unit completed. The most obvious issue will be if the actual measurements differ from those specified on the plans contained in sale particulars.

The creation of a show suite will in itself be a representation of what is on offer where property is being sold off plans.

The sales suite on a typical development will be linked to show home(s) in such a way that visitors can be welcomed and given literature, left then to view the show property and directed back to the sales suite for further discussion and/or information before departing. The sales team will have been trained and fully instructed on all aspects of the development. Amongst those viewing new homes there will be serious buyers, maybe buyers and those out for the afternoon. All can be useful sources of information, but the sales team must concentrate on the more probable buyer. Identification is a simple issue of asking the right questions and listening to the answers. These questions are in turn part of the ongoing market research to identify design faults and other criticisms of the show home.

The sales team must be readily identifiable with the developer and/or the developer's agent. Uniforms or distinguishing scarves and ties seem to be the preferred solution. The sales team must be fully briefed in all aspects of the scheme and the area and trained to sell benefits, not features, but to use the features to sell the benefits, and to be in a position to answer all normal technical questions about the development.

Derek Porter of *Property Forum* considers that to be a successful new homes salesperson the individual needs to be taught or reminded of a number of important skills, namely:

1 How to welcome visitors.
2 How to act upon questions to discover what the customer needs in order to match benefits to needs – How? Why? What? When? Where? Who? are key words.
3 How to listen with interest and how to probe politely for further information to discover the customer's real needs.
4 How to observe reaction.
5 How to sell benefits.
6 How to overcome objections.
7 How to recognize buy signals and how to close a sale.
8 To learn about, understand fully and be up-to-date with all aspects of home purchase finance.
9 How to smile.

On most sites the sales team will still be present when buyers move into their new homes. So in addition the sales negotiators need to know how to handle complaints and how the developer handles after-sales service.

Some of the skills are general marketing skills; others must be combined with 'product' knowledge.

An important point missed by some sales staff is that every visitor to the show home is there because the marketing campaign has been successful. The visitor has seen an advertisement, or the site board, or read about the development in a paper, sent off for particulars or heard about it from a friend. The fact that the visitor is there is part way toward a sale!

The show home will normally be furnished by a specialist interior designer. The show home is the culmination of the market research, so needs to be decorated and finished as the most probable purchaser would wish to see it if it were their own home. The furniture, material, carpets, fixtures and fittings must be of the quality and price range appropriate to that segment of the market expected to pay that price for that home. Thus it is unrealistic to furnish a one-bedroom, bottom-of-the-market starter home with furniture costing thousands of pounds; on the other hand a similar sized home aimed at the single executive might be designer finished at substantial cost.

However furnished, the sales staff must ensure that prospective buyers know which items are included in the price.

Currently valuers are under instruction to exclude from their valuations for mortgage purposes all removable tenants' fixtures and fittings. As a result many of the extras previously provided by the developer are no longer included in the price.

The major developers of residential property are very conscious of the need to project their image as developers of the best new homes. This may be difficult to do if sales are being handled by the town centre office of a local estate agent. The estate agent who wishes to maintain a high profile as a new homes agent must, if the market conditions warrant it, be prepared to set up and run the seven-days-a-week site show home and sales suite and be willing to train sales staff to think solely as agents for that site and that developer. The agent acting for several developers will find this difficult to do from his own office as there will be a conflict and a tendency for staff to participate in the comparative debate of prospective purchasers who have looked at several different developments.

The sales team also has an important after-sales function to perform: first to see that the sale proceeds smoothly, and second to relay to the design team any suggestions made by purchasers which could improve the marketability of the product.

Chapter 8

Mortgages and mortgage valuations

The majority of people purchasing their own home do so with the assistance of a loan, legally termed a mortgage because the property is used as security for the loan. The most common source of such loans are the building societies and high street banks. The principal types of mortgage are the standard repayment mortgage and the endowment mortgage.

A mortgage creates a legal charge on the property offered as security for the loan. As such it will be registered as a land charge and subsequent purchasers will be advised of the charge when they make their searches and enquiries (see Chapter 10). This means that no mortgaged property can be sold without repayment of the mortgage. When signing the mortgage documents the borrower accepts a number of conditions, the most fundamental of which is to repay the whole of the amount advanced (loaned) and all subsequent or further advances and re-advances. The conditions go on to explain the manner in which repayment is to be made (see below). All mortgages also require the borrower to pay interest on all money advanced and outstanding from year to year. Coupled with these requirements are the rights of the mortgagee (lender) to enter into possession of the property if the borrower defaults. Most reputable lenders exercise this power only after all efforts to help a defaulting borrower have failed. Having taking possession, the mortgagee has the power to sell the property in order to recover all outstanding debts. It is in this sense that the property becomes the security for a personal loan made to the borrower(s).

The lenders have therefore two lines of action to recover their loans, one being to sue the borrower on the personal covenant, the other to take possession and sell the property. In the latter case the mortgagee's claim is a prior claim and the sale is made with vacant possession and free of any rights of ownership previously held by the borrower. Any residual sums will be paid to the borrower unless other parties such as a second mortgagee also have a claim against the borrower for which the property was used as security. If the sale proceeds are insufficient to pay off the accumulated debt the lender has the right to recover the balance from the borrower on the personal covenant.

The mortgagee may, under some circumstances, prevent a sale of a mortgaged property unless the net sale proceeds are sufficient to repay the loan or unless the borrower has made alternative arrangements to repay the loan in full. On this point the courts have held that a mortgagor shall not be prevented from selling the mortgaged property solely because the sale proceeds will be less than the accumulated mortgage debt. The problem for the mortgagee is that it removes the security and leaves them with the problem of recovering the balance on the personal covenant. Negative equity transfers on sale and new purchase are being encouraged by government.

In addition to these obvious financial conditions, most mortgage documents also require borrowers to put the property into good repair and to keep it in good repair; to keep the property fully insured – usually by arrangement with one or other specified insurance company by payment of premiums direct to the mortgagee; to comply with all statutory notices served by, say, a local authority and not to lease the property without the consent of the mortgagee.

A mortgage is usually taken out for a term of between twenty and thirty years; rarely for longer, as most mortgagees like to be certain that the borrower will have made the final payment before his or her retirement. A mortgage can, of course, be taken out for shorter periods, thus a borrower might well move home in preparation for retirement and enter into a mortgage for perhaps five or ten years.

It is always sensible for a borrower to retain a small mortgage, as most lenders will then keep the title deeds securely for no charge and the property can then be used as security for personal secured loans or if needed, further advances can be taken out for home improvements.

Before agreeing to a mortgage the lender will first check the personal circumstances of the borrower. This entails taking up references with the prospective borrower's employer and bank. In the case of the self-employed, a check is made of the individual's audited accounts and/or annual tax returns. These checks are to confirm that the borrower will be able to meet the repayments. In order to accelerate the home purchase process many lenders will complete this check at an early stage and issue the prospective borrower with a certificate, to show to vendors and agents, indicating the size or amount of loan that the lender is prepared to lend that applicant.

The amount that lenders are prepared to lend to applicants is based on a multiple of the applicant's income or the joint incomes of joint applicants. Typical multiples are two to three times the gross annual salary of an individual. In calculating this sum lenders will include expected bonuses or portions thereof. For married couples it is usually two to three times the main salary plus one times the second salary; some lenders take a multiple of the joint incomes. Increasingly mortgages are being granted to unmarried couples and to groups of people sharing the same property. The assessment of the total loan in each case will depend upon individual circumstances.

Tax relief at the lower rate of tax is allowed on the interest payable on mortgages for the first £30,000 borrowed per property. Tax relief on loans of £30,000 or less is now handled direct by most lenders under the mortgage interest relief at source scheme, called MIRAS for short.

The MIRAS scheme is an extremely simple scheme for many borrowers. Instead of paying interest on the money borrowed at the borrowing rate, the interest is calculated at a net of tax rate. Thus, if the mortgage rate was 10 per cent and the rate of tax 20 per cent (20p in the £), then the interest actually paid per £100 borrowed would be £8.00 instead of £10.00.

Tax relief on interest payments comes up for discussion every year at or around the time of the budget.

The second factor to be considered by all lenders having vetted the applicant is to vet the property offered as security for the loan. Section 131(b) of the Building Societies Act 1986 states that 'there should be a written report on the value of the land and any factors likely to affect its value made by a person who is competent to value and is not disqualified under this section from making a report on the land in question' (e.g. valuing his or her own property). 'Competent' is not defined, but members of the RICS and ISVA would normally be held to be competent. No similar requirements apply to banks but most do employ valuers to report on the value of the property. This involves the property being inspected by a qualified surveyor employed by the lender or acting on the lender's instructions. The valuer is required to advise on the suitability of the property as security for a loan and upon its value.

REPAYMENT MORTGAGES

The repayment mortgage is the traditional way of borrowing money by way of a mortgage. It requires the borrower to pay the lender a sum of money – usually monthly – which represents both interest on the money borrowed and a small capital repayment. The amount payable will vary from time to time, as almost all mortgages allow lenders to vary the rate of interest in line with movements in money market interest rates. The actual proportion of the payment representing interest reduces over the life of the mortgage as the amount of capital repaid increases over the life of the mortgage. The working of this can be seen in the following illustrative example.

A mortgage of £5,000 over five years has been arranged at a MIRAS rate of 8%*, i.e. this is the basis for the mortgage repayment calculations after netting down the gross rate for tax relief.

The annual repayment can be calculated using the present value of £1 per annum factor for five years at 8%. Sum borrowed ÷ PV of £1 p.a. for five years at 8% = £5,000 ÷ 3.9927 = £1,252.29.

It should be noted that some lenders will calculate the annual sum as here and then divide by twelve to find the monthly sum. This would become £104.36 per month.

* This approach has been adopted to avoid the problem of confusion due to changing interest and tax rates.

Other lenders take a different financial view and would go direct to the monthly sum by taking the term to be sixty months (5 years × 12 = 60) and the interest rate per month to be the monthly amount which would equate with 8 per cent per annum. The two approaches produce marginally different amounts and marginally different annual percentage rates.

Having calculated the annual repayment amount it is simple to illustrate that that amount will, over five years, provide the lender with interest at 8 per cent on the money and the repayment of the £5,000 in full by the end of the term.

Table 8.1 Repayment mortgage over five years at 8 per cent on £5,000

1 Time (years)	2 Capital Owed	3 Annual Payment (2 ÷ 5)	4 Interest @ 8%	5 Capital Repaid (3 − 4)
0	5,000			
1		1,252.29	400	852.29
2	4,147.71	1,252.29	331.82	920.47
3	3,227.24	1,252.29	258.18	994.11
4	2,233.13	1,252.29	178.65	1,073.64
5	1,159.49	1,252.29	92.76	1,159.53*

* rounding error to two decimal places

Table 8.1 shows how the lender charges interest on the amount borrowed or outstanding from year to year, the difference between the interest charged and the annual payment represents capital repaid from year to year. Over the term the amount of interest diminishes and the amount of capital repaid increases.

A few lenders will offer a low start or increasing repayment mortgage. Here the repayment is lower in the early years than for a normal repayment mortgage, but increases substantially in the latter years to make good the initial shortfall.

Mortgage protection policies are offered to borrowers taking on a repayment mortgage. Such a policy protects a borrower's family in the event of the death of the borrower. As with all forms of life assurance the cost or premium will depend upon the policyholder's age and medical record. (Reductions in premium are possible for non-smokers.) They are a relatively cheap form of life policy as the assurance companies' liability is a diminishing one as the term of the mortgage and amount of debt diminishes.

Some lenders insist on borrowers taking out mortgage protection policies, and they are certainly a wise precaution for those with dependants who might otherwise have to sell the family home in the event of the borrower's death.

ENDOWMENT MORTGAGES

Endowment mortgages come in various forms, but the common feature of them all is that they involve a lender, building society or bank, and an insurance/assurance company. The borrower enters into two contractual obligations to secure a mortgage in this way. The lender is the provider of the capital in exchange for interest on the full amount of the loan at a market variable rate for the full term of the loan. The assurance company provides a life assurance policy on the life or lives of the borrower(s) at a premium based on the age of the borrower(s) and their medical record. The policy provides for repayment of the loan in the event of death and for the payment of a sum of money at the end of the term estimated to be sufficient to repay the original loan at that date. The most popular form is the low cost endowment mortgage.

A low cost endowment mortgage offers but does not necessarily guarantee that at the end of the term the policy will have matured to a sum sufficient to pay off the loan and with luck leave a little extra for the borrower.

A non-profit endowment policy guarantees the policyholder a specified sum of money at a specified future date. The conservative investment policy of most assurance companies means that this form of investment will show a very poor rate of return on moneys invested by way of premiums.

Insurance companies also offer with-profits policies. These provide for a specified sum on death and an indicated or expected sum on future maturity. Provided the insurance company's business continues to perform as well in the future as in the past, the profits declared by the company and added to the policy will be sufficient to produce the specified sum. However, underperformance by the insurance company can give rise to a shortfall on the redemption date. A full with-profits policy would provide for a minimum amount equal to the amount of the loan which will usually be guaranteed as for a non-profit policy plus an amount on maturity calculated today on the basis of current bonus or profits. Such policies are very expensive.

The low cost endowment means that the insurance company calculates the level of cover the borrower requires to take out which will accumulate with the continuation of the current level of bonus or profits to the amount required to repay the loan at the end of the term. Again, the conservative nature of such calculations will usually mean that on paper it will over-provide for the repayment, to leave a cash bonus for the borrower. These profit sums cannot be guaranteed.

The cost of an endowment mortgage will vary with the age of the borrower and may or may not be cheaper than a normal repayment mortgage. The real benefit of a paper cash benefit in twenty-five years' time is difficult to assess, as so much depends on the level of profits that a particular insurance company is able to offer and the effect of inflation on the spending power of the pound. Its advantage is that if it does work out as specified on paper it can provide a simple form of saving, but not necessarily a 'profitable' form of saving.

In the *Which?* report on mortgages in May 1986, it was indicated that with mortgage interest rates in excess of 9 per cent, a normal repayment mortgage would tend to be cheapest; below 9 per cent then the cost benefit is in favour of the low cost endowment.

Low cost endowment mortgages can cause administrative and possibly financial problems if a borrower moves home frequently, or if the borrower wishes to repay a mortgage early. Most policies should be transferable when taking out a fresh mortgage on a different property, but it is important to note that the full benefit of such a policy will only be realized if all premiums are paid. Cashing in an endowment policy before maturity or ceasing to pay premiums but leaving the policy to mature will both produce less than proportionate benefits.

The choice between the two may be personal or it may be financial, depending upon mortgage interest rates, but in many instances borrowers are directed toward endowment policies by keen marketing by the insurance companies, banks and building societies.

The legal position of the borrower is no different under an endowment scheme than a repayment scheme. Non-payment of interest or policy premium will lead to the lender seeking redress by foreclosure proceedings and the sale of the property.

PENSION MORTGAGES

The self-employed paying into personal pension schemes can borrow by way of mortgage against their pension. As with an endowment mortgage, interest-only payments are made to the lender. The capital itself is paid out of the lump sum element of the personal pension scheme on maturity of that scheme. The big advantage is that tax relief is claimable (within specified limits) on personal pension contributions. Such mortgages are therefore very suitable for the self-employed.

Current proposals to amend the law on pensions may make this option a real alternative for a larger group of people, provided of course that the double tax-relief element is not reviewed in the same way as tax relief on life insurance premiums was reviewed.

LIBOR SCHEMES

A mortgage can be linked to the London Interbank Offered Rate; such schemes may or may not work out cheaper than normal repayment mortgages.

Independent advice on mortgages is offered by independent intermediaries under the Financial Services Act; some banks and financial advisors are tied agents and will only offer one company's policies. It is a criminal offence to offer specific advice on mortgages, i.e. to recommend a specific company, unless the person or organization giving the advice is authorized by one of the appropriate regulatory organizations such as FIMBRA.

The mortgage business is very competitive and new variations on the repayment and endowment schemes appear almost weekly. The market in 1993 is concentrating on mortgages where the rate is fixed or an upper limit is fixed for up to five years.

MORTGAGE INSPECTIONS AND VALUATIONS

Mortgage valuations and the role of the valuer in the mortgage business receive publicity in the national and the professional press whenever disputes in law occur. There are unsettled cases of valuers being involved in mortgage frauds which clearly bring the property profession into disrepute, but of equal importance is the question of the valuer's responsibility to the borrower.

Until relatively recently, few valuers paused to consider questions of responsibility and liability when carrying out a mortgage valuation. It was generally understood that having received instructions from a building society or bank, liability extended to that party only and that the principal issue was simply whether the property offered adequate security for the loan requested by the applicant. As is the case today, most lenders issued a form to be completed, similar to that illustrated in Appendix IV. If there were obvious major defects these would have been noted and the agreed asking price would have been marked down to a lower value figure for mortgage purposes, to reflect the cost of making good the defects.

This mortgage report was, however, paid for by the mortgage applicant who technically was not permitted to see the valuer's comments. Many applicants resented this and in some instances it was clear that applicants had seen or been told much of the content of the reports. In time, building societies and others decided it would be fairer to applicants to let them have a copy of the reports on the clear understanding that they were not full surveys of the property, that neither the society nor the valuer could accept any responsibility for the condition of the property, nor for the applicant's decision to proceed with the purchase and the mortgage offered.

Such warnings tended to go unheeded and applicants would subsequently return to their building societies complaining that 'this' or 'that' had not been noted by the valuer and that as a result they (the applicants) had been forced to spend large sums of money on repairs. In most cases the applicants had proceeded without obtaining their own full survey reports and the valuer involved would rarely hear of the disagreement because the contract was solely with the society and the society effectively protected the valuer.

This comfortable position was exploded in the case of *Yianni* v. *Edwin Evans & Sons* (1981). The firm of valuers in this case admitted they had been negligent, but held that they were only liable to the lenders, not the purchasers. The courts held that in that case the valuers did owe a duty to the third party, the applicant; they should have foreseen that the applicant would indirectly rely on their opinion; substantial damages were awarded. Following this case the RICS in conjunction with the ISVA issued firm guidance notes for mortgage valuations and many lenders tightened up on their disclaimer clauses. The words used by the Alliance and Leicester Building Society are illustrative of the effort made to forewarn mortgage applicants of the nature of a mortgage valuation and the action prudent purchasers should take. (See Appendix IV.)

In a later case, *Stevenson* v. *Nationwide Building Society* (1984), the plaintiff failed in his action because at the time of his applying for a mortgage he had signed a form which included the statement:

> The inspection carried out by the Society's Valuer is not a structural survey and there may be defects which such a survey would reveal. Should you wish to arrange for a structural survey this can be undertaken by the Society's valuer, at your own expense, at the same time as the Society's Report and Valuation is made . . .
>
> I understand that the Report and Valuation on the property made by the Society's Valuer is confidential and is intended solely for the consideration of the Society in determining what advance (if any) may be made on the security, and that no responsibility is implied or accepted by the Society or its Valuer for either the value or condition of the property by reason of such Inspection and Report.

The plaintiff being an estate agent was felt to have full knowledge of the meaning and intent of such a clause. The clause, in that case, was held to be reasonable under the Unfair Contract Terms Act 1977.

However, in *Smith* v. *Eric S. Bush* (1987), it was held that under different circumstances it was not fair and reasonable to allow the defendants to rely on the disclaimers. In that case, chimney breasts had been removed, leaving the chimney stack unsupported; this could have and should have been noted by the valuer, and the chimney collapsed causing damage to the property. Damages were awarded.

The current legal position is still unclear, but it would seem that even when the applicant(s) sign forms to the effect that they fully understand the limited nature of a mortgage inspection and where such disclaimers are subsequently reprinted on the applicant's copy of the report, the valuer may still be held liable to the applicant, even though the contract is between the lender and the valuer. The case of *Harris* v. *Wyre Forest District Council and Another* (1987) suggests that the liability of the valuer to third parties may be disclaimed under certain circumstances if the applicants do not see the report and the applicants have previously signed a certificate to indicate that they appreciate the report is confidential and for the use of the lenders only (see also *Davies* v. *Parry* (1988)).

Some important points for the residential valuer emerge from these cases. First, the courts do accept that there is a difference between a 'survey' and 'a valuation for mortgage purposes'. In the latter case a surveyor would not be expected to detect hidden defects when the requirement is to carry out a reasonably careful visual inspection. Second, that under normal circumstances the time taken to complete such an inspection and report will be considerably less than for a full survey. Set against this is the implication that as value and condition of property are linked, the courts will consider whether the valuer exercised reasonable care in carrying out the inspection. There is, however, no clear statement as to what that standard is, and therefore on every occasion the extent of the mortgage valuer's responsibility is likely to turn on the specific circumstances of that case. Indeed it has been held that it is the valuer's duty, once alerted, to move furniture to trace as far as possible the extent of a defect (*Roberts* v. *Hampson & Co.* (1988)). In the later case of *Lloyd* v. *Butler* (1990) the judge held that the valuer

> does not necessarily have to follow up every trail to discover whether there is trouble or the extent of such trouble. But where such inspections can reasonably show a potential trouble or the risk of potential trouble . . . it is necessary . . . to alert the purchaser.

Reasonableness causes problems for surveyors and the courts. In *Whalley* v. *Roberts* (1990) it was held to be reasonable for a surveyor not to check floor levels with a spirit level when carrying out a mortgage valuation.

VALUATION GUIDELINES

In an effort to clarify the position, the RICS in conjunction with the ISVA drew up *Mortgage Valuation – Guidance for Valuers* (see Appendix IV).

They have also produced a number of booklets for issue to the general public, the most pertinent of which is *Mortgage Valuations Explained* and their own mortgage valuation report forms.

Unless instructed otherwise, the basis of valuation for mortgage purposes is open market value. In arriving at open market value the residential valuer will be expected to have taken account of and reflected upon most of the factors referred to in Chapter 3. In preparing the report or completing the lender's pro forma the valuer will have had regard to current guidance notes issued by the professional bodies and to any specific instructions issued by the building society, bank or other lender, all of which are too numerous to include here.

Among the more important factors to be considered when inspecting the property will be its age, type (detached, terraced, etc.), design, accommodation, fixtures, construction and condition, subsidence, liability to flooding and other risks, siting, amenities and other environmental factors, known legal and other encumbrances. Removable fittings and sales incentives must be disregarded, as too should the potential for further development. The exception to this might be where a property is being sold with planning consent.

The report must include the main property or building and the other improvements to the site such as garages, workshops, walls, drives, footpaths, etc.

The valuer must report on all facts that might affect value but would not be expected to report on minor matters such as chipped paintwork, unless the sum of such minor defects amounted in total to substantial disrepair which would affect value.

As previously indicated, the extent of the inspection required is still in dispute, although it is accepted that during such an inspection the valuer would not normally move furniture, carpets, etc. nor take up floorboards, nor erect ladders to inspect the outside or roofs, nor carry out drainage tests or test other services. In practice most of these would only be undertaken for a full survey if specifically requested by the client, as they will invariably require the services of a builder and other specialists.

The experienced residential valuer is expected to know the market and to have a broad knowledge of the area in which he or she practises and will therefore bring to each and every inspection knowledge gleaned from other surveys and inspections carried out within a locality. Only the experienced valuer will be aware of issues such as radon gas and the possibility and implications of the land being contaminated.

The inspection

All residential inspections begin as the valuer approaches the property; in a sense they begin the moment the instruction is received and a daytime appointment is made for the valuer to have access to all parts of the property. The valuer should know the area of the town or the village, may know the road and may even know the type of property in that area. Experience in this sense is very important.

On approaching the property the valuer is mentally noting the immediate locality, the amenities, traffic access, environment etc., and whether it is an adopted highway.

On arriving at the property the valuer will note the type of property, its basic design and the extent to which it conforms or fits into the house styles of the immediate locality. Views, open spaces and the good and bad features of the neighbourhood will be noted or known.

The mode of the inspection is a question of valuer's preferences. Some prefer to inspect the outside then the inside, others the inside then the outside. The two are related and it may be necessary for the valuer to retrace his or her steps to cross-check one with the other.

The basic equipment needed for a mortgage inspection consists of a tape measure and measuring rod, screwdriver and sharp probe for checking pointing, rotten timbers etc., a portable ladder, strong torch, binoculars, camera and a moisture meter. In addition some valuers will have with them in their cars a full set of equipment, of which inspection chamber keys may be the most useful additional items for a quick visual check that the drains are running freely.

A walk around the inside gives the valuer a feel for the property, its design in terms of internal layout and the interest that present and previous owners have paid to maintenance and improvements. Obvious or blatant defects will be noted at this stage, such as damp patches on ceilings, peeling wallpaper, excessive condensation and mould, as too will be the details of accommodation and services.

An inspection of the roof space where readily accessible can be useful at this stage, so that in a standard property the valuer is working from top to bottom – in effect, checking on the stability of the property, its ability to keep out the elements, its construction and state of repair. The guidance notes suggest that the valuer need not enter the roof space but must, where accessible, look into the roof space. Many valuers will, however, enter the roof space in order to better observe the whole roof void, condition of timbers, underside of roof coverings, insulation, tanks and electrical services.

Working through the property, the valuer is visually checking for signs of settlement or subsidence – uneven floors, twisted window and door frames, damp penetration, timber rot or infestation, decorative order, condition and functioning of all services. The moisture meter will be used to check for rising and penetrating dampness.

The exterior is checked for condition of walls, timber, rainwater, goods, pointing, painting, chimney stacks, chimney flashings, condition of roof covering. Much is obvious from ground floor level, but more is revealed through binoculars.

All salient factors need to be noted, but it is most important to report on unusual forms of construction – concrete construction such as Airey homes are totally unacceptable to some lenders (see Chapter 2); timber-frame construction must be noted, as too should older flat roofs which were not constructed to acceptable standards; uncorrected continuing movement in the structure caused by soil movements or faulty construction must be reported as it affects the acceptability of the property both as security for mortgage purposes and for insurance purposes.

Tests on services are not expected, but the residential valuer should be able to comment upon the obvious such as very old wiring, lead pipework, whether drains are free-flowing and discharge to the main drainage system or to a septic tank. The lender's attention should be drawn to all essential repairs noted and those items in need of further inspection such as subsidence, penetrating and rising dampness, rot-affected timbers.

On completion of the internal and external inspections the valuer should be able to comment upon the basic construction, e.g. timber frame, cavity walls,[1] solid stone or brick walls, type of roof, wall cladding, decorations, standard of insulation.[2]

Other buildings, walls, paths, drives, should be inspected and reported upon. Other features such as swimming pools should be noted, but clear disclaimers given as to the condition and working order of heating systems, etc.

The property and substantial outbuildings should than be measured externally in order to complete the insurance valuation (see Chapter 15). Plot measurements should be taken and the orientation of the property noted (N/S, E/W).

Knowledge of the area will alert the valuer to the possibility of flooding or other factors which affect value in particular in that area or might affect the value of the subject property. The weather conditions at the time of the inspection should be recorded by the valuer.

On completion of the inspection the specific report form of that lender is checked to see that all questions have been answered, ready for the form to be typed up on return to the office. The valuer will reflect upon the asking price at this stage and make a few notes on his or her feelings before leaving the property. However, it is sometimes better to finalize the insurance and market valuation after further deliberation and where possible after checking for comparables.

The open market value of properties with no defects or outstanding repairs on popular residential estates provides a relatively easy valuation task. More individual properties with defects pose greater valuation problems. In these cases some lenders require guidance as to the probable cost of making good defects and advice as to the open market value subject to the defects and the open market value once the defects have been made good. These are opinions expressed at a moment in time. Many valuers prefer first to answer the question 'What would be the open market value of this property in good condition, in good decorative order and/or where appropriately modernized?' and then to assess the open market value as it stands with all its defects. It is important to realize that the difference between the two is not necessarily the cost of making good all the defects. Cost depends upon the amount of material and labour used to make good the defects, whereas value is a function of market forces. The market can take a very pessimistic view of a run-down house which might cost very little to put right and in good order may have a much higher resale value. In other cases the market may almost totally discount the costs of making good outstanding defects, with buyers over-bidding each other to acquire a defective property at almost its class A value. It is therefore quite impossible to specify how much values in general are affected by condition; that has to be left to the judgement of the valuer in each case.

It is, however, very important to inform the lender of the extent of works needed to put the property into good order and to advise with great care, if asked, as to the likely costs of putting the property in good order and on whether all or some of the works should be made a condition of the loan offer, with or without a retention of some part of the loan pending satisfactory completion of the work (see questions in sample form).

If there are clear legal encumbrances these must be noted and their affect on value included in the valuation. If the highway (road) has not been adopted this must be noted, and in the case of a new road on a new housing estate, it is necessary to check whether a bond has been deposited with the highway authority to cover this cost should the developers fail to meet their obligations. The valuer should also take account of any known planning matters that will adversely affect the value or marketability of the property now or in the future, e.g. road widening, road closures, new developments.

The valuation of leasehold interests in houses for mortgage purposes require the residential valuer to have knowledge of the provisions of the Leasehold Reform Act 1967. This is considered in detail in Chapter 11. The important point for the valuer dealing with mortgage valuations is to be able to assess whether the leasehold interest being valued is one where the leasehold purchaser will be able to exercise rights to buy the freehold or to be granted a fifty-year extension or not. This, together with the unexpired length of lease and the terms and conditions of the lease will be as relevant in assessing market value as the physical condition and other environmental factors.

The general problems of valuing interests in flats and maisonettes are considered in Chapter 11. These same points are equally relevant when valuing interests in such properties for mortgage purposes. The essential point is that the valuer must have regard to the more complex legal relationships and to take account of the physical condition of the whole, not just that of the flat or the maisonette.

In the case of initial reports on new properties at plan stage, great care is needed, as cases have occurred where the finished house or flat is different to that shown on the sales details and/or the architect's plans. A further inspection is required on completion and at that time the valuer needs to check that the product agrees with the plans; if not, the difference must be stated and a comment made on the effect if any that the changes have on value.

FURTHER ADVANCES AND SECOND MORTGAGES

There are two basic reasons why home-owners seek further advances or second mortgages. The first is that they may wish to carry out improvements or substantial works of repair to a property. The second is that they wish to realize part of the capital they have tied up in a property for purposes totally unrelated to the property itself. Additional loans, whether or not required for home improvements, do not qualify for tax relief (1988 budget change).

A further advance by definition is made by the same society or bank as made the original mortgage loan. A second mortgage is generally taken out with another financial institution, usually a finance house. It is the lender's responsibility to satisfy themselves that the borrower can meet the cost of repaying the additional loan as well as the original loan. It is the instructed valuer's task to advise on open market value.

The subject of home improvements is considered in more detail in Chapter 13; here it can be noted that some very costly improvements may add very little to current open market value, whilst on other occasions relatively minor expenditure can add considerably to value. In many cases the lender simply requires a current open market valuation of the property, in others they seek advice on value with the proposed improvements and value without.

In some cases all that is required is a statement of value. Nevertheless, the valuer who provides such an opinion without carrying out a full mortgage inspection is potentially exposing himself to claims for negligence. If a valid claim does arise, the nominal fee accepted for such a valuation will not in itself be a sufficient defence.

OTHER SURVEYS

Clearly the limited inspection and report prepared for mortgage purposes is not sufficient for the prudent buyer, nor is it sufficiently detailed for the valuer to be certain that all defects have been noted. Buyers are strongly advised by all involved in the residential market, including the professional bodies and major lenders, to obtain their own full survey or home buyer's report. Armed with the findings of a full survey the valuer should be that much more certain as to the open market value of a property for mortgage purposes, but even a full survey is not a guarantee that every defect will have been found; a latent defect such as undetected faulty foundations, by definition is something that cannot be observed.

Finally the mortgage valuer must read carefully and adhere to the guidance notes issued by the RICS in the *Manual of Valuation Guidance Notes* and the instructions issued by all instructing lenders. (See Appendix IVC for extracts from the *Manual*.)

NOTES

1 In the case of cavity wall construction, the valuer needs to observe and consider the possible condition of the wall-ties; bulges or iron staining may indicate the failure of one or more ties.
2 Cavity insulation should be noted. In the case of timber frame construction the valuer must state whether the cavity has been filled in, or whether this has not been possible to check; where cavity fill insulation has been introduced into timber frame houses it will invalidate the NHBC guarantee. In the latter case the valuer must check for dampness; if found, then a check in accordance with Building Research Establishment paper ILI/85 must be recommended and until a full check is made it may be very difficult to advise fully on value. If no damp is found the lender must be advised that to further insulate timber frame properties in this way is bad practice and that a detailed survey is essential (see Appendix IB).

Chapter 9

Other residential surveys

The residential agent or valuer, even if qualified (ARICS, ASVA), will not necessarily have sufficient knowledge and experience to undertake the more comprehensive survey work necessary for a Home Buyer's Survey and Valuation (HBSV) or pre-purchase inspection report – colloquially termed a full or structural survey. There are certainly some general practice surveyors who have the right training and experience to undertake this work, but there are those who believe that this work should only be carried out by building surveyors. The man in the street finds it very difficult to distinguish between one type of surveyor and another; indeed, very difficult to distinguish between a non-qualified agent and a qualified surveyor, particularly when they may all be employed by the same firm or company and operate from the same premises. It is equally difficult for the layman to appreciate the difference between an inspection for mortgage purposes, a full survey, and a home buyer's report. In some firms, survey work will be undertaken by a specific division of the firm, whilst in the smaller practice there may be only one qualified surveyor who will undertake all professional work. Here as with mortgage inspections customers seem only too aware of their rights to bring an action for negligence if they believe they have suffered a loss if the report failed to mention a particular point. The case law on negligent surveys is vast, but most cases point to the need for very high standards of professional knowledge on the part of those undertaking survey work. To this end those undertaking such work need a thorough knowledge of domestic construction, both historic and current, and how to keep up to date on all new techniques, materials and legislation. As an added protection, substantial professional indemnity insurance will be arranged, for even under the amended provision of the Limitations Act 1980, as amended by the Latent Damages Act 1986, an action for damages for negligence can be brought at any time up to six years from the date on which the cause for action occurred, or three years from the earliest date on which the plaintiff had both the knowledge and a right to bring such action. A residential survey file may remain active or potentially active for many years, and must therefore contain full documentation in respect of the specific instructions.

The purchase of a residential property is a commitment to invest substantial sums of money to acquire (a) a legal title to a parcel of land and (b) to acquire the bricks and mortar and other improvements attaching to that parcel of land rights at the date of contract. It is also a commitment to maintain, where a loan is involved, and a commitment to maintain and possibly improve if the purchaser wishes to protect that investment over time.

The location of the land together with the improvements primarily dictate value within the pattern of values for an area. The condition of the improvements is a factor determining value in a specific case. So although there is no direct relationship between cost and value, there is in the minds of purchasers a difference between the price paid for a property and the price they would have preferred to have paid when a costly defect is discovered shortly after purchase. Let the buyer beware (*caveat emptor*) is a legal principle of the property market, so for protection the home buyer should employ a solicitor to check all the details of the legal title and a qualified surveyor to check the physical attributes of the bricks and mortar being purchased. Only in the case of fraudulent misrepresentation will it be possible for the buyer to rectify the situation by having the contract set aside or damages awarded. Mortgagees and surveyors do their utmost to protect home buyers from their own foolishness by pointing out the strict limitations of a mortgage report and advising buyers to obtain their own independent survey or home buyer's report on the property.

A full survey provides the buyer with the most extensive report on a property; however, it cannot cover everything. Only by taking a property to pieces down to the foundations would it be possible to say certainly that it did or did not have defects. A surveyor inspecting an occupied property will be restricted by what it is practical and possible for a surveyor to inspect within any limitations agreed by the client or imposed by the vendor. Before carrying out a survey, a surveyor will confirm in writing with the client what exactly will be done and what will not be done, i.e. the surveyor will spell out any limitations which will become part of the report. In most cases the surveyor's report will be restricted to readily accessible parts of the property – a surveyor will not normally take up carpets or floorboards unless the client makes specific arrangements with the vendor, undertakes to arrange for a carpet layer to replace the carpets and undertakes to arrange for a builder to be on site to lift and replace floorboards; inspection of the exterior of the property will be limited to that which is possible from ground level or with ladders of limited height and/or observable with binoculars; inspection of services will be limited to a visual inspection only unless specific instructions are given for services to be tested, in which case the client must meet the additional cost of builders and service engineers needed for these tests. In addition, the client may limit the inspection to, say, the main house and of course, having inspected the property, the surveyor may have to list various parts of the building which physically could not be seen for one reason or another; for example there may be insufficient space between adjoining properties for the surveyor to inspect an end wall properly. Clients must be alerted to these limitations and confirmation as to these limitations obtained in writing from the client and placed in the file. Whilst inspecting the property the surveyor will make extensive notes in writing for the file and in readiness for drafting a report and will also take measurements and photographs to support his or her findings. The file note should contain a reference to weather conditions – a rainy day can reveal defects not so readily visible on a hot summer's day.

A survey report will reflect the surveyor's personal reporting style or the firm's office style and will be influenced by the property itself. It will usually cover construction, condition etc. under the following broad headings:

Address
Description
Location
Accommodation
Construction and condition – External
- Roof and roof coverings
- Chimney stacks and flashings
- Guttering and downpipes
- Walls
- Windows
- Doors
Construction and condition – Internal
- Roof void, tanks, pipes, insulation
- Room by room: ceilings, walls, floors, skirtings, fixtures and fittings, fire openings, flues
- Staircases
- Electrics
- Plumbing
- Heating
Outside
- Other buildings, garages etc., boundary walls, fences, paths
- Drainage and other mains services.
Summary of defects and repairs
Conclusions, with or without valuation.

The length of the report will depend upon the size of the property and the observable factors that need to be reported.

Throughout the report the surveyor must state clearly what has been observed in terms of the nature and materials of construction, their adequacy and current condition, any observed defects and their rectification and, arising from the defects, any possible deterioration that could occur if the defects were not rectified. Health and safety risks will be emphasized, as will any failure of the building to meet current building or planning requirements. The report will be as comprehensive as the building permits, and any technical points will be explained in layman's terms.

If the purchaser intends to extend or improve the property the surveyor may be asked to take such additional measurements and obtain information needed in order to prepare plans and in order to comment upon the purchaser's outline proposals. For example, the purchaser's proposals may involve removal of existing walls, in which case it is important to learn whether they are load-bearing or merely partition walls.

There are many excellent books written on the subject of domestic building surveys, any one of which will give the reader an insight into the technical knowledge needed for such surveys, the provisos needed to be incorporated in survey reports, the equipment needed for such surveys and the liability of the surveyor to the client in law for a negligent survey.

The typical terraced, semi-detached or detached property built by a developer on a housing estate from the 1920s to today may not warrant a full survey and report. The style, construction and condition of the property may, from experience, be such that the surveyor is able to recommend to a purchaser that an RICS HBSV will be sufficient for their purchase requirements. A qualified surveyor will, in the case of a full survey or a home buyer's report, advise on the need for further investigations where necessary.

Since its conception, the home buyer's report has grown in popularity both with surveyors and purchasers and is now produced and operated jointly with the ISVA. The HBSV is a pro forma which may be extended with additional sheets if the space provided on the form is insufficient for all the surveyor's comments. It does succinctly draw the buyer's attention to all subject matters that they may wish to take further advice upon before finalizing on the price and exchanging contracts. A copy of such a report is included in Appendix V.

The surveyor undertaking the survey of a flat or a maisonette has the added problem of reporting on the whole building as well as on the individual residential unit. Such reports may need to be cross-referenced to the terms and conditions of the lease. In the first instance it is important for the buyer to be aware of (a) any defects, issues, etc. relating to the unit being purchased, and (b) any defects to the building as a whole. It is

then important to check (a) on the legal liability for making good such
defects and (b) upon the responsibility for meeting the cost of any repairs.
Finally it is sensible to check on the likelihood of the work being
undertaken and the possible repercussions for the property and the unit
leasehold owner-occupier if the work is not undertaken. In the latter case
it is possible to exercise legal rights to see that repairs to the building are
undertaken, but delays can be both costly and mentally frustrating.

A very simple case illustrates the need for additional care. A ground
floor flat owner had, for his own convenience, replaced all the windows in
his flat with maintenance-free double-glazed replacement units. Unfortunately, all the windows in the block of flats had to be replaced in a similar
manner due to rot in the timber frames. An innocent purchaser of the
ground floor flat then received a bill for his proportionate share of
replacing all the windows in the building, even though those in his recently
purchased unit did not have to be replaced. The cost in such a case could
run into thousands of pounds, on top of a full open-market value purchase
of the flat.

From a surveyor's point of view there are clearly limitations to the extent
of the survey that is possible. It would be impractical to survey every flat
in the building, it may not be possible to gain access to all the shared parts
of the building and indeed the problem may be a leaking waste pipe in an
adjoining flat which encourages the development of rot which takes six
months to spread to the subject flat. So even though the surveyor has taken
all due care, subsequent problems for a purchaser can always occur over
which the surveyor has no control. The RICS specifies the limits of such
an inspection in the HBSV.

As Malcolm Hollis in *Model Survey Reports* points out:

there are three tests that the report must be capable of surviving if
negligence is to be disproved:
1 Omission
2 Projection
3 Construction.

In simple terms, a series of questions have to be asked, the answers
to which will tend to reveal whether on the face of it, a surveyor has
been negligent. Those questions would consider:

1 Is there a defect, failure, etc. that the surveyor has failed to report
upon? If so, was it present at the time of the inspection? If not present
would it have been reasonable to expect a competent surveyor to have
anticipated and forewarned the client about the possibility of the
defect arising in the future?
2 If a defect was noted in the report, was the consequence of ignoring
the defect adequately brought to the client's attention?
3 Should the surveyor have been aware from a knowledge of construction

that a defect or problem could be expected, even though the property was apparently satisfactory at the time of the inspection, and was that possibility brought to the client's attention?

The law of negligence as it affects surveyors and other professionals is still developing, but it is clear that successful actions against surveyors may be brought several years after a report had been submitted and a property purchased. The problem then for the courts is judging whether the defect had emerged or developed, say, due to the ageing of the property, or to work undertaken by the purchaser, or failure to maintain by the purchaser, or whether it was genuinely a defect present at the date of the original report which should have been noted or reported upon.

An additional problem for the surveyor is caused by the nature of the current occupation of the property and the behaviour of that occupier towards a property. Thus a boxed-in beam supporting a load-bearing structure may or may not be of the correct strength for the loads, may indeed be non-existent or may be supported inadequately at the ends. Comments in a report to that effect may be the best a surveyor can offer, but may fall short of the encouraging words a prospective purchaser wishes to read. *Caveat emptor* is a very key term in today's residential market, and no buyer of residential property ought to proceed without an adequate independent survey report.

No residential valuer or agent should accept survey instructions unless they are fully qualified in terms of education and experience for such work, and are adequately protected by professional indemnity insurance.

Chapter 10

The legal process

In England and Wales when offers to purchase residential property are made, if accepted, they are subject to survey and to contract. This process can be misused by vendors and prospective purchasers and there is ongoing discussion by professional surveying bodies, the Law Society and the government (a) to try and evolve a simpler process, (b) to try and evolve a faster process, and (c) by so doing to try and reduce misuse of the subject-to-contract process.

The purpose and intent of subject-to-contract procedures is very simple and sensible. As has already been indicated, two prime forces will have an effect on value, the physical condition of the property, hence the need for the property to be professionally inspected, and the legal title. The subject to survey process means that the prospective purchaser has made an offer subject to the findings of his surveyor. If the surveyor comes back with a poor report itemizing many expensive defects, then the purchaser will wish to withdraw or to renegotiate. Increasingly, although not necessarily stated, on all occasions, offers are also subject to the satisfactory sale of the prospective purchaser's current property and subject to the purchaser being able to arrange the necessary finance for the balance of any purchase monies. The subject-to-contract procedure provides similar protection for the purchaser in respect of defects in title. In practice, purchasers tend to operate on the assumption that they can withdraw at any time until contracts have been signed and exchanged, and will do so at any time for any reason. Similarly, vendors can withdraw their property up until exchange of contracts.

This is the current law and it has its good points and its bad points. Most criticisms relate to the issues of 'gazumping' and 'gazundering'. This means that an otherwise contented vendor backs out of one proposition because he or she has received another higher offer. This can occur at any time and is most frustrating when a purchaser has already incurred costs in having the property inspected for loan purposes, surveyed for his or her own satisfaction and wasted a solicitor's time and money investigating the title. At its very worst the procedure could be used as a threat or bluff by the vendor shortly before contracts are due to be exchanged. In the case of a sole agency instruction in the hands of, say, a chartered surveyor, such a ploy would be contrary to ethical codes unless there really had been a higher offer submitted that the vendor insisted (as is their legal right) on accepting. This practice could be an offence under the Undesirable Practices (No. 2) Order, but an agent cannot stop a vendor using this ploy.

Whatever the truth happens to be, it causes distress and can force a purchaser into making a further higher offer to secure a property which otherwise they might lose. This 'gazumping' process can occur at any time up to exchange of contract. 'Gazundering' is the term used to describe the situation where a purchaser or purchaser's solicitor indicates, shortly before exchange of contracts, that the purchaser cannot proceed at the agreed price but could proceed at a lower price. Sometimes this is supported by an adverse surveyor's report or down valuation by the mortgage valuer, but true gazundering is a tactical ploy to force the vendor to accept a lower price. This can be disastrous if there is a chain of transactions. Here the linked sales can sometimes be saved if all parties are willing to accept a pro-rata reduction in price.

It is equally frustrating for a purchaser when, having expended money on surveys and legal fees, the vendor simply withdraws the property from the market.

For these and other reasons the professions are keen to find an improvement to the subject-to-contract procedure that will prevent its misuse but will still leave the parties free to withdraw for good reason.[1]

It is important for the agent, vendor and purchaser to see that all discussions and correspondence during negotiations and when finalizing the final offer arc made subject to contract, as a document or exchange of documents signed by the parties specifying the property and the purchase price might be interpreted by the courts as an enforceable contract. This would be very unsatisfactory for both parties, but particularly for the purchaser who must, before signing or exchanging a contract, be satisfied that in law he/she is purchasing that which he/she seeks to purchase (but see the Law of Property (Miscellaneous Provisions) Act 1988 for a relaxation of this previously strict interpretation of the law of contract for the sale of property).

From the legal point of view then, 'subject to contract' allows the purchaser (with or without the help of a solicitor) to check the vendor's title to the property to see that he/she does have the right to sell, and to be satisfied that the property can be sold unencumbered and/or that any encumbrance or defects of title are acceptable and have been adequately allowed for in the negotiated price.

It is clearly important to verify whether the property is freehold or leasehold, to check for restrictive covenants which the purchaser will have to abide by and to indemnify the vendor against any subsequent breaches of such covenants. It is important to check that the property is not subject to any local authority notice such as a repair notice requiring works of repair to be carried out. It is important to have time to check that there are no planning, highways or other matters proposed which are likely to affect the property. As well as the official enquiries, it is sometimes sensible for a purchaser to pay a visit to the planning authority or authorities to see if there are any proposals in the pipeline. They may be no more than ideas, but they could be implemented quite quickly and may not show up on the solicitor's official enquiries. The procedure also allows the purchaser time to make enquiries of the vendor on matters relating to the property such as responsibility for repairs to boundaries, whether they, or to their knowledge anyone else, has carried out foundation works to make good subsidence, and whether the vendors are aware of any damp, rot, woodworm etc. in the property. Some of these things should be obvious, but if a vendor has deliberately covered up known defects and then states at this stage that they are unaware of any defects, then it may be held subsequently to be a misrepresentation made falsely to secure the sale.

Pre-contract enquiries are usually made on standard forms produced specially for this purpose and the answers given by vendors and their solicitors are frequently of little real value, but they would, for example, list known restrictive covenants and rights of way. Other standard forms are available for making enquiries or searches of the local authority and other official bodies.

The following (based on Momentum training literature) summarizes the ten usual steps in a conveyancing transaction; the process is simplified in Figures 10.1 and 10.2. References throughout to solicitors should be read to include conveyancers.

1 The vendor's solicitor's first job is to prepare a draft contract. To do this he must have the deeds (e.g. previous conveyances of the property) or sufficient particulars of them, to be able to satisfy himself that the vendor owns the property and can sell it, since this will have to be proved to the purchaser's solicitor in due course. The draft contract will set out such matters as easements and restrictive covenants affecting the property which must be disclosed to the purchaser and will also contain a description of the property (including a list of fixtures and fittings included in the sale) and set out the terms on which the vendor proposes to sell, including any new covenants he wishes to impose. The draft contract which is sent to the purchaser's solicitor for approval, is only a basis for negotiation and is not binding on either party.
2 The purchaser's solicitor examines the draft contract and decides whether its terms are acceptable, having regard to the instructions he

has received from his client. He will then attempt to discover as much information about the property as possible before his client is committed to buy. He will usually do this by sending written questions to the vendor's solicitor (called 'preliminary enquiries') which involve matters likely to be within the knowledge of the vendor through his occupation of the property (e.g. ownership of fences, availability of gas, electricity, local authority and council tax, etc.) as well as proposed date of completion. He will also make a search for local land charges with the local council and make additional enquiries of the council to discover whether any matters within its jurisdiction affect the property (e.g. road widening schemes, compulsory purchase orders, planning restrictions).

3 When both sides are agreed on the terms of the contract and the purchaser's solicitor is satisfied with the answers he has received to his searches and enquiries, a fair copy ('engrossment') of the contract is prepared by each party's solicitor for signature. A binding contract only comes into existence when these two parts of the contract have been signed and exchanged. Before the purchaser's solicitor sends his client's signed contract to the vendor's solicitor, he checks that if his client needs a mortgage, a satisfactory mortgage offer has been received. The contract usually provides that the purchaser shall pay a percentage of the purchase price by way of deposit on exchange of contracts.

4 When contracts have been exchanged, the vendor's solicitor must prove his client's title to the property by sending to the purchaser's solicitor (if he has not already done so) an 'abstract of title', i.e. a copy of the deeds or summary of their contents showing recent dealings with the property. If the title is registered, it is proved by obtaining a copy of the entries on the register from the appropriate District Land Registry and sending this to the purchaser's solicitor.

5 The purchaser's solicitor examines the abstract of title or copy entries to check that the vendor owns the property and that there are no third party interests affecting the property which were not disclosed in the contract. If any matter is unsatisfactory or needs clarification, he will send written questions (called 'requisitions on title') to the vendor's solicitor. If the purchaser is obtaining a mortgage, his solicitor may in turn have to prove the title to the property to the mortgagee's solicitor and answer any queries raised by him, if necessary by consulting the vendor's solicitor. Frequently, however, the same solicitor will be acting for both the purchaser and the mortgagee.

6 The purchaser's solicitor also has to prepare the conveyance or transfer i.e. the deed which will pass the vendor's interest in the property to the purchaser. A draft of this is sent (usually at the same time as the requisitions on title) to the vendor's solicitor for approval and he will check that it complies with the requirements of the contract (e.g.

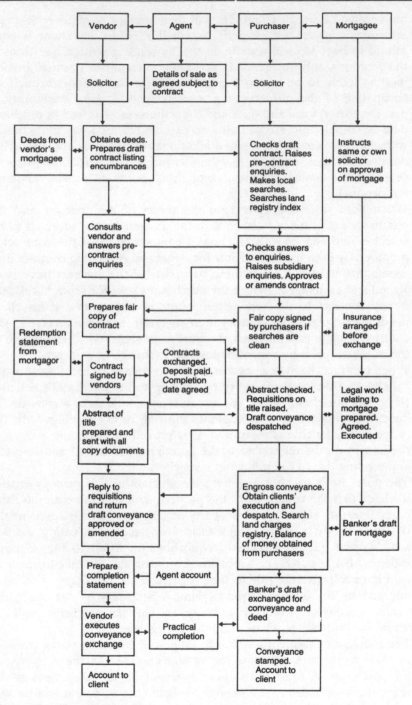

Figure 10.1 Unregistered title

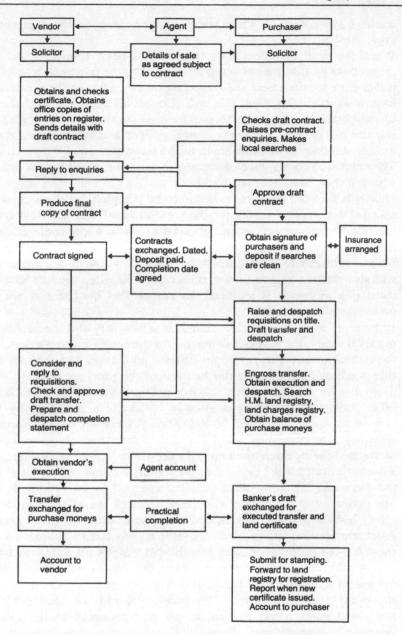

Where a mortgage or loan is involved then as with unregistered title there is the added complication of redemption and the documentation needed for the new mortgage. In chain transactions the process is multiplied and all transactions usually have to dovetail on the same day.

Figure 10.2 Registered title

contains any covenants which the purchaser agreed in the contract to enter into).

7 When the draft conveyance or transfer has been approved and the requisitions on title are answered satisfactorily, the purchaser's solicitor will engross the document and (if it contains covenants by the purchaser) have it signed by his client. He will also ask his client for the balance of the purchase money. If the purchaser is obtaining a mortgage, his solicitor will get him to sign the mortgage deed and will arrange for the mortgage money to be available in time for completion of the purchase. The engrossed conveyance or transfer is sent to the vendor's solicitor, who will then have it signed by his client.

8 Shortly before the transaction is due to be completed, the purchaser's solicitor will make a search (at the Central Land Charges Registry if the title to the property is unregistered or at the appropriate District Land Registry if the title is registered) to make sure that there are no adverse interests registered which he does not know of or expect. He will also make a search of the Bankruptcy Register against his own client if a mortgage is required, to ensure that his client is not an undischarged bankrupt.

9 If the reply to the appropriate search is satisfactory and the necessary money is ready, the parties will make arrangements for completion, i.e. the occasion when the purchaser obtains possession and receives the title deeds in exchange for the balance of the purchase money. This could involve the purchaser's solicitor going to the vendor's solicitor's office (unless the property is already subject to a mortgage by the vendor, in which case it will be the office of the vendor's mortgagee's solicitor). The purchaser's solicitor makes sure that any outstanding mortgage is being discharged and, if everything is in order, hands over a banker's draft for the balance of the purchase money in exchange for the deeds and the conveyance or transfer signed by the vendor. If the title is unregistered, he may also have to check the original deeds to satisfy himself that they correspond with the abstract he already has.

10 After completion, the vendor's solicitor merely has to account to his client for the proceeds of sale, but the purchaser's solicitor may have to deal with certain further matters. First, he must have the conveyance or transfer stamped by the Inland Revenue, which involves both paying stamp duty (unless the price of the property does not exceed £30,000) and also giving certain particulars of the transaction to the Inland Revenue Commissioners. Second, if the title is registered or, if unregistered, the land is in an area of compulsory registration, the transaction will have to be registered at the Land Registry, who will issue a Land Certificate (which contains a copy of the entries on the register of the title) unless the property is subject to a mortgage when instead a Charge Certificate will be issued to the mortgagee.[2]

This formal process has been amended in operational terms to accelerate the process. It is now a common practice for the vendor's solicitor or conveyancer to undertake local and other relevant searches to pre-prepare answers to standard preliminary enquiries and to forward these with the draft contract. The transfer of funds for completion is generally dealt with through the banks' direct transfer systems, thus avoiding the need for a physical exchange of documents and money. These arrangements are critical where there is a chain of sales, each dependent upon another and where buyers are all trying to move house on the same day. The longer the chain, the more complex the process.

An agent should regularly update his knowledge on typical costs associated with buying and selling property, the most important being solicitors' fees, land registry fees, search fees, valuation and survey fees, stamp duty and VAT.

NOTES

1 Firms of solicitors such as Nabarro Nathanson have sought to overcome aspects of gazumping by the use of pre-contract contracts or 'Exclusivity Agreements'. These are basically agreements of trust between the parties, binding for a limited period during which both parties will proceed with utmost diligence to bring the sale to contract stage and during which the vendor will not deal with any other party. Their efficacy remains to be tested.
2 This extract is as previously printed, with apologies to female readers.

Chapter 11

Leasehold residential property

The owner of a freehold property enjoys maximum ownership rights in perpetuity. The owner of a leasehold property enjoys restricted ownership rights for a limited term, namely for the length of the lease. The owner of a leasehold property is in effect a tenant of that property, bound by the terms and conditions of the lease and required to pay rent for those restricted rights. The value of a leasehold estate in a specific property will generally be less than the value of a freehold estate in a similar property, the actual difference will depend upon the length of the lease, the extent to which the ownership rights are restricted by the terms and conditions of the lease and according to how much rent is payable to the landlord or freeholder as a condition of the lease and upon the relationship of that rent to the open market rent that would be paid for the right to occupy that property.

Similar freehold properties in an area will have similar values. However, if some of the properties are held leasehold their value will differ according to the amount of the freehold estate that has in each case been transferred by the lease to the leaseholder. If the freehold estate is thought of as a rectangle, as in Figure 11.1, then it can be seen that the total value could be divided between the freehold and leasehold according to the size of each in terms of time and rights.

Clearly the total value can be divided in a hundred and one ways. In the property market the position is complicated by imperfections in the market and by statutes which can materially affect the enforcement of contractual terms and conditions as between freeholder and leaseholder. Thus in many cases the combined value of freehold and leasehold will be less than the value of the freehold in possession.

This chapter only considers the complications relating to the valuation of long leasehold residential properties, i.e. those originally granted for over twenty-one years, offered for sale (assignment) with vacant possession or valued on a vacant possession basis. The valuation of freeholds subject to occupational tenancies are considered in Chapter 14 dealing with investing in residential property. In other cases such as leases coming

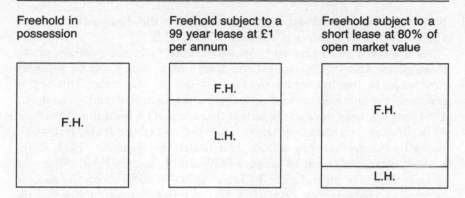

Freehold in
possession

Freehold subject to a
99 year lease at £1
per annum

Freehold subject to a
short lease at 80% of
open market value

F.H.

F.H.

L.H.

F.H.

L.H.

Figure 11.1 Diagrammatic division of value between freehold and leasehold
estates in a property

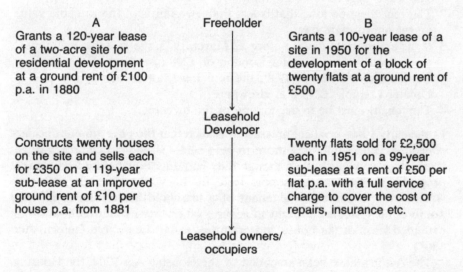

A
Grants a 120-year lease
of a two-acre site for
residential development
at a ground rent of £100
p.a. in 1880

Freeholder

B
Grants a 100-year lease of a
site in 1950 for the
development of a block of
twenty flats at a ground rent of
£500

Leasehold
Developer

Constructs twenty houses
on the site and sells each
for £350 on a 119-year
sub-lease at an improved
ground rent of £10 per
house p.a. from 1881

Twenty flats sold for £2,500
each in 1951 on a 99-year
sub-lease at a rent of £50 per
flat p.a. with a full service
charge to cover the cost of
repairs, insurance etc.

Leasehold owners/
occupiers

Figure 11.2 Typical building lease arrangements

under the protection of the Rent Acts, it is illegal to sell (assign) at a
premium (price).

HISTORY OF LEASEHOLD ESTATES IN LAND

For many years owners of land and developers of land for residential
purposes were reluctant to part with the freehold in the land itself. The
practice developed of disposing of the land on a building lease at a ground
rent (substantially in excess of the previous agricultural rent) to a builder
or developer. The developer would then sell on the completed homes on
an improved ground rent, the purchaser paying the market price for the

property which would approximate closely to the equivalent freehold value. The typical process is shown in Figure 11.2.

As a lease draws to an end, questions arise as to the position of the leaseholder who legally (under the terms of a lease) should offer up possession to the freeholder on the last day of the lease. This social/ political problem was covered initially by the Landlord and Tenant Act 1954 Part I. Under the Act the tenant (leaseholder) is permitted to remain in occupation as a statutory tenant after the end of the lease, but would today be required to pay a 'fair' rent under the Rent Act 1977, if the tenancy expires between 14 January 1989 and 14 January 1999. Where the tenancy comes to an end after 14 January 1999 it will become an assured tenancy under the Housing Act 1988. So the leaseholder will not necessarily lose the right to live in his or her home merely because the lease has come to an end. The conditions that have to be satisfied are that:

1 The lease must have been granted for twenty-one years or more.
2 The rent must be low, that is less than two-thirds of the rateable value on the appropriate day.
3 If the appropriate day is before 22 March 1973, the rateable value must not exceed £400 in Greater London or £200 elsewhere. For a tenancy created after 31 March 1990, the rent must not exceed £1,000 p.a. in Greater London, £250 p.a. elsewhere.
4 The tenant must be in occupation of the dwelling.

In the early 1960s political pressure was such that the government decided it needed to do something more to help such leaseholders who regarded themselves as owners, even though they had only ever held a lease to the property. In 1967 the Leasehold Reform Act was passed, the effect of which was: 'to confer on a tenant of a leasehold house, occupying the house as his residence, a right to acquire on fair terms the freehold or an extended lease of the house and premises' (s.1(i) Leasehold Reform Act 1967).

The Act has since been amended by the Housing Act 1969, the Housing Act 1974, the Leasehold Reform Act 1979, the Housing Act 1980 and the Leasehold Reform, Housing and Urban Development Act 1993.

The interpretation of this law and its application is complex and resulted in many early cases being referred to the Lands Tribunal, and latterly to Leasehold Valuation Tribunals and on points of law to the High Court. Agents and valuers concerned with such leasehold houses are referred to the further reading recommended at the end of the book; that which follows outlines the basic elements of the provisions. In most cases the valuer is advised to consult with the leaseholder's solicitor before formalizing any opinion on the ability to enfranchise and on the enfranchisement price. An action for negligence against a professional valuer would certainly follow if a client was incorrectly advised to buy a leasehold property because it would be possible to buy the freehold, when in fact it was clear that such rights did not exist; similarly if an agent were to advise to sell at the wrong time (say with less than three years of the lease to run), resulting in the loss for ever of the valuable enfranchisement rights. The first step is to check that the tenant qualifies under the 1967 Act or under the extended provisions of the 1974 and 1993 Acts and that the tenant is not disqualified for any of the specified reasons.

To qualify, the following conditions must be satisfied:

1 The property must be a house, namely

'any building designed or adapted for living in and reasonably so-called, notwithstanding that the building is not structurally detached, or was or is not solely designed or adapted for living in, or is divided horizontally into flats or maisonettes; and
(a) where a building is divided horizontally, the flats or other units . . . are not separate 'houses' . . . though the building as a whole may be; and
(b) where a building is divided vertically, the building as a whole is not a 'house', though any of the units into which it is divided may be.

Basically this means that owners of leasehold flats and maisonettes have no rights under the 1964 legislation to either an extension or to buy the freehold. Their only protection at the end of the lease will be the limited protection provided by the Landlord and Tenant Act 1954 or such other 'rights to buy' as enacted by Parliament in the Leasehold Reform Housing and Urban Development Act. (The Landlord and Tenant Act 1987 does provide extensive rights to tenants of a block of flats to first refusal of a freehold where landlords other than resident landlords are disposing of their rights in the building.)

2 The house must be the tenant's principal residence and must have been so for the last three years or for three years within the last ten years.
3 The lease must be for more than twenty-one years.
4 The ground rent must be less than two-thirds of the rateable value as at 23 March 1965 or if later, the first day of the tenancy or as amended by the 1993 Act.
5 The rateable value of the house must fall within certain rateable value limits:
(a) Under the Leasehold Reform Act 1967 the rateable value on the appropriate day (i.e. the later of 23 March 1965 or the first date of entry in the valuation list) must not exceed £400 in Greater London, £200 elsewhere.
(b) Under the Housing Act 1974 the limits are £1,500 and £750 respectively where the lease was granted before 19 February 1966 and

listed in the valuation list before April 1973, and £1,000 and £500 where the lease was granted after 18 February 1966.

(c) If the tenancy was created after 31 March 1990 the rateable value condition is replaced by a formula the product of which must not exceed £25,000:

$$\frac{\text{Premium} \times 0.06}{1 - 1.06^{-n}}$$

where n is the number of years granted by the original lease.

6 *Note*: The 1993 Act extends the right to enfranchise. It provides that where the tenant would qualify 'but for the fact that the applicable financial limit specified in $SS(1)(a)(i)$ or (ii) or as the case may be $ss(5)$ or (6) of that section is exceeded, this part of this Act shall have effect to confer on the tenant the same right to acquire the freehold of the house and premises as would be conferred by $SS(1)$ of that section if that limit were not exceeded.' These subsections in the 1967 Act as amended are those relating to Rateable Values etc., so the 1993 Act effectively extends the right to all long leases at low rents of houses subject to the principal residence requirement. The 1993 Act amends the low rent test to read 'less than two-thirds of the rateable value at the time of the grant of the lease if entered into on or after 1 April 1963 but before 1 April 1990 or if the tenancy was entered into before 1 April 1963 less than two-thirds of the letting value or in other cases less than £1,000 in Greater London or £250 elsewhere.'

There are additional provisions under Schedule 8 of the Housing Act 1974 whereby a tenant who has carried out improvements, the value of which is reflected in the rating assessment, can apply to the Inland Revenue for a notional reduction in the rateable value for the purposes of the Act. In this way tenants who satisfy all the conditions for enfranchisement other than the rateable value limit may be able to slip into the net and may also slip into the 1967 Act provisions rather than the 1974 provision – the importance here is that the enfranchisement price under the 1967 Act is usually lower than under the 1974 provisions.

A qualifying tenant under the 1967 Act has the right to a fifty-year extension or to purchase the freeholder's interest. None of the legislation sets down any rules for assessing the enfranchisement price, but precedent set by the Land Tribunal has in effect produced an accepted (if disputable) formula for the majority of cases.

The valuation problem in an individual case is likely to fall within one of the following four sets of circumstances:

1 Qualifying under the 1967 Act: (a) with no development value attaching to the site.
                                    (b) with development value attaching to the site.

2 Qualifying under the amended
   legislation in the higher rateable
   value bands and under the 1993
   Act:

(a) with no development value
     attaching to the site.
(b) with development value
     attaching to the site.

The issues can become complex, and readers wishing to know more are referred to the further reading listed at the back of the book; the following examples deal in outline with the most straightforward problems.

Example 11.1   A tenant occupying a house outside London qualifies for enfranchisement under the 1967 Act. The lease has twenty-two years of a ninety-nine year term to run at £20 per annum. The freehold vacant possession value would be £80,000. The tribunal's guidance suggests that an underlying principle is that the freeholder owns the site and the tenant the buildings. On this basis the freeholder has the right to receive the current ground rent for a notional fifty-year extension, plus the right to the full value of the house thereafter. Because the latter is deferred some fifty or more years, a frequent short-cut is to treat the reversionary ground rent as an income in perpetuity, even though there is provision in the legislation for a review of the rent after twenty-five years. The tribunal's findings also suggest that the new ground rent can be assessed directly – if comparables are available, or by apportioning the open market value of the freehold property between land and buildings and then by converting the land value element into an annual equivalent – i.e. the ground rent. The effect of these rulings is to produce the following fairly standard enfranchisement price valuation model.

Enfranchisement price calculation

Present ground rent	£20.00 p.a.	
PV £1 p.a. for 22 years at 7%	11.06	£221
Reversion in 22 years' time to modern ground rent.		
Freehold value	£80,000	
Site value, say	40%	
	£32,000	
Annual equivalent at 7%	£ 2,240	
(32,000×0.07)		
PV £1 p.a. in perp. at 7%		
PV £1 in 22 years at 7%	3.22	7,212
		£7,433

or	£2,240			
PV £1 p.a. for 50 years at 7%				
PV £1 in 22 years at 7%	3.12	£6,986		
Plus reversion to	£80,000			
PV £1 in 72 years at 7%	.0076	£608	£7,594	
			£221	
			£7,815	

Notes

1 The increase in house prices in the 1980s has had an effect on enfranchisement prices and the 'or' approach may produce the higher figures.

2 The use of 7% throughout the calculation has arisen out of case decisions and has rarely been successfully defeated.

Example 11.2 Assessment of enfranchisement price in accordance with s.9(1)A of the Housing Act 1974. Under these circumstances precedent has again established an accepted approach (although this can always be challenged) which holds that regard must be had to the potential additional value of merging the freehold and leasehold estates into that of a freehold in possession. A number of alternative interpretations of this approach have been held to be acceptable; that which follows is but one of these models. (Facts as in Example 11.1.)

(i) Ground rent	£20	
PV £1 p.a. for 22 years at 7%	11.06	£221
(ii) Reversion after 22 years to a fair rent[1] under Landlord and Tenant Act 1954 Part I		
Fair rent, say	£2,500	
less landlord's repairing liabilities etc.	£500	
Net of expenses income	£2,000	
PV £1 p.a. in perp. at 9%		
× P.V. of 1 in 22 years at 9%	1.67	£3,340
		£3,561

(iii) Plus marriage value given
the vacant possession value of   £80,000
FH subject to the tenant's rights
under the Landlord and Tenant
Act 1954 Part I   £3,561
LH value for next 22 years from
market comparison   £20,000

Sum of FH and LH	£23,561	–23,561
Marriage value potential		£56,439

Allowing 50 per cent[2] share of marriage value between FH and LH following the precedent in *Norfolk* v. *Trinity College Cambridge* (1976) produces an enfranchisement price of:

	(i)	£221
+	(ii)	£3,340
+ 50% of	(iii)	£28,219
		£31,780[3]

Notes

1 The provisions in the Housing Act 1988 as amended by the Local Government and Housing Act 1989 are such that a statutory tenancy arising under the Landlord and Tenant Act 1954 Part I after 15 January 1989 but before 15 January 1999 will be at a fair rent under the Rent Act 1977; after that date it will be an assured tenancy at market rent. In example 11.2 the reversion to a fair rent must now be a reversion to a market rent in all cases arising after 15 January 1989 where the tenancy is due to expire after 15 January 1999.
2 S.66 of the 1993 Act restricts the tenant's share of marriage value to 50 per cent.
3 To this figure should be added costs, and under s.66 of the 1993 Act other losses or diminution in value of other property held by the landlord.

Summary

The residential valuer and agent need to fully appreciate the workings of the Leasehold Reform Act 1967 as amended as it relates to 'houses', if they are to advise on the sale or purchase of leasehold homes and/or on the probable price that a leaseholder will have to pay to acquire the freehold or on the price that a freeholder should seek either when a leaseholder serves notice to enfranchise or seeks to acquire by negotiation knowing that it will be possible to fall back on the law if the freeholder is unwilling to sell. This consideration is in addition to all the other factors discussed elsewhere such as age, condition etc.

The first step is to check whether the leaseholder or subsequent purchaser of the leasehold is or will be entitled to rights under the 1967 Act as amended; this should be confirmed by the client's solicitor. If not, then care is needed when valuing the leasehold by comparison to see that it is comparable with other similar non-enfranchisable leaseholds.

If the right to enfranchise is established in principle then the leaseholder with a valuer's guidance needs to consider whether to sell the leasehold before or after exercising the enfranchisement rights. It must be borne in mind that a subsequent purchaser will have to satisfy the three years' residence requirement before they in turn will be able to exercise such rights. In many cases the decision will be a personal one dictated by the need to sell, the speed with which a sale must be concluded and possibly the length of the unexpired term of the lease. In theory the sale price of a leasehold with enfranchisement rights should approximate to freehold vacant possession value less the enfranchisement price and associated costs – a leaseholder enfranchising will be required to meet most of the freeholder's costs as well as his or her own costs, other than the free-holder's leasehold valuation tribunal costs. In practice the difficulty of raising finance to purchase, say, a ten-year lease linked with the need to wait three years before seeking to enfranchise together with all the associated niggles of such an exercise may depress the sale price. Clearly, when the lease has as little as five years to run it would make more sense to enfranchise first and then to sell the freehold. An important considera-tion is the size of the marriage value involved – the reason being that if this is potentially a substantial sum from the leaseholder's point of view, then the leaseholder should seek to maximize on that potential.

Market comparison is still important in the valuation of vacant possession leasehold estates in residential property. In the absence of leasehold comparables an idea of the leasehold value can be found as suggested by reference to comparable freeholds and deducting the enfranchisement price and costs.

At one time there were a number of loopholes in the enfranchisement legislation, but all the known loopholes have now been blocked, including the much-publicised concept of seeking a fifty-year extension prior to seeking to enfranchise before the expiry of the original lease. Specific rules under the Housing Act 1980 cover the problem of a 'minor superior tenancy', that is with a reversion of no more than a month and a profit rent of no more than £5 per year.

LONG LEASEHOLD FLATS AND MAISONETTES

The agent/valuer/surveyor dealing with leasehold properties of this nature must take account of the terms and conditions of the lease. In the case of both purpose-built blocks of flats and in the case of houses converted into flats the lease will indicate (not necessarily clearly) the liability of the leaseholder in respect of the individual unit and the whole building.

Most leases will make the leaseholders liable jointly for meeting the costs of repair, maintenance and renewal of the whole structure including all common areas, grounds and services. A common practice is to provide for the recovery of these costs on a proportionate basis through a service charge or maintenance charge. Although some owners will supervise such works themselves, many appoint managing agents to collect the rents and service charges and to oversee all matters relating to the building. The agent/valuer should inspect the lease to ascertain the facts and make enquiries of the owners or managing agents to obtain details of the current service charges per annum. Such information as is provided in these cases should be confirmed in writing. It is also important to inspect not only the flat being valued or sold but also the whole building and to find out whether any major capital expenditures have just been undertaken or are planned.

Where the ownership of the building is in the hands of a management company the flat owner as a shareholder should have details of the annual maintenance account and minutes of the annual general meeting. The object of the enquiries is to check both the quality of the general maintenance and management, the normal cost and any substantial expenses due in the near future.

If it were possible to make a strict comparison then the value of leaseholds where the leaseholders are also shareholders in the company owning the freehold would be greater than those where the ownership of the freehold is in the hands of an independent owner.

The problem of surveying flats has already been considered, but as condition affects value so the valuer and agent must be as alert in their inspection of the whole as they are in respect of the subject flat. The RICS in their *Mortgage Valuation* leaflet make the same point when they state that:

> It would be impracticable to derive guidance notes that could be relied upon when taking account of the common parts of converted or purpose-built flats or maisonettes, but it should be borne in mind that the management and maintenance arrangements for the building(s) of which the flat or maisonette forms part are relevant factors for valuation purposes.

Comments here can go little further on the difficulties associated with valuing leasehold properties of this type, other than to emphasize the need for additional care in surveying, in valuation and in preparing sale details. The length of the lease and its terms and conditions will have a major impact on value, and as leases differ between properties on almost every lease term, valuation by comparison becomes even more complex.

Currently public opinion has focused on two main aspects of this class of leasehold property. The first is the problem of tenant control over the standard of repairs and services provided by landlords and the charges made for such services. Tenants now enjoy substantial rights under the Landlord and Tenant Act 1985, one effect of which is to take away from the landlord and/or the landlord's agents the total discretion to do as little or as much as they felt was necessary and the discretion to accept whichever estimate they preferred for works without, in many cases, even seeking competitive estimates. The second issue is that relating to the right to buy. The Landlord and Tenant Act 1987 is stated to be:

> An act to confer on tenants of flats rights with respect to the acquisition by them of their landlord's reversion; to make provision for the appointment of a manager at the instance of such tenants and for the purchase of long leases held by such tenants; to make further provisions with respect to service charges payable by tenants of flats and other dwellings.

Although this gives power to leaseholders to influence the way in which their building might be managed, especially in the case of difficult or absentee landlords, there are many who feel it does not go far enough and that a right to buy should be granted to individual unit holders. The underlying argument is the same as that postulated prior to the Leasehold Reform Act 1967, namely that the leaseholder owns the flat and the freeholder the land, structure and common parts. For this reason the government has extended the 'right to buy' to certain groups of lease-holders (see below). In addition the 1993 Act provides for the establishing of codes of good practice in property management and allows tenants to audit management accounts.

The enfranchisement provisions in the 1993 Act give leaseholders a right to buy collectively the freehold of their block of flats. Briefly these proposals apply to long leaseholds (over twenty-one years) at no rent or a low ground rent (less than two-thirds of the letting value if entered into before 1 April 1963 or less than two-thirds of the rateable value on the grant of the lease if entered into between 1 April 1963 and 31 March 1990 (inclusive) or, if let after 1 April 1990, less than £1,000 (London) or £250 (elsewhere). At least two-thirds of qualifying tenants must collectively agree to enfranchise, at least two-thirds of the flats must be held on long lease and one-half of the qualifying tenants must satisfy the residence condition. These proposals will only apply to buildings containing two or more flats where not more than 10 per cent of the internal floor area is, or can be, used for non-residential purposes. If the landlord is resident in a flat in the building then the building will be exempt if the building contains four or fewer flats. Long leaseholders are entitled to a ninety-year extension to their lease.

The enfranchisement price (and the price to be paid for a ninety-year extension) will be based on normal market valuation principles and will include:

1 the open market value of the freeholder's interest assuming the tenants are not in the market, plus
2 at least half the marriage value, plus
3 any additional amounts to cover the landlord's injurious affection, plus
4 the landlord's costs.

These rights are in addition to and separate from the prior rights to buy set out in the Landlord and Tenant Act 1987 as amended by the 1993 Act. The calculation of enfranchisement prices must be left to the specialist. The author advises all agents to obtain a statement from the vendors' solicitors whenever a long leasehold property is to be sold, setting out clearly the nature of the original lease and the current position and indicating in the case of flats and maisonettes whether:

1 a collective approach to enfranchise has been proposed and the outcome of discussion and any notices served on the landlord, and
2 if not, whether collective long leasehold enfranchisement could apply to the block.

It seems essential to clarify these points of detail, accurately, for the benefit of all potential purchasers.

The changing nature of the market for leasehold flats and maisonettes and the legislation relating to such properties requires the agent/valuer to be doubly alert to the potential effects on this segment of the market of all relevant new legislation.

Chapter 12

The desirable plot

The valuation of a plot of land suitable for constructing a single residential unit and the valuation of an area of land suitable for development as an estate of houses both lend themselves to a more precise scientific method of appraisal. However, throughout the exercise the valuer will be juggling so many conflicting and complimentary variables that in the end, market experience may count for as much as the mathematics in formulating a final opinion of value. In practice the larger the site and/or the larger the potential scheme of development, the greater will be the number of variables and imponderables and the greater will be the complexity of the appraisal exercise.

Comparison acts as a backstop to all residential development appraisals. Sale records provide the valuer with information needed to establish a general level or likely band of value for the single plot and for the multiple unit scheme. Thus, right from the moment of instruction the residential valuer will sense from their knowledge and experience that a plot of land should sell for £20,000 or £50,000, or an acre for £250,000 or whatever. Many valuers may be content that their sense from comparison with known sales is correct, but others involved in residential development work may require additional proof. Thus the vendor may need supporting calculations to arrive at a reserve price for an auction. Financial backers may need a full appraisal before guaranteeing both short-term funds for the development and long-term mortgage facilities for the eventual home buyers. A bank manager may need a proper appraisal to approve a loan to allow an individual to purchase a site to build a home of their own.

Residential development work for the residential agent and valuer breaks down into site finding, research, legal enquiries, physical investigations and financial analysis.

SITE FINDING

The national firms of home builders and the larger local firms tend to employ their own site finders. Site finding and market research go hand in hand, as developers are intent upon satisfying the demands of the general public for the right property in the right place at the right price. The site finder must therefore be aware of significant shifts in demand, be they shifts in terms of quality of end product desired or shifts in locational preference. They need to be as fully informed as possible of the dynamic nature of the housing market.

Sites suitable for developing may be (a) brought to the attention of the site finder by local agents, by advertisements and by personal contact with landowners, or (b) by analysis and investigation of registers held by local authorities, nationalized industries and the like who may hold surplus land or (c) by personal survey of a local land market to identify sites which might not yet be ripe for development but look hopeful for future development. In many cases it is the site finder who creates the residential development opportunity by working with a landowner or landowners and the local planning authority, and overcoming legal and physical difficulties and possible local opposition.

In London the home buyers market was so buoyant in the 1980s that site finders were creating opportunities out of sites already developed for other land uses. Thus existing industrial and warehouse uses have been found to be more valuable for redevelopment as residential schemes than in their existing uses. The site finder with the development team creates the opportunity from an apparently insoluble mixture of land ownership, land uses, legal constraints and physical restrictions. The position in the 1990s is very different, however, with major residential developers holding large land banks which have been substantially down-valued. But whilst there have been enormous changes in market activity, the process remains unchanged, with even more emphasis now being placed on market research.

MARKET RESEARCH

Market research both precedes and follows site finding. Market research is an ongoing activity which identifies consumers' needs and then seeks to provide a route by which those needs can be satisfied. Market research in the housing market occurs at various interrelated levels.

At one level it involves monitoring major population changes to identify new or changing markets. This monitoring may reveal a change in locational preferences caused by improvements to road and rail communications. Thus the rapid change in the residential market in East Anglia occurred following trunk and motorway improvements and electrification of rail systems. New and faster train services can bring an attractive but non-commuter town or region into commuting distance. Such changes are firstly reflected in an acceleration in the local homes market, both in the volume of sales and in the rise in house prices, and then by a growth in demand from developers for sites for new homes. The end result may be the destruction of all the features that previously made it an attractive location. Reduction in travel times seems to be a major force behind the changing pattern of home location.

Change in the composition of the population must also be researched, as it signals changes in the type of housing required by the nation, but more specifically it may highlight shortages of certain types of accommodation of certain qualities in particular areas.

Market research in the broad sense is essential to the housebuilding industry. It is also very important at the local and site-specific scale.

Once land has been identified or purchased for residential development, the success of the scheme of development will depend upon how successful the developer has been in accurately identifying the market. This level of research is at its most sophisticated at the top end of the market, but is increasingly essential where developers with similar schemes are in competition within a given geographic area.

Part of market research is to identify unsatisfied segments of the market. Thus over recent years there has been a move by major housebuilders to provide homes for first-time buyers, single people and for the retired. In different areas of the country and in different parts of London very different markets can be identified. Coupled with this identification of market segments is the identification of users' requirements and the level of price that that type of purchaser is prepared to pay for that quality of property where he or she or they expect to find it.

In the housing market there is a tendency to assume that the buyer will be an owner-occupier. This is not always the case, and although the requirements of the end user (the occupier) need to be foremost in the developer's plans, the re-emergence of the residential investor cannot be ignored, nor can the emergence of the speculator who buys to resell on a rising market at a quick profit.

For many years the quality developer has endeavoured to sell to build. Provided they have identified the right market, secured a site in an area acceptable to that market, correctly identified the price the market will bear and the quantity and quality of space required at that price, then the development will sell itself often phase by phase, before the units are built. To accelerate this process developers will thoroughly market the scheme, creating the right reflective image, using promotional literature and advertising to sell that image and unit mock-ups to convey the quality of the planned home environment. A complete package of facilities will sometimes be needed to include landscaping, security, leisure facilities, services. All of this will flow from that ongoing research, so that wherever possible, the developer brings together the right product, in the right place, at the right time, at the right price, and that the whole package of benefits matches as accurately as possible the expectations of the end user.

Where a site has been found the process is the same, but here the analysis of opportunity must flow from the site. The exercise is essentially the same, that is to alight upon the highest and best use for that site, having full regard to all the variables. In practice, when demand exceeds supply as it did in the period up to 1989, it is necessary for the developer to secure future development opportunities for the development company before completing the whole analysis and research into the highest and best use. To do this, developers enter into 'option agreements' or 'partnership contracts' with landowners. These arrangements effectively secure the site or first refusal to buy a site, but may be extremely complex, involving some degree of equity participation. A very simple arrangement might be for the developer to offer to pay the landowner 35 per cent of the sale price of every completed unit, rather than a capital purchase of the whole site on completion of formalities. Such arrangements can secure a much better cash flow for the developer than the traditional buy and build arrangement.

The less user-conscious developers still build to sell – often building to old designs and without proper regard to the market. Without sufficient forethought they find that buyers will only inspect once the home is completed, at which point the developer will have stamped his image on the property and removed any opportunity for the new owner to express his or her preference for finish and fixtures. Instead of being occupied immediately upon completion these units remain empty for weeks or months, at a cost to the developer.

Market research and site finding are interrelated; once a site is found then the exercise becomes site specific and must have regard to the legal and physical factors that relate to that specific site.

PHYSICAL CONSTRAINTS

The local market must be thoroughly analysed and the highest and best use for the site determined having regard to all the factors. This requires an appreciation of the location of the property in relation to the immediate area, communications – road, rail and air, schools, hospitals, leisure facilities, shopping facilities, proximity to the nearest major centre and major employment opportunities, and assessment of the general environment quality. The area analysis should take account of the state of the local housing market, current values, and should identify any over- or under-supply of property types and the quantity and quality of homes being offered by competitors. Out of this might come answers to questions such as, 'Which socio-economic group is most likely to want to live in homes to be built on the site?', 'What sort of homes would they most like to own?', 'What price are they best able to pay?', 'What quality and quantity of space needs to be provided to achieve sales at that price?'

At the same time, the suitability of the site for development will be considered. The nature of the soils and subsoils will be checked, bore holes may be necessary at some stage to check load-bearing capability, investigations made to check that the site is not made-up ground or subject to mining subsidence or flooding. Some such 'contaminated' sites may in the future be noted on registers held by District Authorities, but for the moment sound local knowledge is essential. Height above sea level, topography, water-table and aspect will be checked and enquiries made of any extreme weather conditions or micro-climate. Natural features will be noted in case they may enhance the development or have to be removed to provide for the development; this could include ponds, lakes, streams and wooded areas. Such enquiries will also elicit whether there is likely to be a major public outcry once the scheme is announced which could lead to delays of one form or another.

The object of these investigations is to discover whether there are any physical factors that could give rise to increased construction costs or reduced sale prices.

Enquiries of various public bodies and authorities are also needed. The developer must sound out the planning officers for the area and the local highways department. Problems of access must be resolved, even if it is a single plot of land. Checks on the availability of mains water, the costs of connection and the ability of the system to cope with the anticipated increase in consumer demand will have to be made. (Separate arrangements will be necessary for a water supply for the contractors during the construction process.) Similar checks have to be made in respect of electricity and gas supplies.

In order to gain the necessary planning consents it may be essential to enter into an agreement with the authority to provide certain facilities by way of planning gain. On the highways side this could include the widening of approach roads and construction of roundabouts, bus lay-bys and the like. The planners may be looking for the provision of community facilities over and above that which a developer would have included for the successful marketing of the scheme.

LEGAL CONSTRAINTS

There are also legal points to be checked. The land may be the subject of covenants restricting it to agricultural use. Such restrictions can be lifted after reference to the Lands Tribunal, but whether they are or not will depend upon the circumstances and the arguments put to the Lands Tribunal. Previous owners may have granted leases to the whole or part of the land which will have to be bought out or allowed to terminate. In the case of business tenancies, compensation may be payable. The presence of protected residential tenants may severely restrict development unless satisfactory arrangements can be made with the tenants for rehousing.

There could be rights of way over the land which will have to be protected, i.e. a scheme of development worked out which will provide users with similar rights from A to B across the site.

There may be building or tree preservation orders in force. There is no order to the discovery of all the information needed before proceeding with the financial considerations. However, anything missed may become a major issue during a development scheme, and could swing a profitable operation into a loss-making exercise or at worst, bankruptcy for the builder or developer.

Development land being offered for sale by auction or by tender poses the additional problem that all investigations must be undertaken by a specific date, but the developer does have the opportunity to make all enquiries openly. In other cases the developer is juggling with time, the landowner's patience, shareholders' capital, the planning authority, solicitors and financiers; hoping that no other developer comes along to upset negotiations by offering a better, purely speculative price whilst the first developer tries to dot the i's and cross the t's. It is for this reason that many developers, after an initial assessment of an opportunity, will agree to buy subject to contract, survey and the grant of outline planning permission, or will enter into a partnership arrangement, or will seek an option to purchase, securing more time to complete the investigations.

This stage of the development process is very complex, and although some of the principal points have been touched upon in outline, it is not a series of discrete chronological events; everything happens as an on-going process for a number of sites at the same time, overlapping with market research. Similarly, whilst it is possible to detail the financial process as a simple model the reader should appreciate that the valuer's task becomes extremely complex when dealing with major schemes of redevelopment or refurbishment.

RESIDENTIAL SITE VALUATION

The single plot

The valuation of residential development sites is possibly the most logical of valuation exercises. For those active in this market, initial analysis and valuation will often be based on direct comparison rather than on the theoretically sound cash flow analysis. However, at later stages in negotiations, initial approximations will be checked against results obtained from cash-flow models. Once a scheme is under way, the discounting process of valuation is replaced by cash-flow accounting so that targets can be monitored and maintained. Without this development control, profit margins would be eroded. This accounting process perfectly illustrates the valuation exercise needed at the preliminary appraisal stage. For example,

Table 12.1 Summary of builder's accounts and analysis for constructing one
house

August	Site purchase	£25,000	Interest at 1% per month × 1.01
	Legal fees	250	
		£25,250	
September			252.50
October	Planning etc.	2,000	255.03
November	Site works	1,500	277.58
December	Foundations etc.	6,000	
	Materials on site	5,000	295.35
January	Problems, Christmas break, bad weather		
	Labour	1,200	408.30
February	Brickwork etc.	5,000	424.39
March	Brickwork/roof	4,000	478.63
April	Subcontract, heating, electrics etc.	6,000	523.42
May	Finishes	2,000	588.65
June	Fencing, drives etc.	3,000	614.54
July	House sold		650.68
		£60,950	£4,769.07
	Total costs and interest	£65,719.07	
	Sale at £75,000 less fees	£73,000	
	Profit	£ 7,280.93	
	Profit as return on gross development value	£ 7,280.93 × 100 = 9.71%	
		£75,000	

assuming that a local builder has purchased a small infill site for one house
in an established residential location at a cost of £25,000, the final account
for this development might appear as set out in Table 12.1.

The figures used are illustrative and represent an approximate summary
of a builder's accounts: in the real world the labour charges, material
invoices, VAT statements etc. would be far more complex. Indeed the
payment of many amounts would be deferred several months and the
whole picture complicated by the builder's other contracting activities
which might take his labour off-site for a few days or weeks. Nevertheless
the figures help to emphasize several points.

First is the importance of allowing for interest charges. Whether a
builder uses his own money or borrows all the money, an allowance must
be made for interest payable or notional interest lost if an accurate picture
is to be found of the cost of building a house. The interest column
illustrates how these costs rise over the construction period to be a
significant element, and again assist in understanding the need for 'creative
accounting'. Thus a shrewd builder should be weighing the discounts for
prompt cash payments against the increased interest payable on money

used for such payments for, say, four to eight weeks ahead of final demands.

Here the total charge to interest is approaching £5,000, which represents some 7.5 per cent of the costs. It also illustrates the need to defer site purchase until all the preliminaries are completed. If site purchase can be deferred until detailed consent is obtained, then the date of purchase can become the date of commencement of construction. The amounts here are small, but they can be very significant on a major scheme. Thus as far as possible developers will transfer this burden to the existing landowner.

Second, delays during the construction period are costly. Most can be avoided through sound project management; some, however, cannot, such as the discovery of important archaeological remains.

Third, it illustrates a golden rule, which is 'sell to build', not 'build to sell'. Speculative development is risky, but some risk elements can be reduced to acceptable levels: one such is associated with finding a buyer. A careful balance has to be struck between achieving a sale too soon at current prices against the cost of a delay beyond completion but achieving a future sale price. At this scale, builders still tend to put the property on the market too close to practical completion – they build to sell – and it can take several months for the buyer to complete. Such delays after the bargain has been made will be costly for the builder.

Finally, it illustrates why the Lands Tribunal and others are so keen to criticize development appraisals and how keen the media is to criticize the level of development profits. Here the builder has taken a calculated risk and has achieved a profit of 9.71 per cent over and above his allowances for overheads etc. If he had based his bid on an expected sale of £75,000 and over the ten-month construction period sale prices had risen by 10 per cent his profit would have risen to say £16,500, to show a return on costs of 25 per cent. This is completely outside the builder's control as it is a function of the housing market. If, on the other hand, he failed to achieve a sale at £75,000 and after a three-month delay had to accept a sale at £72,500, his profit margins would be eroded. The latter has happened to a greater extent between 1989 and today, but the media will soon forget this in the next period of inflationary house prices.

In inflationary periods the market can become so competitive that a part of the inflation in house prices has to be reflected in the site bids. In addition, owners of the larger residential sites will expect to participate in the equity of the large schemes by gearing the price of the sites to the sale price of the houses (see above). This is unlikely to find favour with landowners in times of falling prices.

Residential site valuation is this contractor's account in reverse, as the object of the exercise is to assess a sensible bid price for the site – see Table 12.2.

In Table 12.1 interest at 1 per cent per month was added. Alternatively, each month's total could have been multiplied by $1 + i$, here by $1 + 0.01$, that is by 1.01. So in Table 12.2 to allow for this element the cash flow needs to be discounted back month by month by dividing by 1.01.

These two tables demonstrate the simple difference between accounting over time and discounting over time. At this level of the residential land market most competent builders can go direct to plot value by comparison or by the simple process of deducting an estimate of construction from the expected sale price, such as £75,000 less £50,000 equals £25,000 for the site. In the case of larger sites it becomes more complicated, as one must allow for the phasing of the scheme and for the complex flows of money in and out. A full cash flow analysis is in effect Table 12.2 accumulated on a timescale 10, 20 or 100 times, according to the size of the development. In some cases it will be useful to repeat the exercise (a) to check for the sensitivity of any of the variables and (b) to incorporate estimated inflation in house prices and building costs.

The two tables help to illustrate the nature of the market for single plots and some of the strange prices paid in the market by potential owner-occupiers. Single plots tend to attract the small local builder and the owner-occupier keen to build a home to an architect's interpretation of their own design. The larger builder may not be able to compete because of larger overheads. However, at an increased density it is the small builder who cannot compete because of their inability to reap the economies of scale enjoyed by the national housebuilders. The apparently high prices paid by the future owner-occupier can be explained in part by a lack of understanding and an element of DIY. The owner-occupier will rarely reflect interest charges in his or her calculations and will forget to allow for a profit margin.

Fortunately for many in the past, inflation in house prices provided a sufficient margin at the end for the mortgage valuation to support the decision to build and to provide the necessary long-term funds to repay short-term borrowings plus interest. In addition the owner-occupier has a tendency to account differently to a builder and ignores the cost of his or her own labour when undertaking the non-contracted works. Finally, as the owner-occupier tends to subcontract most of the construction work, he or she will avoid some of the overheads that a builder has to include. The result is that at auctions, individuals may carry on bidding after the local builder has withdrawn. The local builder relies more on their knowledge of the area and site finding skills to maintain a flow of small sites outside the auction room.

Crucial to all residential site valuation work is the skill of the appraiser in assessing demand, the level of demand, the highest and best use for a site, the costs of development including interest and acceptable profit margins, and the price people will pay for completed units. Without this skill there would be insufficient accurate information to complete the

Table 12.2 Developer's assessment to find site value

End month		
12	House sold for	£75,000.00
	Less costs	2,000.00
		73,000.00
	Allowance for profit at 9.71% say	7,282.50
	− 1.01 for monthly discounting	65,717.50÷1.01
		65,066.83
11	Site works, fencing, drives etc.	3,000.00
		62,066.83÷1.01
		61,452.31
10	Finishes	2,000.00
		59,452.31÷1.01
		58,863.67
9	Electrics, heating etc.	6,000.00
		52,863.67÷1.01
		52,340.27
8	Brickwork, roof etc.	4,000.00
		48,340.27÷1.01
		47,861.65
7	Brickwork, etc.	5,000.00
		42,861.65÷1.01
		42,437.28
6	Wages, no progress	1,200.00
		41,237.28÷1.01
		40.828.99
5	Foundations and materials on site	11,000.00
		29,828.99÷1.01
		29,533.65
4	Site clearance etc.	1,500.00
		28,033.65÷1.01
		27,756.09
3	Planning etc.	2,000.00
		25,756.09÷1.01
2		25,501.08÷1.01
1		25,248.59
	Less fees	
		£24,998.10*

* 25,248.59 = Site value X + fees at 1% 1.01X = 25,248.59
X = 24,998.61 (two decimal place rounding error)

appraisal; thus, as always, experience and the valuer's art has to blend with the science of valuation to produce supportable opinions of worth.

Multiple unit sites

As with any development appraisal exercise, the financial calculations must follow detailed preliminary investigations and enquiries. These investigations must cover all legal, physical, planning, highway, services matters.

The list is almost endless, but the investigations need to be as thorough as possible to avoid unscheduled delays in the construction process once the site has been acquired. Although such delays will be post the acquisition, the possibility of there being delays must be built into the appraisal if the developer is to acquire the site at a price that will provide profit at a level commensurate with the risks involved.

At this initial stage of the appraisal exercise the valuer should be able to determine a 'best estimate' of all the costs and benefits of the scheme at current price levels. It should also be possible to judge the phasing of the development in terms of the likely market take-up for new homes in that locality and the related best phasing of construction to meet that demand, having regard to any (and all) site, servicing, labour and construction issues.

Subsequently a view may be taken and figures amended if, over the projected development period, it is felt that either costs or benefits are likely to change owing to real or inflationary price movements. The extent to which a particular developer is prepared to do this is debatable. Competition in the London land market in the mid-1980s was so great in some districts that land owners appeared to be able to ask almost any price for their land; developers in turn being able to ask whatever price was necessary to cover their land and other costs. At a period when house prices in London were rising at £50 or more per day this may have been a case of buying with inflation fully discounted in the calculation. The problem with this desperate approach is that an abrupt downturn in home prices can bankrupt the over-enthusiastic developer (precisely the situation that occurred immediately after publication of the first edition of this book in 1989).

The nature of the cash flow valuation needed to handle the larger more complex multiple unit site is well illustrated by Diane Butler in her book *Applied Valuation* (Macmillan, 1987). An amended version of her example is shown below, which can of course be changed to derive any one of the main variables. Thus, given the site asking price it can be used to calculate the profit, or the minimum sale price needed to achieve an acceptable profit, or to calculate the maximum sum available for construction, given all the other variables.

Example

A site with outline consent for 110 units is to be offered for sale by tender. It is estimated that it will take one year to complete the whole scheme and that thirty units would be sold after six months, fifty more after nine months and the last thirty after twelve months. The following assumptions have been made:

Acquisition costs of the land to be taken at 4 per cent on purchase price;
Gross area of each unit to be 82m^2;
QS and architect's fees to be taken at 10 per cent of building cost with 60
   per cent payable on commencement and 40 per cent upon completion;
Estate agency and legal fees etc. to be taken as 4 per cent of sale price;
Financing costs to be at 1 per cent per month;
Sale price per unit to be £35,000;
Developer's profit of £500,000 to be taken out by the developer.

   Certain initial calculations are necessary to provide the data for the DCF
solution in order to arrive at a tender price.

Building costs
110 × 82m^2 × 250 = £2.255m
evenly spread ÷ 12 = £187,916 per month

QS and architect's fees
10% of costs   = £225,500
60% now   = £135,300
40% on completion = £90,200

Sales proceeds
After 6 months   = 30 × £35,000 = £1.05m
After 9 months   = 50 × £35,000 = £1.75m
After 12 months = 30 × £35,000 = £1.05m

Estate agents' and legal fees at 4%
After 6 months   = £42,000
After 9 months   = £70,000
After 12 months = £42,000

The DCF monthly calculations on these assumptions are set out in Table
12.3. From this it is possible to calculate the maximum tender price that
the developer can afford to submit with the tender document.

   Totalling the monthly figures, having due regard to the plus and minus
signs, produces a figure of £1,049,506.

   This represents profit of £500,000, purchase price and acquisition costs
thus:
Total   £1,049,506
Less profit   500,000
                £ 549,506

Letting x = Site value and $0.04x$ = acquisition costs then:
1.04 x = £549,506
and x = £528,871

   Thus offering in the region of £525,000 would produce the desired level
of profit on the assumptions made. This would not necessarily succeed as a
tender, however; clearly, a more optimistic developer would be able to

Table 12.3 DCF monthly calculations

Item	0	1	2	3	4	5	6	7	8	9	10	11	12
Fees	−135,000												−90,200
Building costs		−187,916	−187,916	−187,916	−187,916	−187,916	−187,916	−187,916	−187,916	−187,916	−187,916	−187,916	−187,916
Sales							+1.05m			+1.75m			+1.05
Agents' & legal fees							−42,000			−70,000			−42,000
Totals	−135,000	−187,916	−187,916	−187,916	−187,916	−187,916	+820,084	−187,916	−187,916	+1,492,084	−187,916	−187,916	+729,884
PV at 1% per month*	1	0.990	0.980	0.971	0.961	0.951	0.942	0.933	0.923	0.914	0.905	0.896	0.887
Discounted totals	135,000	−186,037	−184,158	−182,466	−180,587	−178,708	+772,519	−175,326	−173,446	+1,363,745	−170,064	−168,373	+647,407

* to 3 decimal places

offer a higher price. These figures are illustrative and must be assumed to include every cost item including contingencies that every respectable developer would normally allow for on an item-by-item basis. Additionally, the assumptions of timing are gross simplifications of the housebuilding process in the real world.

Many trainee valuers find it difficult to appreciate that in a DCF exercise such as this there is no need to add on the interest charges before discounting. For example, why, if £135,000 is to be paid out immediately, is there no apparent provision for interest at 1 per cent per month for twelve months? The more astute will, however, see immediately that if interest were to be added, the expenditure in period 0 would be moved forward to period 12 compounded at 1 per cent per month, only to be brought back to period 0 by discounting at 1 per cent per month. It is simple to demonstrate that the DCF exercise as set out fully reflects the nature and incidence of interest charges at 1 per cent per month by testing the residual result by accounting forward from period 0 to period 12 – see Table 12.4.

Acquiring at a figure of £528,371 produces after-interest charges (note sign changes in Table 12.4) both for interest payable and interest receivable of £564,154. The profit allowed for was for a present sum of £500,000 and therefore a future sum of £564,154 represents the result after allowing for interest at 1 per cent per month.

$$£500,000 \times (1 + 0.01)^{12} = \text{say } £564,000$$

As with any set of calculations, the results are totally dependent on the inputs. Therefore clear thinking is needed if a DCF calculation is to produce meaningful results. Thus profit could be expressed as a return on cost or as a percentage of sale price or taken out in period 12. The timing and the amounts will influence the final conclusion. If in fact the figure for profit of £500,000 had been taken out in period 12 then the developer's bid could have gone up to £582,505. Altering the variables this way and testing to see the effect on the results is very much simpler if the basic tabulation is set up in the form of a spreadsheet calculation.

It is argued that DCF is a better technique for the appraisal of development sites than the traditional residual – in particular for large residential schemes, where (as here) cash inflows can at times exceed accumulative cash outflows. This allows the developer effectively to deposit money. A simple residual cannot allow for this factor; a DCF can in fact allow for differences in interest between that payable and that receivable.

The ever-improving standards of project management which have led to ever-faster construction schedules mean that valuers have to bring their appraisal techniques into line with the tight schedules and cash-flow controls exercised by the project managers. Naturally, there remains a

Table 12.4 Development funding account on a purchase price of £528,371

	£				£	
Period 0	528,371	Site purchase			883,425	
	21,135	costs at 4%	Period 7		187,916	Construction
	135,000	Fees			1,071,341	
	684,506				10,713	Interest at 1%
	6,845	Interest at 1%			1,082,055	
	691,351		Period 8		187,916	
Period 1	187,916	Construction			1,269,971	
	879,267				12,699	Interest at 1%
	8,792	Interest at 1%			1,282,670	
	888,059		Period 9		−1,492,084	Sales
Period 2	187,916	Construction			−209,413	
	1,075,975				2,094	Interest at 1%
	10,759	Interest at 1%			−211,507	
	1,086,735		Period 10		187,916	Construction
Period 3	187,916	Construction			−23,591	
	1,274.651				235	Interest at 1%
	12,746	Interest at 1%			−23,827	
	1,287,397		Period 11		187,916	Construction
Period 4	187,916	Construction			164,088	
	1,475,313				1,640	Interest at 1%
	14,753	Interest at 1%			165,729	
	1,490,067		Period 12		−729,884	Net sales
Period 5	187,916	Construction			**−564,154**	Profit
	1,677,983					
	16,779	Interest at 1%				
	1,694,762					
Period 6	−820,084	Sales				
	874,678					
	8,746	Interest at 1%				
	883,425					

(All figures adjusted to nearest £1 as per calculator computation.)

place for the quick initial residual calculation to support the developer's 'hunch' or 'feel' for a good prospect. But after that the valuer needs to adopt a more complex cash flow approach.

Multi-unit single structure residential development

Residential development is not always undertaken on greenfield sites, nor is it in structural terms restricted to simple domestic low rise schemes. In concentrated urban areas it is sometimes the case that the developer will create the site by the piecemeal acquisition of a block of existing large family homes, or by acquiring a mixture of land uses from a multiplicity of land owners, or by acquiring sites vacated by relocating central land users such as electricity boards, local education school sites, bus depots and old warehouses.

The development process in these cases becomes more complex. It also becomes that much more difficult to assess market demand through market research, and in some cases the developer is tapping latent demand. In other words, it is the creative skill of the developers in their design or refurbishment work and their marketing that moves or shifts demand from more conventional locations to these refurbishment or redevelopment schemes. Where the design solution is to construct flats or complexes of residential units in a single structure, there is a change in the cash flow that has to be accounted for.

It is not possible to release flats on an individual basis in a major complex. Though detailed consideration at the design stage may make it possible to release units in blocks or phases, clearly before occupation can occur most of the communal elements must be complete. Staircases, lifts and other essential shared areas must be finished before occupation. The financial effect is that there is a longer period of waiting before any cash inflows occur. This difference in phasing of costs and benefits must be reflected in the cash flow calculations.

When demand is very high it is possible to sell from plan. This usually requires the launch of a major marketing campaign with studio mock-ups of interior finishes etc., to whet the buyers' appetites – the aim being to secure contracts on all or most units in each phase before commencing any construction work. These contracts usually require the deposit of 10 per cent of the purchase price, and so in this way the developer can recover perhaps 20 per cent of the construction cost at the commencement of the project. Unfortunately, to secure this in month one requires an agreement at that stage on the final purchase price. Few buyers are prepared to be bound by an open-ended contract, although in some cases a building cost index-linked contract might be possible. In such a case the prospective buyer might agree to purchase a specified flat upon completion for £300,000; such price only to be varied if a specified building cost index increases by more than 5 per cent. Provision would then be made for the way in which the price could be amended. What is more important to the developer is to see that each phase of the scheme is sufficient in itself to attract substantial interest but small enough to allow for rapid completion. Thus during the total construction period it is possible to release phases at intervals to maintain a flow of money receipts.

The general prosperity in the London area during the 1980s allowed many developers to operate in this way at the top end of the market. As a result schemes attracted not only end-users but also investors and speculators. A typical speculator would pay £30,000 now to secure a £300,000 unit due for completion in twelve months' time. Over that twelve-month period values in London rose by, say, 20 per cent. Thus the next phase of units and the speculator's unit in twelve months would have a market value of £360,000. The speculator then sold-on the contract for

£60,000 and thus achieved a return on capital of 10 per cent in twelve months. If at the end of the twelve months the market had not risen enough, then the speculator might complete the purchase and let the unit for a further twelve months at an economic market rental on a shorthold basis, prior to selling at a future date.

Achieving the right balance for the developer between cash in hand today in the form of 10 per cent deposits and fixed sale prices, and deferring sales for six months to achieve a hoped-for even higher price is all part of the complexity of the development process and careful market research and marketing.

A somewhat similar but nevertheless different issue occurs in the case of sheltered housing schemes. Here the attraction to buyers is the convenience, help and security provided by the presence of a warden. Because of this purchasers require the assurance that the scheme is totally finished and has a warden on site before they move in. So again, although very similar to a normal housing development, the cash flow may be negative for a little longer than for a commensurate normal scheme. There is less opportunity in such schemes for securing early contracts because of the more cautious nature of retired purchasers.

The recession following the 1980s property boom has bankrupted some residential developers and left others holding land banks purchased at prices in excess of current values. These economic changes have not affected the rationale of the residual method. The method would currently support the market view that the costs of development exceed the value of the homes that could be built on certain sites.

The developer's dilemma is being able to gauge the state of the market. Thus in a rising market over-bids may be compensated by further rises in house prices. In a falling market, falling house prices will erode profit. The next uplift is likely to be slow starting until purchasers' confidence is returned through stable or rising prices. Rising land prices will only occur when once more effective demand is seen to be in excess of available supply, and that is not likely to occur before a strengthening of the UK economy has permeated through the labour market and renewed the individual's desire to move, or to purchase for the first time.

Chapter 13

Home improvements

Those who earn a living from home improvement contracts have a tendency to overstate the benefits to the home-owner – in particular creating a mistaken view that money spent on residential property improvements will always be recoverable on the resale of the property. Unfortunately there is no set of rules to guide the unwary; merely a number of points that should be checked before embarking on works.

As a generality, prospective buyers will endeavour to negotiate prices down to reflect what they perceive to be, or have been professionally advised to be, items of disrepair. Their own eye also alerts them to the decorative order of a property and again both buyers and residential agents tend to place a lower price on a property in poor decorative order than one in good decorative order. It is therefore possible that expenditure on repairs and redecoration alone will affect the value or price of a property. The extent to which the need for such works affects price is for the market to determine. Thus the alert and active agent will know at a point in time which of the following scenarios will apply to properties in a poor order:

The property is in poor order but in a very popular residential area. The competition between buyers is such that sale prices are very close to the market value of similar properties in good order.

The property is in a reasonably popular area but with market alternatives available to buyers the price will have to be reduced by an amount roughly approximate to the cost of making good the defects in condition and decoration.

The property is in a depressed area and prices for all properties are low and no amount of expenditure by an individual on a single property will have any effect on values. The difference in value between the poorly maintained and the better maintained is marginal. However in some such areas, area improvement by a number of owners could so alter the area that relatively minor expenses could have a significant impact on appearances and on values.

These are just three examples to illustrate that the difference between good and bad properties in a given area may or may not be reflected by a variation in value equal to the cost of making good, greater than the cost of making good, or less than the cost of making good. Value and cost are not synonymous.

The position here as with home improvements is clouded by the stories of Mr and Mrs X who only paid £A thousand pounds for a property, spent £B on redecoration and repair, and resold for £D thousand pounds. In these stories it is important to separate increases in market value due to changes in market conditions from increases due to owner's expenditure and to be aware of the difference between monetary costs and real costs. Few home-owners add on to the monetary cost their own labour costs when they have managed to do most things themselves. DIY is then an added complication in the residential market when considering the economic justification for home improvements and similar expenditures.

In the case of home improvements the problems are very similar, as value is a function of market forces but cost is an absolute sum made up of materials and labour, overheads and profit. Thus there will always be examples of low-cost improvements resulting in substantial value changes, high-cost improvements resulting in marginal value changes, some improvements at whatever cost which have no effect on value or in extreme cases may reduce value, and other cases where value and cost tend to be in balance.

VIABILITY

Before embarking on improvement work, the home-owner should try to answer these questions: 'If my house was improved in accordance with my plans overnight, what would be the new value? Would that change in value cover the costs involved? Does this allow for the disturbance time? Does it produce a profit? If it is clear that the change in value will not cover the costs, then the individual must be satisfied that the added benefit to themselves justifies the expenditure.

The residential agent/valuer ought to be able to give some guidance on the value implications, whilst most competent builders can advise on the costs, subject to unexpected contingencies.

There are a number of obvious cases where value judgements can be accurately made. For example, terraced houses with no proper bathroom or hot water supply etc. can be compared to those in the same street that have been improved, and simple cost/value judgements made. On certain housing estates one finds standard extensions have been added to some but not all the properties. Thus a number of three-bedroom units may have been enlarged to four bedrooms by building over the garages (foundations etc. permitting). So here again a reasonable cost/value judgement is possible.

The effect of installing central heating to property A on an estate where some properties have central heating and some do not is also assessable.

Improvements in the form of modern, i.e. current, kitchens, or recently refitted bathrooms, may improve a property in the eyes of buyers and accelerate the sales process but may add very little to value. In these cases over-expenditure will virtually never be recovered. Spending £10,000 on kitchen units in properties normally selling for £30,000 will have almost no effect on value. Spending £5,000 on new kitchen units in properties selling for £200,000 may prejudice the attitude of purchasers in that price range to that property.

There are some clues to sensible home improvements, the principal of which is that the improvement needs to conform to the property and to the market if it is to be reflected by a sufficient change in value to recover all costs. This means that it is necessary to know what price people are prepared to pay in the market for what quantity and quality of property in the area of the subject property.

Thus an attractive three-bedroom house on a good-sized plot in a street dominated by similar four-bedroom houses may be capable of enlargement and by such improvement may release sufficient latent value to cover all the costs. A similar exercise in an area dominated by inferior two- and three-bedroom houses is very unlikely to show an adequate change in value.

The whole subject of improvements and value change is also naturally linked to the quality of the architect, building surveyor or designer used to advise on the possibility of home improvements in general or specifically to meet an owner's desire. Subsequently the quality of the design solution and choice of materials, finishes and builder will have the result in the right combination producing the right solution at an economic cost, i.e. value of improvement exceeding total cost; or in the wrong combination possibly producing a complete disaster, to which the market-place reaction will be one of 'well the only thing to do is to knock it all down and start again'.

Where the improvements involve additions to the exterior of the property the general consensus is that the proposals must match the existing in terms of design and materials. Roof lines and roofing materials are very important. At long last, most people seem to have recognized the ugliness of the flat roof extension, so that some form of pitched roof is now insisted upon by planning officers for two-storey extensions and preferred, even if only monopitch, for single-storey extensions. This rule seems to apply to all properties, not just period properties. A few believe that where it is not possible to follow the existing, then it is better to go for a complete contrast. Again on completion there will be those in the market-place who will say, 'What a pity, I wonder why they did not try to match up with the original structure?'.

The warning is that although it might be cheaper to go for a non-conforming design solution, it may have an adverse effect on value.

No single chapter in a book can cover all the do's and don'ts of home improvement work. Fortunately, there are many good books on the subject, an increasing number of good examples to look at in all areas and an increasing number of professional experts to guide the home-owner. There is also an increasing expertise in planning offices. In this field the local residential agent/valuer will need to develop his or her skills to be able to advise accurately on the value changes associated with home improvements.

Extensions to a property may be costly but can be financially rewarding where the result is to move a property into a different value range. This is not a function of the size of the extension, nor of its cost; it is a market measure. Indeed, in a number of cases the latent value potential of a location may be such that the best solution is to demolish the existing property which is under-utilizing the site and to replace it with a property that fulfils the potential of the site. A typical example might be the replacement of a two-bedroom bungalow in a non-bungalow location with a four-bedroom detached house. In each case, the market dictates values and value changes, not costs.

More typically, improvements may involve alterations to the internal layout. This may involve, in a proper and workmanlike manner, the removal of walls, the relocation of a bathroom, the creation of an en-suite shower area to a master bedroom, provision of fitted wardrobes, the redesigning of bathroom or kitchen. Fashions change, styles change, preferences change, so that here again capturing the tone of the market-place may produce good financial returns at low cost. Equally the charm and character of a property can be destroyed by bad taste satisfied at high cost with negative value impact. Market awareness and market research helps the good agent/valuer to improve his or her advisory skills in this specialist area, where even the choice of the right colour for the bathroom fittings can make or break a design concept.

A final word of warning for the unwary on the subject of conversions. The original design of a builder may lend itself to convert unused space into useful space. If such additional space will add to the marketability of the property then the cost of conversion may be justified. If to do so involves major structural changes, however, then costs may not be matched by value changes. Media advertisements that proclaim it is cheaper to convert a roof than to move to a larger property may be correct in certain cases, but this does not mean that such costs will be recovered by immediate value changes.

Thus:

Two-bedroom house value	£30,000	Three-bedroom house value	£40,000
Roof void conversion	(10,000)	Costs to sell and buy	
Two-bedroom house with		including removal	(2,000)
third bedroom in			
roof value now	**£32,000**	Total cost	**£42,000**

The advertisement is correct in that the additional space can be created for £10,000, whilst a move would have cost £12,000. The result, however, is that the unwary will now own a non-conforming three-bedroom unit in a two-bedroom locality with a marginally increased market value of £32,000. In these specific circumstances the home-owner would have been better advised to move upmarket. The abolition of tax relief on home improvement loans may be a further incentive to move rather than to improve.

BUYING FOR GAIN

It is possible to develop an expertise in this area and to buy judicially to improve and subsequently sell, realize the gain (which is untaxed in the case of a principal residence) and move on to another improvable opportunity. Improvement in this sense may mean alteration, conversion or extension. It should, however, be clear from the foregoing section that this is extremely problematic and in many cases is linked with movements in house prices, keeping ahead of the market and moving upmarket toward the luxury homes sector. It may also involve risks such as the purchase of property with a protected tenant in occupation of part and having to find that tenant alternative accommodation of an acceptable standard and in an acceptable location, or waiting for the tenant to move out. Similarly, gains can be made under the correct circumstances by obtaining planning permission on a separate part of the garden or for converting a single family residence into flats and indeed, in the right market, by converting a multi-occupied property back to a single family residence. Those individuals who have the time and the patience to operate in this way in the market-place make their gains from a combination of everything. The skills required are those of the entrepreneur, valuer and market analyst, plus good luck; otherwise the market can turn against the tide at the wrong time. Success is achieved by buying that which can be improved and which will produce a value gain over and above the associated costs. This involves recognizing market trends and buying ahead of those trends by purchasing properties at low cost in areas which subsequently increase in popularity with resultant increases in value. All of this involves risk; if it did not and if the market were perfect, then the potential to gain by purchase and improvement would be eroded to the point where costs equated with value change.

There are no firm rules about the effect of improvements on value, as it is a question of the market's reaction post the event that dictates the value change. The valuer's duty, if asked, is to advise on the probable outcome pre the event; the approach is that of before and after valuation. Bryan J.D. Spain and Leonard B. Morley in their book *Home Improvement Price Guide* (E. & F.N. Spon, 1987) estimated that the percentage of construction costs recovered from resales within two years of completion for the following standard works of improvement might be:

Central heating	50–75	per cent of costs
Garage	50–75	" " " "
Double glazing	40–50	" " " "
Loft conversion	20–40	" " " "
Basement conversion	20–40	" " " "
Sun lounges	10–30	" " " "
Bathroom extension	0–20	" " " "
Kitchen extension	0–10	" " " "
Porch	0–10	" " " "

On the other hand, every agent, valuer and builder can quote supportable cases where costs have been fully recovered by value changes within twelve months. Overall costs and value are rarely the same; the successful residential improver has to identify those circumstances where immediate value change will exceed the costs of alterations and improvements by 15 per cent or more.

PLANNING PERMISSION AND BUILDING CONTROL APPROVAL

Some local authorities issue booklets explaining the need for planning permission and setting out the process in simple terms.

Almost all extensions and alterations to residential property will require building regulation approval. There are limited exceptions in the case of open-sided car ports, porches and conservatories not exceeding 30m² in area. Certain similar-sized free-standing buildings may be erected if they are not intended for use as a bedroom.

All substantial extensions or additions to a residential property will require planning permission. If work is undertaken without planning permission the authority can exercise their powers to insist on a retrospective application, or if necessary, use their enforcement procedures to require the property to be reinstated. Where permission is granted, the works must be completed in accordance with the approved plans; if not, the authority can require additional works, including renewal and reconstruction.

An application for planning permission must also be made in the following cases:

1 To separate part of a house to create a separate home.
2 To use a caravan in a garden as a home for someone else.
3 To use part of a house for business or commercial purposes, or to use part of the gardens for parking a commercial vehicle or taxi.
4 To undertake any works in contravention of any conditions imposed by the original planning permission.
5 Where the work may obstruct the view of road users.
6 Where the work involves a new or wider access to a major road.
7 To make additions or extensions to a flat or maisonette.

Certain classes of improvement work are classed as permitted development; in these limited cases permission is declared to have been granted. However, in some areas the classes of permitted development are restricted, so it is essential to check the position with the relevant planning authority. Where the property is in a conservation area, a national park, an area of outstanding natural beauty, or in the Norfolk or Suffolk Broads, or is a listed building, the planning position is more complex and consultation with local planners is essential before commencing any works. Agents operating in such areas should obtain copies of advisory leaflets from their planning offices for the benefit of prospective purchasers.

In some areas the local council may have restricted some of the permitted developments by means of an Article 4 direction.

The following types of work are included in the list of permitted development under the general development order:

1 The construction of a porch provided it is 2 metres away from any boundary, is less than $3m^2$ in area and does not exceed 3 metres in height.
2 Extensions which add less than $70m^3$ or 15 per cent of the volume to the original house – that is the property as at 1 July 1948 or as first built – up to a maximum of $115m^3$ measured externally. It must not be for use as a separate dwelling, it must not occupy more than half the existing garden, if it is less than 2 metres to a boundary it must be less than 4 metres high, it must not extend beyond any existing wall fronting a highway, it must not exceed the highest part of the original roof. In practice most two-storey extensions will exceed the volume tolerance and most planning authorities now require all two-storey extensions to be constructed under a pitched roof. The specified areas are reduced to $50m^3$, or 10 per cent of the volume in the case of terraced houses and all houses in conservation areas, national parks and areas of outstanding natural beauty and the Norfolk Broads. (The position in Scotland is different.)

A check with the planning authority and the building control office prior to drawing up plans and submitting applications is a sensible precaution.

Early advice can often be obtained on important points such as foundation depths and type of materials.

A fee is payable on submission of a planning application and when submitting for building regulation approval. Further fees are payable when the building inspector carries out inspections, generally at foundation level and on completion.

Home-owners who have purchased with a mortgage will also need to obtain the permission of the relevant bank or building society.

GRANTS

Owner-occupiers may be entitled to grants from the local authority to help with certain home improvement works. There are strict tests to be applied by the local authority and it is essential that no work is begun until all the requirements of the authority have been satisfied and written approval of the grant issued by the authority.

Details of the various grants are set out in *House Renovation Grants*, a booklet produced by the Department of the Environment and the Welsh Office.

Local authorities are required to apply a test of financial resource when assessing eligibility for a grant. For the majority of purchasers, their eligibility for mortgages is probably a measure of their ineligibility for grants. Owners on income support are more likely to be eligible.

Agents need to be aware of any areas designated for 'Group Repair Schemes'. Here the authority will meet 50 per cent of the cost of specified repairs to the external fabric of a group of houses. This could be a useful selling point for a property.

FITNESS FOR HABITATION

Agents and valuers need to be aware of the standard test of fitness for human habitation. The provisions of the Property Misdescriptions Act are such that an agent may need to indicate where a property clearly fails to meet the standard test.

A property is fit for habitation unless it fails to meet one or more of the following requirements and because of that failure is not reasonably suitable for occupation:

1 it is structurally stable;
2 it is free from serious disrepair;
3 it is free from dampness prejudicial to the health of the occupants (if any);
4 it has adequate provision for lighting, heating and ventilation;
5 it has an adequate supply of wholesome water;

6 there are satisfactory facilities in the dwelling-house for the preparation and cooking of food, including a sink with a satisfactory supply of hot and cold water;
7 it has a suitably located water-closet for the exclusive use of the occupants (if any);
8 it has, for the exclusive use of the occupants (if any), a suitably located fixed bath or shower and wash-hand basin, each of which is provided with a satisfactory supply of hot and cold water; and
9 it has an effective system for the draining of foul waste and surface water.

Chapter 14

Investing in residential property

Residential property has always offered investment opportunities for private individuals, builders, speculators and the small to medium-sized property company. As an investment, property is similar to many other types of investment where a capital sum is paid out today in exchange for future benefits. In the case of property the future benefits may be income in the form of rents, and/or capital in the form of future sale monies which may or may not be greater than the sum paid out today to acquire the property. In each case the investor endeavours to assess the level of future benefits and the probability of actually receiving those benefits, relates those benefits to the total acquisition cost, measures the relationship between benefits and cost to ascertain the probable rate of return from the investment and decides whether that return is sufficient to compensate for the risks involved in making the investment.

THE RISKS

The particular risks of investing money in residential property are:

1 Risk to income – Will the tenant(s) pay the rent?
– Will they pay it on time?
– Will it keep pace with inflation?
– Will it be subject to fluctuation due to the owner's responsibility at law or under the lease to spend money on the property on repairs etc.?
– Is it or will it be restricted by legislation?
– Will it be subject to voids when tenants vacate?

2 Risk to capital – Will it be maintained in money and real terms?
– Will it be possible to realize the capital by resale, without undue delay or cost?
– If vacant possession value exceeds investment value will it be possible to release the higher value, or is possession restricted, or will it be restricted, by legislation?

                – Will the capital value be eroded by the tenants' wear
                   and tear of the fabric?

3 Management
  risk   – Will it prove to be expensive to manage?

In addition, because property has a fixed location and can only be used
and enjoyed at that location, the investor must be conscious of the effect
that changes in the local economy and the local environment may have on
the investment, as well as an awareness of the way the national economy
influences all UK-based investment opportunities.

Opportunities to speculate in the residential market have already been
referred to, thus it is possible to purchase freehold land and freehold
residential units merely to hold and to speculate on their capital value
rising over one or more years. (Where an individual makes such a
purchase, the return may be treated solely as a capital gain for tax purposes
– in which case it will be index linked (see Chapter 15), and taxed at the
individual's marginal tax rate.) In periods or areas of excess demand it may
be possible to sign a contract to purchase upon completion at a fixed price
and to resell the contract at a price reflecting the increase in property value
before the new home is completed. However, the normal interpretation
of investing in property implies the purchase of already tenanted rent-
producing property, or the purchase of property with the intention of
leasing. This form of investment in residential property is the subject of
considerable legislative interference, and only fools purchase without
taking the advice of solicitors with expertise in landlord and tenant law.

The position in the nineteenth century for the residential investor was
far simpler. A residential property could be purchased and leased to a
tenant at a market-based occupational rent and the investment would have
been created. Provided the purchase was of the freehold, then the initial
relationship could be measured by expressing the net of expenses property
income as a rate of return on acquisition cost, thus:

$$\frac{\text{Net income}}{\text{Acquisition cost}} \times 100 = \text{rate of return}$$

This rate of return could then be compared to other investment
opportunities, and having considered the relative risks a decision could
have been taken as to whether such a return was a sufficient reward for
the risks. An important feature of the market at that time was that the
owner would have remained free to deal with that property subject only
to the contractual terms of the occupier's lease. If the lease came to an
end through the passage of time or by the service of notice in accordance
with the lease, the tenant would have vacated the property unless another
lease were signed. If the tenant failed to pay the rent, the landlord could
have exercised the right to use bailiffs to distrain upon the tenant's

possessions to recover the rent, and could recover possession for non-payment of rent. The position since 1915 has been complicated by successive legislation designed to protect some or all tenants by restricting the landlord's rights to recover possession at any time for any reason and by making provision at various times for legislative control over the level of rent that could legally be recovered from a tenant.

The letting of residential property for twenty-one years or less before 14 January 1989 may have created a protected tenancy under the Rent Act 1977; if let for longer than twenty-one years it may convey rights under the Leasehold Enfranchisement Act 1967 on tenants of houses, rights under the Landlord and Tenant Act 1954 part I on all other tenants, and collective enfranchisement rights on certain long leasehold flat tenants under the Leasehold Reform, Housing and Urban Development Act. Any letting of residential property may imply in law that that property is fit for human habitation. Any letting for less than seven years after 24 October 1961 will impose certain repairing liabilities upon the lessor (landlord) under ss. 11–14 of the Landlord and Tenant Act 1985, even if in the lease the tenant has covenanted to repair. The same Act also covers 'information to be given to a tenant', 'the provision of rent books and the information to be contained in rent books', 'fitness for human habitation', and 'matters relating to service charges, namely accounts, reasonableness, estimates and consultations'. If this was not enough, the Landlord and Tenant Act 1987 also:

> confer(s) on tenants of flats rights with respect to the acquisition by them of their landlord's reversion; to make provision for the appointment of a manager at the instance of such tenants and for the variation of long leases held by such tenants; to make further provision with respect to service charges payable by tenants of flats and other dwellings; to make other provisions with respect to such tenants.

The Act became law in May 1987, and most parts of it are now operative; this Act and the 1993 Act are of real importance to those considering investing in freeholds or head leaseholds in blocks of flats. Their provisions are understood only by a small number of surveyors and solicitors specializing in this type of property.

The popular concept of investing in houses and flats is one that is confused by legislation. To the private individual in this market a major issue is that of the protection afforded to pre-January 1989 tenants by the Rent Act 1977, be they tenants of unfurnished or furnished accommodation. A property or tenancy will qualify for protection under the 1977 Act if the tenancy is contractual and is of a separate dwelling house and has a rateable value on 'the appropriate day' within one or other of the rateable value limits set out in the Act. These conditions need careful checking by a solicitor, but reference needs to be made to the following rateable values.

The first figure refers to properties in London; the figure in brackets to properties outside London:

Appropriate day	Rateable value limits not to exceed		
Pre-22 March 1973	£400	(£200)	
	£600	(£300)	(on 22 March 1973)
22 March 1973 to			
1 April 1973	£1,500	(£750)	(on 1 April 1973)
After 1 April 1973	£1,500	(£750)	

In addition the rent must exceed two-thirds of the rateable value on the appropriate day. In the case of post 31 March 1990 tenancies, the rent must be between £1,000 (£250) and £25,000. A few anomalies to this may exist which may require research into the history of the tenancy. The effect of the protection provided by the Act is to (a) extend the tenancy beyond any contractual or lease agreement, with the possibility of the tenancy passing on death, i.e. possibly from husband to surviving wife, from wife to surviving son or daughter, subject to an occupation qualification. A tenancy passing on death after 14 January 1989 will, in most cases, become an assured tenancy (see below); (b) make provision for the determination of a maximum recoverable rent, known as a 'fair rent' by a rent officer – such rent must exclude any scarcity element in its determination and for unfurnished lettings this can result in levels of rent substantially below economic or market levels, a rent so determined remains fixed, saving for exceptional circumstances for two years; (c) restrict a landlord's rights to repossession to the grounds set out in the Act, most of which are at the discretion of the court.

Absentee owners, owners of property purchased for retirement, and owners of property let for holidays are the few owners who will be able to recover possession, provided the procedures set out in the legislation are followed to the letter.

In order to try to circumnavigate these restrictions, particularly those relating to rent and recovery of possession, some landlords drew up extremely complex 'licences to occupy'; however, these have been held by the courts to be for all intents and purposes leases, and therefore within the 1977 Act.

In an endeavour to encourage more owners to release space for letting, the Housing Act 1980 created a new concept of 'shorthold' tenancies. These were subject to the fair rent provisions but provided the proper process of notices under the legislation was followed, repossession had to be granted by the courts.

The only group of investors to escape from this labyrinth were those 'approved landlords' such as building societies who were able to create 'assured tenancies' under the Housing Act 1980. These were lettings at market rental where the tenant had rights to renew the lease but where the approved landlord could recover possession for non-payment of rent or for redevelopment.

The position was amended by the Housing Act 1988. Tenancies granted prior to 14 January 1989, if 'protected', continue to be 'protected' tenancies under the 1977 Act. However, any new tenancy created after 14 January 1989 will be either an 'assured tenancy' or an 'assured shorthold tenancy'. In addition, most 1980 'assured tenancies' have been converted into Housing Act 1988 'assured tenancies'. An assured tenant enjoys security of tenure but pays a market rent; an assured shorthold tenant has limited protection over the level of rent but has no security of tenure. Again the legislation links a number of conditions that have to be satisfied for a residential tenancy to be classed as assured or assured shorthold. Mandatory (automatic) and discretionary grounds for possession are set out in the Act. The mandatory grounds are briefly:

Ground 1   Owners seeking to repossess their principal house;
Ground 2   Mortgagees exercising their powers of sale;
Ground 3   Holiday lettings;
Ground 4   Lettings to students;
Ground 5   Lettings to Ministers of Religion;
Ground 6   Housing Association lettings;
Ground 7   Death of the tenant;
Ground 8   Non-payment of rent.

The specific requirement for service of notices set out in the Act must be followed precisely.

The warning for all owners of residential property and the warning to be given by all residential agents is clear: 'Don't let residential property furnished or unfurnished without first discussing the matter with an experienced residential property manager and a solicitor.'

Nevertheless, there are still opportunities for investors to obtain good returns from residential property if committed to understanding the law and prepared for the very high cost (in time and money) of management, and when existing tenanted properties can be purchased at a price reflecting all the risks of investing in this sector, thus:

Maximum recoverable rent	£2,000 p.a.
Less costs of repairs,	
property insurance and management, say	500
Investment income	£1,500
× P.V. £1 p.a. in perpetuity at 10%	10
Capital value	**£15,000**

If the freehold vacant possession value is £50,000, then an investment value for a protected tenanted freehold property representing 30 per cent of the freehold vacant possession value is quite realistic.

The very active investors in this market built up portfolios of such properties and over a number of years (a) the fair rents rose slowly; (b) some tenants died and vacant possession sales occurred; (c) some elderly tenants were rehoused – suitable alternative accommodation being a ground for recovering possession and with a willing tenant it may be possible to transfer a protected tenancy of a house to similar rights in a smaller, possibly cheaper to rent and run property – and the valuable freehold sold; (d) some sitting tenants offered to buy the freehold at a price reflecting their bargaining strength as tenants, say half-way between the illustrative £15,000 and £50,000. The returns thus achieved represented an acceptable overall return to an investor.

There are also those investors who are prepared to buy and to let for multiple occupation with a preference for letting furnished to students. Thus a large Victorian house might be let to 10 students in a provincial city at £25 each per week (25 × 10 × 52 = £13,000 gross per annum); the problems are many, the risks are high, but if purchased for £80,000 the return may again be acceptable.

In this chapter it has only been possible to provide an insight into the dangers, difficulties and benefits of investing in residential property. Professional advice to investors can only be offered after a detailed study has been undertaken of all the current housing, landlord and tenant, Rent Act and taxation laws. Recent announcements from the government have indicated a growing support for more properties to be made available for letting. This is likely to occur if house prices remain stable and if rents remain high enough to provide an adequate return to investors.

Chapter 15

Valuation for other purposes

VALUATION FOR INSURANCE

The valuation of residential property for insurance purposes is simple in theory, somewhat less simple in practice and in both cases can only be understood given a reasonable appreciation of the nature of buildings insurance. It is essential to distinguish between an insurance valuation and an open market valuation. The latter might be defined as the best price one would hope to achieve on the sale of a specific estate in the land and buildings if offered for sale under normal market conditions. An insurance valuation in most instances is an estimate of the amount it would cost to rebuild everything on the land if the existing buildings were totally destroyed. As such it can be a figure which is the same as, greater than or smaller than the market value.

Why insure?

Owners of property can suffer losses in a number of ways. The sensible owner and/or occupier will take all reasonable care to ensure that such losses are minimized and that as far as possible they are compensated for such losses through adequate insurance.

The cover provided by most insurers under a domestic buildings policy extends to loss or damage caused by:

1 Fire, smoke, explosion, lightning or earthquake.
2 Riot, civil commotion, strikes or labour disturbances.
3 Malicious acts and vandalism.
4 Subsidence and/or heave of the site on which the buildings stand, or landslip.
5 Storm and flood.
6 Theft or attempted theft.
7 Collision by aircraft or by any vehicle or animal.
8 Escape of water from domestic plumbing, plumbed fittings and heating installations.

9 Leakage of oil from fixed oil-fired heating installations.
10 Falling branches and trees.
11 Falling TV and radio aerials.

This schedule, which will vary between one insurer and another, gives some idea of the ways in which a home-owner could suffer loss, and the comprehensive nature of a good insurance policy. Most policies contain reservations and exceptions. Thus in many cases the insured is dissuaded from making minor claims by various excess clauses which require the insured to meet the first – say £20 – of every loss. Special provisions usually apply to periods when the building is unoccupied and specific exclusions may apply to certain items such as storm damage to fences.

In those cases where the insurance cover is arranged by mortgagees such as building societies and banks, it will often be in the form of a block policy. In most cases an extract of the policy is issued so that the home-owner can judge the adequacy of the cover provided. In some cases it is important for the valuer to have sight of the policy, because it may affect the valuation.

Policies usually cover accidental damage to the buildings, to the statutory undertakers' pipes and cables serving the buildings and to accidental breakage of fixed glass, fixed wash basins, sinks, baths, showers etc., but not swimming pools forming part of the buildings. Here again the specific policy must be checked for exceptions and reservations and cross-checked with any policies taken out to insure contents.

In addition owners and occupiers have a responsibility to third parties. Property owners' liability is provided for under most buildings policies, whilst occupiers' liability to third parties comes under the contents policy.

Building insurance covers the cost of replacement and/or repair and resultant additional costs or losses. These additional items include architects', surveyors', engineers' and legal fees that may be incurred. For example, if a house is completely destroyed by fire it will be necessary to have plans prepared and approved for planning and building purposes. Cover also includes the cost of site clearance and certain other expenses, notably the cost of rented accommodation if the building has to be vacated whilst insured damage is made good.

Buildings

The phrase 'buildings' in most residential buildings insurance policies will include the dwelling itself and:

1 domestic outbuildings;
2 garages;
3 permanent swimming pools;
4 tennis courts;

5 paved terraces, paths and drives;
6 service tanks (cold water tanks), drains, pipes, cables;
7 oil storage tanks;
8 walls, gates and fences;
9 fixtures and fittings.

As already mentioned there may be exceptions from parts of a policy. Thus a fence destroyed by fire might be an allowable claim, one blown down in a storm may be excluded. A damaged garden wall on the other hand is probably covered under all possible heads of claim.

The insured sum

When assessing the amount of the insured sum the valuer must have regard to the actual or (where not available) the probable terms of the policy, the most important of which is the proviso that 'the sum insured must at the time of the loss or damage represent the full cost of rebuilding the buildings'. This statement may then be qualified to include or exclude some or all additional costs. Currently insurers seem to favour inclusion of all additional costs. The cost of rebuilding implies or may be qualified to mean the cost of rebuilding the actual buildings in the same form, size, style and condition as when new.

The importance of the proviso cannot be overstated. It represents what is called 'the average' or 'averaging' provisions. If for example a dwelling would cost £50,000 to rebuild but is only insured for £25,000 then the insurers will only pay out a maximum of 50 per cent of any claim

$$\frac{25,000}{50,000} \times 100 = 50\%$$

The problem with this proviso may become particularly pronounced in the case of listed buildings – those of historic or architectural interest, and with old, inefficient and/or badly designed buildings. In the case of a listed building the insured might be required to rebuild or to replace with replica materials and style – possibly very costly in terms of the open market value of the buildings. In the case of a badly designed or inefficient building the insured might in the event of total destruction take advantage of the situation and rebuild with a modern efficient building at a much lower cost. Nevertheless it would normally be essential to be insured for a sum sufficient to rebuild the actual building, otherwise a lesser claim for partial damage might only be met in part.

A second point to consider relates to those properties where replacement in the case of total loss may not be practical or possible. Examples of this type of property are the old 'back to back' houses and some 'mews' properties, where local authorities would not permit their rebuilding. In such cases the insurers might pay out on the basis of the reduction in market value, but in any event the sum would not exceed the cost of making good if replacement or repairs had been possible.

These sorts of issues may give rise to a conflict between the insured and the insurers arising from a major difference between rebuilding cost and open market value. The problem arises when rebuilding costs grossly exceed open market value, or when open market value grossly exceeds rebuilding costs.

Thus a very old, badly designed Victorian house may have a rebuilding cost of £80,000 and an open market value of £35,000, whilst another more unique property may have an open market value of £80,000 and a rebuilding cost of £35,000. Most policies require the buildings to be insured for their full rebuilding cost. In the first case the insurers may limit a total loss claim to £35,000 but to provide cover for partial claims an insured sum of £80,000 is necessary. In the latter case if for any reason the building cannot be rebuilt the insurers may seek to limit the claim to the sum insured of £35,000. Whether the land value would make up the difference between £35,000, the maximum insurance claim on a £35,000 cover, and the £80,000 actual loss suffered would be crucial to the insured.

There is no single solution to these difficult cases. In most instances it would be advisable to negotiate special cover with the insurance company.

The third point that has to be considered is that of inflation. An insurance policy is for a period of one year and the sum insured must be sufficient to cover the cost of rebuilding in the event of total destruction on the last day of the insured term. Some policies now cover this in the terms of the insurance, but in other cases it is still necessary to see that the cover is sufficient for future costs, not today's costs. It is therefore essential to check how the policy copes with the inflation element. A number of policies are now index-linked, the index most commonly used being the *House Rebuilding Cost Index* published by the Building Cost Information Service of the Royal Institution of Chartered Surveyors, Paragraph II. The BCIS is also responsible for the *Guide to House Rebuilding Costs for Insurance Valuation*, which is published annually on behalf of the British Insurance Association. Increasingly it is this guide that provides the valuer with the base data for many residential insurance valuations.

THE INSURANCE VALUATION

The sum to be insured is the current cost of rebuilding the buildings covered by the policy; this is generally based on a cost per square metre or square foot of gross floor area.

The cost of rebuilding a house, flat or other residential property will vary with size, type, age, quality and location. In addition, account must be taken of the additional costs of demolition and fees. All these factors are explained in some detail in the RICS guide, but the following main points can be noted.

Size

Building costs per unit area tend to decrease as size increases. Part of this is because fixed costs are spread over a larger area; for example, the cost of fittings such as kitchens and bathrooms, unlike, say, the cost of flooring which increases approximately in direct proportion to area. Building costs per unit area increase with the complexity of design and layout. A simple square house represents the cheapest design and any indentations or additions will add to the cost, even though there may have been no change in total size. Building costs per unit area increase with increased storey height and with every increase in the quantity and quality of the accommodation. For example, a totally open plan dwelling is cheaper than the same space divided up with partitions and doors into a number of separate rooms.

Type

Bungalows tend to be more expensive because to accommodate the same space as a two-storey house requires double the amount of foundation and roofing, which is not compensated by the reduction in wall heights and staircase provision. Terraced houses tend to be cheaper than semi-detached houses, which are cheaper than detached houses, due to the savings in shared foundations and walls.

Age

Older properties tend to have higher rebuilding costs per unit area because floor to ceiling heights are greater and finishes and materials used in older properties are more expensive than the modern equivalents.

Quality

The higher the quality of design, fittings and finishes, the higher will be the cost per unit area.

Location

The cost per unit may be higher in some areas than others. Thus the cost of rebuilding in Central London is likely to be high compared to other areas due to problems of construction in high-density areas and higher labour rates.

THE RICS 'GUIDE TO HOUSE REBUILDING FOR INSURANCE VALUATION'[1]

The costs given in the guide cover demolition, clearance, rebuilding to the original design in modern materials using modern techniques, and allow for fees at 12 per cent of the construction cost. The guide provides tables of house rebuilding costs for four regions; five house types – detached, semi, terraced, bungalow and semi-detached bungalow; three age bands – pre-1920, 1920–45, 1945 to date; three sizes – small, medium and large; and three quality bands – basic, good and excellent.

Such a guide can only hope to cover the estate and conventionally designed individual house, but provided the property to be valued fits reasonably comfortably into one of the descriptions then a simple valuation can be carried out.

The costs in the guide are expressed in terms of gross external floor area, that is the total of all floors measured to the external face of the external walls or to the centre of party (shared) walls, and include the area of integral garages. Attached and detached garages are measured separately and costed separately. The guide also contains instructions for dealing with three-storey buildings and buildings with basements.

Example Value for insurance purposes a semi-detached house built in the 1980s. It is of medium size and good quality with a gross external floor area of 105m² and a separate garage of 16m². The BCIS cost is given as £450 per m².

Gross external floor area	105m²
RICS (BCIS) rate per m²	450
	£47,250
Separate 16m² garage	£5,000
Insurance value	£52,250

If the policy is not index-linked then the sum of £52,250 will need to be increased by an amount in line with the current building costs inflation rate to cover a possible two-year rebuilding period before the sum is entered on the insurance proposal form.

Non-guide properties

In the case of properties that fall outside the BCIS guidelines, the valuer must turn to other rebuilding cost information, and in such cases a valuation might be better prepared by a building surveyor.

To assess rebuilding cost in non-guide cases the full quantities approach or the cost per unit area approach can be adopted. The latter method which follows the RICS guide is the more common but it requires considerable experience of building types, methods of construction and building costs in order to arrive at the correct rebuilding cost per square metre or square foot gross external floor area. In estimating this rate care is needed to avoid being over influenced by current costs of constructing new estate properties. In the latter case considerable cost savings are enjoyed through the scale of the operation. The fire insurance rebuilding cost figure assumes a one-off rebuilding exercise.

The eighteenth-century timber-frame thatched cottage, the twentieth-century architect-designed split-level steel and glass structure, the solid stone, or stone-faced cottage, and every residential property over 2,000 square feet are likely to pose insurance valuation problems which can only be solved by perhaps one or two valuers or building surveyors working in that region and experienced in the specific type of construction of that area.

In addition to the rebuilding cost for the main dwelling and garage, figures must be included or added to cover all outbuildings, swimming pools, tennis courts, garden sheds, patios and garden walls. If excluded from the total they may affect the averaging provisions in the case of every claim.

The home-owner must make adequate provision for fire insurance, must pay premiums on time and must review the cover provided regularly; even when index-linked, figures can become out of date. In some cases it is sensible to be insured for the open market value of the property, but open market value is not the same as insurance value, being a reflection of people's attitudes towards a property, whereas in most cases insurance value must be the full cost of reinstating the actual buildings.

TAXATION

Property has been a source of revenue for central and local government for centuries. The Statute of Elizabeth in 1601 was the foundation for the rating system. Currently, income arising from property by way of rent to an individual is taxed under Schedule A (Part III of the Taxes Act 1970) and capital gains realized on the sale of residential property may be taxable under the Capital Gains Tax Act 1974. On the death of an owner the value of all residential property will be assessed and added in with the deceased's estate for the calculation of inheritance tax – this may also include gifts of property made during the deceased's life.

Income from residential property

Individuals receiving income or rent from residential property must declare that income to the Inland Revenue. If an individual owns a number of properties then he or she may be considered to be in business and the profits will be taxed accordingly. Income arising from properties owned by a company will be subject to corporation tax.

An individual letting property can set against the gross income (rent plus service charges etc.) certain items of allowable expenditure including:

All rents payable to a superior landlord, ground rents and, if not redeemed, rent charges (see Appendix I).
All expenditure on repairs and maintenance but not capital items, e.g. a new boiler, nor sums paid out on accrued dilapidations existing at the time of purchase.
The cost of insuring the property and the cost of any insurance valuation.
Management expenses, including agents' letting fees.
The cost of any services provided by the landlord.
Payments such as council tax and water rates may be allowed in appropriate circumstances.

The gross receipts less the allowable expenditure produces the net income on which the taxpayer will be required to pay income tax at his or her tax rate.

In certain circumstances and where the law permits, a lump sum known as a premium may be paid by a tenant instead of part of the rent. Premiums are treated for tax purposes as part capital, part income. The capital element may amount to a part disposal for capital gains tax. The tax rules governing premiums are contained in ss. 80–2 of the Taxes Act 1970. The residential agent/valuer must be aware that premiums are taxable, but must leave the assessment of tax payable to a client's accountant. Surveyors involved in residential management must keep proper accounts for their clients in accordance with the rules and regulations laid down by the professional societies. As managing agents for absentee owners they will be required to account to the Inland Revenue for tax payable on a client's property rents.

Capital gains tax

CGT is payable on gains arising from the disposal of assets. Residential property is an asset for CGT purposes, but one of the main exemptions is the principal or main residence of an individual, including land held with the residence as a garden. Up to one acre of garden is normally accepted, and more where that would be appropriate.

To qualify, the individual must have used the property as his or her main residence throughout the ownership, except that they need not have so used the property for the last twenty-four months of ownership.

In addition, certain periods of absence from the property are permitted, provided that before and after the specified absences, the property was the main residence. These permitted periods of absence are up to three years for any purpose, up to four years in the UK due to employment away from home, and any period of time absent whilst working abroad.

Where more than one residence is owned, the individual must indicate to the Inland Revenue within two years of purchasing the second home which one is to be treated as the main residence for CGT purposes. As always, husband and wife count as a single individual for tax purposes, but separated couples may each own a main residence for CGT purposes. Once the nominated house is sold the second may then be occupied and gains from that later date will be exempt if it has then become the main residence.

Full exemption may be reduced in the following cases:

If a second home is built in part of the garden and then sold.

If part or all of the property is let (other than to a sharing lodger); however, considerable relief in the case of part-let properties can be obtained – see Inland Revenue leaflet CGT4.

If part is used exclusively for work.

If the absences exceed the stated limits.

If the house is one of a series bought and sold with the object of making a profit.

In all other cases the sale of residential property will give rise to a charge for CGT when a gain is realized. The amount of the chargeable gain is, however, considerably reduced in the following manner.

First the disposal price is reduced by the amount of all costs incurred in the sale, such as legal and agents' fees. Second, the sum is reduced by the purchase price and all associated costs and by the amount of any sums expended on improvements (not repairs) that have enhanced the value.

The next adjustment is for indexation. All gains arising from 1982 must be indexed-linked; this is to reflect that much of the capital value increase of an asset is only an inflationary increase. In the case of properties purchased before 6 April 1982 the value as at April 1982 may be substituted for purchase price as the base value for CGT calculations. The indexation adjustment is made by multiplying each allowable expenditure by a figure expressed as a decimal found from the formula:

$$(RD - RI)/RI$$

RD is the retail price index for the month in which the disposal occurred and RI is the retail price index for March 1982 or the month in which the expenditure was incurred (whichever is the later).

Finally, the chargeable amount will be reduced by the whole or unused element of the individual's permitted chargeable gains allowance or tax-free slice. The remaining sum will be taxed at the individual's marginal tax rate.

The residential valuer is not qualified to undertake tax calculations on behalf of a client; however, they may be called upon to provide supportable opinions of value as at 1982 to assist a client or client's accountant.

Inheritance tax

When an individual dies, inheritance tax is payable if the total wealth of that individual – his or her estate – is greater than the 'nil-rate' band current at the date of death. A residential valuer will be called upon, in all save the simplest cases, to provide an open-market valuation of any residential properties owned as at the date of death – sometimes referred to as probate valuations.

Such valuations are normal open market valuation exercises, but the valuer needs to be clear that the figure required is that which would have applied immediately prior to death. Any diminution in title and hence in value arising directly from the deceased's death must be discounted.

For very many people, inheritance tax will automatically become payable because of the very high property values.

The valuer needs to be aware of the point at which the inheritance tax becomes payable. This figure is generally revised annually in the Budget. A small change in value in combination with the deceased's other assets may make the difference between the whole estate being above or below the break point. It must, however, be a proper valuation, reflecting all the circumstances such as age, condition, location etc., but may often be less than a subsequently achieved sale. Where property is sold shortly after death it will be offered at a figure above the probate level (notwithstanding any changes due to a rising market), to allow for negotiation. If a very much higher figure is achieved in a very short time the Inland Revenue may require the sale price to be substituted for the probate figure. If not, then capital gains tax may be payable on the difference between the probate value and the realized figure.

LOCAL TAXATION – COUNCIL TAX

Up until relatively recently, one of the main sources of revenue for local authorities was from the rates. In 1990 residential rates were replaced by the community charge, or poll tax. This proved to be such an unpopular way to raise revenue that the government had to again review the whole subject of local taxation. The result is the replacement of the community charge with the council tax. The choice of name may be political, because in effect it is a tax to be levied on the 'value' of all 'dwellings' as defined by s. 115 of the General Rate Act 1987.

The valuations required for the council tax are not valuations in the normal sense, as the requirement placed on the listing officer for each billing authority is to place each dwelling in an appropriate value band. The value bands for England are:

Band	£		£
A		less than	40,000
B more than	40,000	and less than	52,000
C " "	52,000	" " "	68,000
D " "	68,000	" " "	88,000
E " "	88,000	" " "	120,000
F " "	120,000	" " "	160,000
G " "	160,000	" " "	320,000
H " "	320,000		

The bands for Wales and Scotland are different. The valuations are based on information available to the Inland Revenue and on external inspections, the valuation date being 1 April 1991. See Appendix VI for the basis of valuation.

The tax payable varies between bands. A 25 per cent discount is available to single residents and a 50 per cent discount is available for unoccupied dwellings and second homes.

Taxpayers have a limited opportunity to appeal against the initial valuation. For such an appeal to succeed it will be necessary to produce good evidence of comparable sale price at, or close to, 1 April 1991.

COMPENSATION FOR COMPULSORY ACQUISITION

The residential valuer should always advise clients with compensation issues to consult their solicitors. Any advice on values should be given only on specific instructions from a compensation expert. However, a residential valuer should be able to reassure a client and advise that client in broad terms on their rights to be compensated if their land or buildings are to be compulsorily acquired in whole or in part.

The first indications an owner may receive that his property is required for road widening, highway construction, channel tunnels, airports, etc. is generally a brief statement in the local press indicating that the local authority or some nationalized industry is planning to build on certain land, including land on which the client's property stands. The formal procedure is strict and all acquiring authorities must follow the specified procedures.

Typical proceedings would follow the pattern of:

1 Identifying the land needed by the acquiring aurthority.
2 Referencing the land, that is, checking each parcel and identifying the interests in each parcel that will need to be acquired.

3 Making the compulsory purchase order (CPO) in accordance with the general act, e.g. Housing Act or under a special Act of Parliament passed for the specific purpose.
4 Submitting the order to the Minister for confirmation.
5 Holding a public inquiry, which allows those affected to express views against the proposed scheme.
6 Confirmation of the order followed by service of notices, that is notices to treat and notices of entry.

Once an order has been confirmed and notice served, there is no further legal action that an owner can take to prevent his or her property from being acquired, but they are entitled to compensation and should seek professional advice to ensure that they claim all the compensation to which they are entitled at law.

Freeholders and leaseholders with an interest greater than a year, and persons enjoying the benefit of a contract or option to purchase are entitled to claim compensation under one or more of the following headings:

1 Compensation for the land taken.
2 Compensation for severance and injurious affection.
3 Compensation for disturbance.

The essential rules for the assessment of compensation are set out in ss. 5, 6–9 and 14–16 of the Land Compensations Act 1961 as amended by the Planning and Compensation Act 1991. Section 5 of the Land Compensation Act 1961 requires that in assessing compensation:

  (i) No allowance shall be made on account of the acquisition being compulsory.
 (ii) The value of land shall subject as herinafter provided be taken to be the amount which the land if sold in the open market by a willing seller might be expected to realize.
(iii) The special suitability or adaptability of the land for any purpose shall not be taken into account if that purpose is a purpose to which it could be applied only in pursuance of statutory powers, or for which there is no market apart from the requirements of any authority possessing compulsory purchase powers.
(iv) Where the value of the land is increased by reason of the use thereof or of any premises thereon in a manner which could be restrained by any court, or is contrary to law, or is detrimental to the health of the occupants of the premises or to the public health, the amount of that increase shall not be taken into account.
 (v) Where land is, and but for the compulsory acquisition would continue to be, devoted to a purpose of such a nature that there is no general demand or market for land for that purpose the compensation may, if the Lands Tribunal is satisfied that reinstatement

in some other place is *bona fide* intended, be assessed on the basis
of the reasonable cost of equivalent reinstatement

(vi) The provisions of rule (ii) shall not affect the assessment of
compensation for disturbance or any other matter not directly
based on the value of land.

In addition the claimant may make appropriate planning assumptions as
provided for in ss. 14–16. These assumptions include existing use (excluding
any assumptions in relation to Part II of Schedule 3 of the Town and Country
Planning Act 1961), or use for which planning permission has been granted,
or for the purposes for which the land is being acquired or for the purpose
indicated by a Certificate of Appropriate Alternative Development.

Thus, in the case of a freehold interest in a home being compulsorily
acquired, the freeholder could claim compensation based on the open market
value of the house, but if it was being acquired in order to facilitate the development of a new shopping centre, it might be possible (circumstances are
all-important in each case) to base the claim on the value for retail purposes.

Under appropriate circumstances the owner occupier of a house is
entitled to claim compensation for disturbance; it has been held that this
can include removal costs, the cost of altering carpets and other fittings or
the loss on forced sale because they cannot be adapted, abortive costs
incurred in the search for a new home and the legal and surveyor's fees in
acquiring the new property. Such a claim is in addition to the claim for
the acquisition of the house itself at open market value and the payment
of fees incurred by the professional advisors to the claimant on the claims.
Such claims for disturbance are not appropriate where the claim is based
on a higher value planning assumption.

In some cases all that the acquiring authority requires is part of an
owner's property. Two points must be noted here: the first is that if the
other land is increased in value because of part being taken, then
compensation will be reduced by the amount of betterment. The second,
which is more normal in the residential market, is that if the loss in value
to the remainder is greater than the value of the small area of land actually
acquired, the claim may cover such losses. An approach to this problem
is to assess the value of the whole before acquisition and the value of the
property left after acquisition. Deducting the value of the land actually
taken leaves a figure to cover the loss due to severance.

Open market value of freehold interest	£100,000	Before
" " " " " "	£80,000	After
Total loss suffered	£20,000	
Value of strip of land acquired	£2,000	
Compensation for severance	£18,000	
Compensation for land taken	£2,000	
Total claim	**£20,000**	

In these cases it may also be valid to ask for accommodation works to be undertaken by the acquiring authority, for example the erection of a fence, or realignment of a drive.

Under the Airports Authority Act 1963 and other special acts, an acquiring authority may be required to insulate a property and the Secretary of State may make insulation a requirement under s. 20 of the Land Compensation Act 1973. The latter Act also extended the rights of owners to claim compensation in circumstances where losses are suffered but no land is actually acquired. These claims are particularly relevant to the use of land for highways and aerodromes where an owner may be able to claim compensation for depreciation in value caused by noise, vibration, smell, fumes, smoke, artificial lighting, etc. The Planning and Compensation Act 1991 has improved the position of people who find their properties are seriously affected by proposals to construct or alter public works such as highways. Authorities may now purchase by agreement land which in their opinion will be seriously affected and to do so in advance of actual requirements.

It is essential when advising a client to see that they claim for all losses under all possible heads, and for this reason the matter is best left to valuers with compensation experience.

Clearly, the rights to compensation extend to landowners and thus if residential building land is compulsorily acquired, the freeholder can claim full residential development value.

In some instances the acquisition arises from action taken by an authority under the Housing Act 1985. This could include the acquisition of unfit property deemed incapable of being made fit at reasonable expense and made subject to a closure order. The basis of compensation depends upon whether the property is acquired as an unfit property or not. An unfit property basically has no value other than the value of the land itself, and in the 1950s very many – as then defined – slum properties were acquired at nominal site values. Currently it is essential to check whether the claimant will have a right to claim: (a) well-maintained allowances, (b) owner-occupiers supplements, (c) severance and/or injurious affection compensation, or (d) disturbance payments. The regulations for home loss payments and their amounts have been amended by the 1991 Act.

Properties acquired under the Housing Acts which are not unfit will be acquired in accordance with the normal rules for compensation as set out under the Land Compensation Act 1961 as amended by the 1973 Act.

COMPENSATION UNDER THE TOWN AND COUNTRY PLANNING ACTS

Compensation may also be claimable under the Town and Country Planning Acts as a result of decisions taken by a planning authority. This is an extremely complex area of law, but without going into details an owner of residential land or buildings may have a right to claim compensation if:

1 Existing planning permission is modified or revoked.
2 The Secretary of State confirms an order for the discontinuance of an established use, or for the continuance of the use subject to conditions.
3 As a result of planning decisions land is rendered incapable of reasonable beneficial use, i.e. effectively rendered valueless, then a purchase notice may be served on the authority requiring them to acquire the property.
4 It becomes impossible to dispose of certain property because of planning proposals, i.e. if the property becomes blighted, it may be possible to require the authority to acquire the land by serving a blight notice – compensation will be in accordance with the Land Compensation Act. However, when planning permission is refused for new development there is no right to claim compensation.

Other rights to compensation may arise out of other acts of planning authorities but these are very specialist and unlikely to be raised by clients of residential valuers.

NOTE

1 The RICS *Guide to House Rebuilding for Insurance Valuation* can be purchased from the Building Cost Information Service, 85/87 Clarence Street, Kingston upon Thames, Surrey, KT1 1RB.

Appendix IA

Assessment of cost to redeem a rent charge – the Rent Charges Act 1977

The Rent Charges Act 1977 provides that subject to a number of exceptions no new rent charges may be created (s. 2). The 1977 Act defines a rent charge as any annual or other periodic sum charged on or issuing out of land (s. 1) and thus distinguishes it from the usual meaning of rent as a payment between tenant and landlord for the use and occupation of property.

In the case of existing rent charges the Act provides for their total extinguishment by July 22 2037, that is a period of sixty years beginning with the passing of the Act (s. 3).

The owner of land subject to a rent charge may apply to the Secretary of State for a certificate certifying that the rent charge has been redeemed (s. 8). This means that either the owner of land can continue to pay the rent charge or the charge may be redeemed at any time by paying the redemption price.

Although rent charges are effectively an annual expenditure which could be met out of the income from property, now that their life has been reduced to a future sixty years and as the discount rate for calculating the redemption price will invariably differ from that used for capitalizing rental income, it is suggested that they should be treated as a capital deduction for valuation purposes.

In s. 10 the Act sets out the following formula for calculating the redemption price:

$$P = \pounds\frac{R}{Y} - \frac{R}{Y(1 + Y)^n}$$

where P = redemption price

R = annual amount of rent charge

Y = the yield, expressed as a decimal fraction, from 2.5% Consolidated Stock.

n = period for which the rent charge would remain payable if not redeemed

In this formula the yield is to be found from the middle price on the last trading day of the week immediately preceding the week in which redemption takes place.

Cavity insulation of timber frame houses

The following general advice for valuers was issued by the RICS in February 1988 and is reprinted with permission from *Chartered Surveyor Weekly* of 4 February 1988.

TIMBER FRAME HOUSES

Cavity fill insulation

Following developments in Scotland some general advice has been prepared for valuers about cavity fill insulation in timber frame houses and the consequent effect on value.

Although there is no evidence of the long-term effect of the installation of cavity fill insulation in the cavity of timber frame houses, there is general agreement that the cavity should not be filled. Further information on the subject can be obtained from the Building Research Establishment information paper IP1/85. In fact, where cavity fill insulation has been introduced into timber frame houses less than ten years old, National House Building Council Guarantees are withdrawn in relation to the timber frame.

There has been a wide divergence of views among lending institutions in the past, but recent, strong advice from the Building Societies' Association to its members is that they should consider each property on its merits and that consequently it is important that the valuer should supply correct information. The following advice will, however, be of assistance in reporting on these types of houses:

*It is important to check in every valuation (a) whether the house is timber framed (which must be ascertainable in any inspection); and (b) if so, whether it has cavity insulation. If necessary enquiries should be made of the vendor, in which case the source of information must be stated in the report.

*If you ascertain that the house is timber frame, but cannot find out whether or not there is cavity insulation, you should include the following in your report:

A statement that it has not been possible, within the scope of the inspection for which you have been instructed, to ascertain whether or not the house has cavity insulation; a reference to the difficulties to which cavity insulation have given rise, as indicated above; the recommendation that further investigations should be carried out, either by you or by a separate specialist, to establish whether the house has cavity insulation; a statement that your report is made on the assumption that there is no cavity insulation and that, unless you are instructed to give a further report, you accept no liability for any loss or depreciation in value that may arise on a subsequent discovery that the house does have cavity insulation.

*In reporting on timber frame properties with cavity insulation, it is recommended that you adopt an approach as follows:

Where your inspection reveals no surface evidence of dampness
In the general remarks section of the report include a comment to the effect that the applicant should be advised that insulation of cavities in this type of property is contrary to good practice and that it would be prudent for him to obtain a more detailed survey.

The valuation figure should be qualified to the effect that it is prepared on the assumption that a detailed inspection of the timber frame would not reveal significant defects.

Where your inspection does reveal surface evidence of damp penetration and you suspect the cause to be the infill material
Your report should include a statement that it should be made an essential condition of the mortgage that the cause of the moisture penetration is identified, and that the condition of the timber frame is checked – and where necessary repaired – with the infill material being removed if this is found to be the cause of the defect.

Should you be instructed to specify the check to be carried out on the timber frame attention is drawn to BRE information paper IL1/85 which covers this subject.

*Where properties are less then ten years old, it will also be necessary to advise the applicant/lender that, as a result of the installation of the infill material, the NHBC cover on the property may be wholly or partly invalidated.
*Should you ever be approached for advice about installing cavity insulation in timber frame houses, it is recommended that you advise the property-owner of the professional and scientific view and the likely effect on future value and sale.

Source: Chartered Surveyors Weekly, 4 February 1988

The nature and use of valuation tables

A wide selection of financial tables for investors and analysts is now available. *Parry's Valuation and Conversion Tables*, edited by A. Davidson and published by the *Estates Gazette* in conjunction with the College of Estate Management are probably the best known valuation tables.

The illustrative tables in this Appendix have been prepared by Peter Byrne using a spreadsheet on an IBM personal computer from the formula shown below. This is a simple illustration of the use of spreadsheets which are increasingly being used to solve directly (i.e. without reference to valuation tables) all the investment arithmetic calculations, including morgage calculations, illustrated in the text.

Amount of £1 $\qquad\qquad (1 + i)^n$

Amount of £1 per annum $\qquad \dfrac{(1 + i)^n - 1}{i}$

Annual sinking fund $\qquad \dfrac{i}{(1 + i)^n - 1}$

Present value of £1 $\qquad \dfrac{1}{(1 + i)^n}$

Present value of £1 per annum (or year's purchase single rate) $\qquad \dfrac{1}{\dfrac{1 - \dfrac{1}{(1 + i)^n}}{i}}$

Annuity £1 will purchase $\qquad \dfrac{i}{1 - \dfrac{1}{(1 + i)^n}}$

Year's purchase dual rate $\qquad \dfrac{1}{i + \left(\dfrac{s}{[1 + s]^n - 1}\right)}$

Year's purchase dual rate
adjusted for tax

$$\dfrac{1}{i + \left(\dfrac{s}{(1 + s)^n - 1} \times \dfrac{1}{(1 - t)} \right)}$$

where i = rate of interest per interest earning period expressed as a decimal
n = interest earning period
s = rate of interest earned within a sinking fund
t = rate of tax

Amount of £1, no income tax

Example:

If a person deposits £1,000 in a savings account earning interest at 10 per cent for ten years and leaves the interest to accumulate, how much money will there be at the end of ten years?

	£1,000
Amount of £1 for ten years at 10%:	2.5937
	£2,593.70

If tax is payable at 25p in the £1 this will accumulate at 7.5 per cent to produce:

	£1,000
Amount of £1 for ten years at 7.5%	2.0610
	£2,061.00

Amount of £1

Rate %	7.50	8.00	9.00	10.00
Period				
1	1.0750	1.0800	1.0900	1.1000
2	1.1556	1.1664	1.1881	1.2100
3	1.2423	1.2597	1.2950	1.3310
4	1.3355	1.3605	1.4116	1.4641
5	1.4356	1.4693	1.5386	1.6105
6	1.5433	1.5869	1.6771	1.7716
7	1.6590	1.7138	1.8280	1.9487
8	1.7835	1.8509	1.9926	2.1436
9	1.9172	1.9990	2.1719	2.3579
10	2.0610	2.1589	2.3674	2.5937
11	2.2156	2.3316	2.5804	2.8531
12	2.3818	2.5182	2.8127	3.1384
13	2.5604	2.7196	3.0658	3.4523
14	2.7524	2.9372	3.3417	3.7975
15	2.9589	3.1722	3.6425	4.1772

Rate %	7.50	8.00	9.00	10.00
16	3.1808	3.4259	3.9703	4.5950
17	3.4194	3.7000	4.3276	5.0545
18	3.6758	3.9960	4.7171	5.5599
19	3.9515	4.3157	5.1417	6.1159
20	4.2479	4.6610	5.6044	6.7275
21	4.5664	5.0338	6.1088	7.4002
22	4.9089	5.4365	6.6586	8.1403
23	5.2771	5.8715	7.2579	8.9543
24	5.6729	6.3412	7.9111	9.8497
25	6.0983	6.8485	8.6231	10.8347
26	6.5557	7.3964	9.3992	11.9182
27	7.0474	7.9881	10.2451	13.1100
28	7.5759	8.6271	11.1671	14.4210
29	8.1441	9.3173	12.1722	15.8631
30	8.7550	10.0627	13.2677	17.4494
31	9.4116	10.8677	14.4618	19.1943
32	10.1174	11.7371	15.7633	21.1138
33	10.8763	12.6760	17.1820	23.2252
34	11.6920	13.6901	18.7284	25.5477
35	12.5689	14.7853	20.4140	28.1024
36	13.5115	15.9682	22.2512	30.9127
37	14.5249	17.2456	24.2538	34.0039
38	15.6143	18.6253	26.4367	37.4043
39	16.7853	20.1153	28.8160	41.1448
40	18.0442	21.7245	31.4094	45.2593
41	19.3976	23.4625	34.2363	49.7852
42	20.8524	25.3395	37.3175	54.7637
43	22.4163	27.3666	40.6761	60.2401
44	24.0975	29.5560	44.3370	66.2641
45	25.9048	31.9204	48.3273	72.8905
46	27.8477	34.4741	52.6767	80.1795
47	29.9363	37.2320	57.4176	88.1975
48	32.1815	40.2106	62.5852	97.0172
49	34.5951	43.4274	68.2179	106.7190
50	37.1897	46.9016	74.3575	117.3909
51	39.9790	50.6537	81.0497	129.1299
52	42.9774	54.7060	88.3442	142.0429
53	46.2007	59.0825	96.2951	156.2472
54	49.6658	63.8091	104.9617	171.8719
55	53.3907	68.9139	114.4083	189.0591
56	57.3950	74.4270	124.7050	207.9651
57	61.6996	80.3811	135.9285	228.7616
58	66.3271	86.8116	148.1620	251.6377
59	71.3016	93.7565	161.4966	276.8015
60	76.6492	101.2571	176.0313	304.4816
61	82.3979	109.3576	191.8741	334.9298
62	88.5778	118.1062	209.1428	368.4228
63	95.2211	127.5547	227.9656	405.2651
64	102.3627	137.7591	248.4825	445.7916
65	110.0399	148.7798	270.8460	490.3707
66	118.2929	160.6822	295.2221	539.4078

Rate %	7.50	8.00	9.00	10.00
67	127.1649	173.5368	321.7921	593.3486
68	136.7022	187.4198	350.7534	652.6834
69	146.9549	202.4133	382.3212	717.9518
70	157.9765	218.6064	416.7301	789.7470
71	169.8247	236.0949	454.2358	868.7217
72	182.5616	254.9825	495.1170	955.5938
73	196.2537	275.3811	539.6775	1051.1532
74	210.9727	297.4116	588.2485	1156.2685
75	226.7957	321.2045	641.1909	1271.8954
76	243.8054	346.9009	698.8981	1399.0849
77	262.0908	374.6530	761.7989	1538.9934
78	281.7476	404.6252	830.3608	1692.8927
79	302.8787	436.9952	905.0933	1862.1820
80	325.5946	471.9548	986.5517	2048.4002
81	350.0142	509.7112	1075.3413	2253.2402
82	376.2652	550.4881	1172.1220	2478.5643
83	404.4851	594.5272	1277.6130	2726.4207
84	434.8215	642.0893	1392.5982	2999.0628
85	467.4331	693.4565	1517.9320	3298.9690
86	502.4906	748.9330	1654.5459	3628.8659
87	540.1774	808.8476	1803.4550	3991.7525
88	580.6907	873.5555	1965.7660	4390.9278
89	624.2425	943.4399	2142.6849	4830.0206
90	671.0607	1018.9151	2335.5266	5313.0226
91	721.3902	1100.4283	2545.7240	5844.3249
92	775.4945	1188.4626	2774.8391	6428.7574
93	833.6566	1283.5396	3024.5747	7071.6331
94	896.1808	1386.2227	3296.7864	7778.7964
95	963.3944	1497.1205	3593.4971	8556.6760
96	1035.6489	1616.8902	3916.9119	9412.3437
97	1113.3226	1746.2414	4269.4340	10353.5780
98	1196.8218	1885.9407	4653.6830	11388.9258
99	1286.5835	2036.8160	5072.5145	12527.8294
100	1383.0772	2199.7613	5529.0408	13780.6123

Amount of £1 per annum

Example

If a person deposits £1,000 at the end of every year in a savings account earning interest at 10 per cent for ten years and leaves the interest to accumulate, how much money will there be at the end of ten years?

£1,000

Amount of £1 per annum for ten
years at 10%   15,9374
                             £15,937.40

Amount of £1 per annum

Rate %	7.50	8.00	9.00	10.00
Period				
1	1.0000	1.0000	1.0000	1.0000
2	2.0750	2.0800	2.0900	2.1000
3	3.2306	3.2464	3.2781	3.3100
4	4.4729	4.5061	4.5731	4.6410
5	5.8084	5.8666	5.9847	6.1051
6	7.2440	7.3359	7.5233	7.7156
7	8.7873	8.9228	9.2004	9.4872
8	10.4464	10.6366	11.0285	11.4359
9	12.2298	12.4876	13.0210	13.5795
10	14.1471	14.4866	15.1929	15.9374
11	16.2081	16.6455	17.5603	18.5312
12	18.4237	18.9771	20.1407	21.3843
13	20.8055	21.4953	22.9534	24.5227
14	23.3659	24.2149	26.0192	27.9750
15	26.1184	27.1521	29.3609	31.7725
16	29.0772	30.3243	33.0034	35.9497
17	32.2580	33.7502	36.9737	40.5447
18	35.6774	37.4502	41.3013	45.5992
19	39.3532	41.4463	46.0185	51.1591
20	43.3047	45.7620	51.1601	57.2750
21	47.5525	50.4229	56.7645	64.0025
22	52.1190	55.4568	62.8733	71.4027
23	57.0279	60.8933	69.5319	79.5430
24	62.3050	66.7648	76.7898	88.4973
25	67.9779	73.1059	84.7009	98.3471
26	74.0762	79.9544	93.3240	109.1818
27	80.6319	87.3508	102.7231	121.0999
28	87.6793	95.3388	112.9682	134.2099
29	95.2553	103.9659	124.1354	148.6309
30	103.3994	113.2832	136.3075	164.4940
31	112.1544	123.3459	149.5752	181.9434
32	121.5659	134.2135	164.0370	201.1378
33	131.6834	145.9506	179.8003	222.2515
34	142.5596	158.6267	196.9823	245.4767
35	154.2516	172.3168	215.7108	271.0244
36	166.8205	187.1021	236.1247	299.1268
37	180.3320	203.0703	258.3759	330.0395
38	194.8569	220.3159	282.6298	364.0434
39	210.4712	238.9412	309.0665	401.4478
40	227.2565	259.0565	337.8824	442.5926
41	245.3008	280.7810	369.2919	487.8518
42	264.6983	304.2435	403.5281	537.6370
43	285.5507	329.5830	440.8457	592.4007
44	307.9670	356.9496	481.5218	652.6408
45	332.0645	386.5056	525.8587	718.9048
46	357.9694	418.4261	574.1860	791.7953
47	385.8171	452.9002	626.8628	871.9749
48	415.7533	490.1322	684.2804	960.1723
49	447.9348	530.3427	746.8656	1057.1896

Rate %	7.50	8.00	9.00	10.00
50	482.5299	573.7702	815.0836	1163.9085
51	519.7197	620.6718	889.4411	1281.2994
52	559.6987	671.3255	970.4908	1410.4293
53	602.6761	726.0316	1058.8349	1552.4723
54	648.8768	785.1141	1155.1301	1708.7195
55	698.5425	848.9232	1260.0918	1880.5914
56	751.9332	917.8371	1374.5001	2069.6506
57	809.3282	992.2640	1499.2051	2277.6156
58	871.0278	1072.6451	1635.1335	2506.3772
59	937.3549	1159.4568	1783.2955	2758.0149
60	1008.6565	1253.2133	1944.7921	3034.8164
61	1085.3058	1354.4704	2120.8234	3339.2980
62	1167.7037	1463.8280	2312.6975	3674.2278
63	1256.2815	1581.9342	2521.8403	4042.6506
64	1351.5026	1709.4890	2749.8059	4447.9157
65	1453.8653	1847.2481	2998.2885	4893.7073
66	1563.9052	1996.0279	3269.1344	5384.0780
67	1682.1981	2156.7102	3564.3565	5923.4858
68	1809.3629	2330.2470	3886.1486	6516.8344
69	1946.0652	2517.6667	4236.9020	7169.5178
70	2093.0200	2720.0801	4619.2232	7887.4696
71	2250.9966	2938.6865	5035.9533	8677.2165
72	2420.8213	3174.7814	5490.1891	9545.9382
73	2603.3829	3429.7639	5985.3061	10501.5320
74	2799.6366	3705.1450	6524.9836	11552.6852
75	3010.6094	4002.5566	7113.2321	12708.9537
76	3237.4051	4323.7612	7754.4230	13980.8491
77	3481.2104	4670.6620	8453.3211	15379.9340
78	3743.3012	5045.3150	9215.1200	16918.9274
79	4025.0488	5449.9402	10045.4808	18611.8201
80	4327.9275	5886.9354	10950.5741	20474.0021
81	4653.5220	6358.8903	11937.1258	22522.4024
82	5003.5362	6868.6015	13012.4671	24775.6426
83	5379.8014	7419.0896	14184.5891	27254.2069
84	5784.2865	8013.6168	15462.2021	29980.6275
85	6219.1080	8655.7061	16854.8003	32979.6903
86	6686.5411	9349.1626	18372.7324	36278.6593
87	7189.0317	10098.0956	20027.2783	39907.5253
88	7729.2090	10906.9433	21830.7333	43899.2778
89	8309.8997	11780.4987	23796.4993	48290.2056
90	8934.1422	12723.9386	25939.1842	53120.2261
91	9605.2029	13742.8537	28274.7108	58433.2487
92	10326.5931	14843.2820	30280.4348	64277.5736
93	11102.0876	16031.7446	33595.2739	70706.3310
94	11935.7441	17315.2841	36619.8486	77777.9641
95	12831.9249	18701.5069	39916.6350	85556.7605
96	13795.3193	20198.6274	43510.1321	94113.4365
97	14830.9682	21815.5176	47427.0440	103525.7802
98	15944.2909	23561.7590	51696.4780	113879.3582
99	17141.1127	25447.6997	56350.1610	125268.2940
100	18427.6961	27484.5157	61422.6755	137796.1234

Annual sinking fund

Example

If a person wishes to raise £10,000 in ten years by regular saving in a deposit account earning interest at 9 per cent, how much must be saved at the end of each year?

	£10.000
Annual sinking fund for ten years at 9%	.065820
	£658.20

Proof:	£658.201
Amount of £1 per annum for ten years at 9%	15.1929
	£9,999.99*

* rounding error

Annual Sinking Fund

Rate %	7.50	8.00	9.00	10.00
1	1.000000	1.000000	1.000000	1.000000
2	0.481928	0.480769	0.478469	0.476190
3	0.309538	0.308034	0.305055	0.302115
4	0.223568	0.221921	0.218669	0.215471
5	0.172165	0.170456	0.167092	0.163797
6	0.138045	0.136315	0.132920	0.129607
7	0.113800	0.112072	0.106891	0.105405
8	0.095727	0.094015	0.090674	0.087444
9	0.081767	0.080080	0.076799	0.073641
10	0.070686	0.069029	0.065820	0.062745
11	0.061697	0.060076	0.056947	0.053963
12	0.054278	0.052695	0.049651	0.046763
13	0.048064	0.046522	0.043567	0.040779
14	0.042797	0.041297	0.038433	0.035746
15	0.038287	0.036830	0.034059	0.031474
16	0.034391	0.032977	0.030300	0.027817
17	0.031000	0.029629	0.027046	0.024664
18	0.028029	0.026702	0.024212	0.021930
19	0.025411	0.024128	0.021730	0.019547
20	0.023092	0.021852	0.019546	0.017460
21	0.021029	0.019832	0.017617	0.015624
22	0.019187	0.018032	0.015905	0.014005
23	0.017535	0.016422	0.014382	0.012572
24	0.016050	0.014978	0.013023	0.011300
25	0.014711	0.013679	0.011806	0.010168
26	0.013500	0.012507	0.010715	0.009159
27	0.012402	0.011448	0.009735	0.008258
28	0.011405	0.010489	0.008852	0.007451
29	0.010498	0.009619	0.008056	0.006728
30	0.009671	0.008827	0.007336	0.006079

Rate %	7.50	8.00	9.00	10.00
31	0.008916	0.008107	0.006686	0.005496
32	0.008226	0.007451	0.006096	0.004972
33	0.007594	0.006852	0.005562	0.004499
34	0.007015	0.006304	0.005077	0.004074
35	0.006483	0.005803	0.004636	0.003690
36	0.005994	0.005345	0.004235	0.003343
37	0.005545	0.004924	0.003870	0.003030
38	0.005132	0.004539	0.003538	0.002747
39	0.004751	0.004185	0.003236	0.002491
40	0.004400	0.003860	0.002960	0.002259
41	0.004077	0.003561	0.002708	0.002050
42	0.003778	0.003287	0.002478	0.001860
43	0.003502	0.003034	0.002268	0.001688
44	0.003247	0.002802	0.002077	0.001532
45	0.003011	0.002587	0.001902	0.001391
46	0.002794	0.002390	0.001742	0.001263
47	0.002592	0.002208	0.001595	0.001147
48	0.002405	0.002040	0.001461	0.001041
49	0.002232	0.001886	0.001339	0.000946
50	0.002072	0.001743	0.001227	0.000859

Present value of £1

Example:

Calculate how much money a lender should lend today against a guaranteed future sum of £10,000 due for settlement in five years' time at a rate of 8 per cent.

	£10,000
Present value of £1 in five years at 8%	.6806
	£ 6,806

Proof:	£ 6,806
Amount of £1 in five years at 8%	1.4693
	£10,000

Present value of £1

Rate %	7.50	8.00	9.00	10.00
Period				
1	0.9302	0.9259	0.9174	0.9091
2	0.8653	0.8573	0.8417	0.8264
3	0.8050	0.7938	0.7722	0.7513
4	0.7488	0.7350	0.7084	0.6830
5	0.6966	0.6806	0.6499	0.6209
6	0.6480	0.6302	0.5963	0.5645
7	0.6028	0.5835	0.5470	0.5132

Rate %	7.50	8.00	9.00	10.00
8	0.5607	0.5403	0.5019	0.4665
9	0.5216	0.5002	0.4604	0.4241
10	0.4852	0.4632	0.4224	0.3855
11	0.4513	0.4289	0.3875	0.3505
12	0.4199	0.3971	0.3555	0.3186
13	0.3906	0.3677	0.3262	0.2897
14	0.3633	0.3405	0.2992	0.2633
15	0.3380	0.3152	0.2745	0.2394
16	0.3144	0.2919	0.2519	0.2176
17	0.2925	0.2703	0.2311	0.1978
18	0.2720	0.2502	0.2120	0.1799
19	0.2531	0.2317	0.1945	0.1635
20	0.2354	0.2145	0.1784	0.1486
21	0.2190	0.1987	0.1637	0.1351
22	0.2037	0.1839	0.1502	0.1128
23	0.1895	0.1703	0.1378	0.1117
24	0.1763	0.1577	0.1264	0.1015
25	0.1640	0.1460	0.1160	0.0923
26	0.1525	0.1352	0.1064	0.0839
27	0.1419	0.1252	0.0976	0.0763
28	0.1320	0.1159	0.0895	0.0693
29	0.1228	0.1073	0.0822	0.0630
30	0.1142	0.0994	0.0754	0.0573
31	0.1063	0.0920	0.0691	0.0521
32	0.0988	0.0852	0.0634	0.0474
33	0.0919	0.0789	0.0582	0.0431
34	0.0855	0.0730	0.0534	0.0391
35	0.0796	0.0676	0.0490	0.0356
36	0.0740	0.0626	0.0449	0.0323
37	0.0688	0.0580	0.0412	0.0294
38	0.0640	0.0537	0.0378	0.0267
39	0.0596	0.0497	0.0347	0.0243
40	0.0554	0.0460	0.0318	0.0221
41	0.0516	0.0426	0.0292	0.0201
42	0.0480	0.0395	0.0268	0.0183
43	0.0446	0.0365	0.0246	0.0166
44	0.0415	0.0338	0.0226	0.0151
45	0.0386	0.0313	0.0207	0.0137
46	0.0359	0.0290	0.0190	0.0125
47	0.0334	0.0269	0.0174	0.0113
48	0.0311	0.0249	0.0160	0.0103
49	0.0289	0.0230	0.0147	0.0094
50	0.0269	0.0213	0.0134	0.0085
51	0.0250	0.0197	0.0123	0.0077
52	0.0233	0.0183	0.0113	0.0070
53	0.0216	0.0169	0.0104	0.0064
54	0.0201	0.0157	0.0095	0.0058
55	0.0187	0.0145	0.0087	0.0053
56	0.0174	0.0134	0.0080	0.0048
57	0.0162	0.0124	0.0074	0.0044
58	0.0151	0.0115	0.0067	0.0040

Rate %	7.50	8.00	9.00	10.00
59	0.0140	0.0107	0.0062	0.0036
60	0.0130	0.0099	0.0057	0.0033
61	0.0121	0.0091	0.0052	0.0030
62	0.0113	0.0085	0.0048	0.0027
63	0.0105	0.0078	0.0044	0.0025
64	0.0098	0.0073	0.0040	0.0022
65	0.0091	0.0067	0.0037	0.0020
66	0.0085	0.0062	0.0034	0.0019
67	0.0079	0.0058	0.0031	0.0017
68	0.0073	0.0053	0.0029	0.0015
69	0.0068	0.0049	0.0026	0.0014
70	0.0063	0.0046	0.0024	0.0013
71	0.0059	0.0042	0.0022	0.0012
72	0.0055	0.0039	0.0020	0.0010
73	0.0051	0.0036	0.0019	0.0010
74	0.0047	0.0034	0.0017	0.0009
75	0.0044	0.0031	0.0016	0.0008
76	0.0041	0.0029	0.0014	0.0007
77	0.0038	0.0027	0.0013	0.0006
78	0.0035	0.0025	0.0012	0.0006
79	0.0033	0.0023	0.0011	0.0005
80	0.0031	0.0021	0.0010	0.0005
81	0.0029	0.0020	0.0009	0.0004
82	0.0027	0.0018	0.0009	0.0004
83	0.0025	0.0017	0.0008	0.0004
84	0.0023	0.0016	0.0007	0.0003
85	0.0021	0.0014	0.0007	0.0003
86	0.0020	0.0013	0.0006	0.0003
87	0.0019	0.0012	0.0006	0.0003
88	0.0017	0.0011	0.0005	0.0002
89	0.0016	0.0011	0.0005	0.0002
90	0.0015	0.0010	0.0004	0.0002
91	0.0014	0.0009	0.0004	0.0002
92	0.0013	0.0008	0.0004	0.0002
93	0.0012	0.0008	0.0003	0.0001
94	0.0011	0.0007	0.0003	0.0001
95	0.0010	0.0007	0.0003	0.0001
96	0.0010	0.0006	0.0003	0.0001
97	0.0009	0.0006	0.0002	0.0001
98	0.0008	0.0005	0.0002	0.0001
99	0.0008	0.0005	0.0002	0.0001
100	0.0007	0.0005	0.0002	0.0001

Present value of £1 per annum

(or year's purchase single rate)

Example:

Calculate the value today of the right to receive an income of £1,000 at the end of each year for the next ten years if a return of 10 per cent is to be received from the purchase.

	£1,000
PV of £1 per annum for ten years at 10%	6.1446
	£6,144.60

Proof:

	Income	Interest at 10%	Capital recovered
£6,144.60	£1,000	£614.46	£385.54
£5,759.06	£1,000	£575.90	£424.09
£5,334.97	£1,000	£533.49	£466.51
£4,868.46	£1,000	£486.85	£513.15
£4,355.31	£1,000	£435.54	£564.46
£3,790.85	£1,000	£379.09	£620.91
£3,169.94	£1,000	£317.00	£683.00
£2,486.94	£1,000	£248.70	£751.30
£1,735.64	£1,000	£173.57	£826.43
£ 909.21	£1,000	£ 90.93	£909.07*

* rounding error due to use of two decimal places

Example:

On an 8 per cent basis, assess the value of a freehold property currently worth £15,000 a year but let at £10,000 a year for the next five years.

Term

		£10,000	
PV £1 p.a. for five years at 8 per cent		3.9927	3,992.70
Reversion		£15,000	
PV £1 p.a. in perpetuity at 8 per cent	12.5		
× PV £1 in five years at 8 per cent	.6805	8.51	127,593,75
			£131,586,45

Present value of £1 per annum

Rate %	7.50	8.00	9.00	10.00
1	0.9302	0.9259	0.9174	0.9091
2	1.7956	1.7833	1.7591	1.7355
3	2.6005	2.5771	2.5313	2.4869
4	3.3493	3.3121	3.2397	3.1699
5	4.0459	3.9927	3.8897	3.7908
6	4.6938	4.6229	4.4859	4.3553
7	5.2966	5.2064	5.0330	4.8684
8	5.8573	5.7466	5.5348	5.3349
9	6.3789	6.2469	5.9952	5.7590
10	6.8641	6.7101	6.4177	6.1446
11	7.3154	7.1390	6.8052	6.4951
12	7.7353	7.5361	7.1607	6.8137
13	8.1258	7.9038	7.4869	7.1034
14	8.4892	8.2442	7.7862	7.3667
15	8.8271	8.5595	8.0607	7.6061
16	9.1415	8.8514	8.3126	7.8237
17	9.4340	9.1216	8.5436	8.0216
18	9.7060	9.3719	8.7556	8.2014
19	9.9591	9.6036	8.9501	8.3649
20	10.1945	9.8181	9.1285	8.5136
21	10.4135	10.0168	9.2922	8.6487
22	10.6172	10.2007	9.4424	8.7715
23	10.8067	10.3711	9.5802	8.8832
24	10.9830	10.5288	9.7066	8.9847
25	11.1469	10.6748	9.8226	9.0770
26	11.2995	10.8100	9.9290	9.1609
27	11.4414	10.9352	10.0266	9.2372
28	11.5734	11.0511	10.1161	9.3066
29	11.6962	11.1584	10.1983	9.3696
30	11.8104	11.2578	10.2737	9.4269
31	11.9166	11.3498	10.3428	9.4790
32	12.0155	11.4350	10.4062	9.5264
33	12.1074	11.5139	10.4644	9.5694
34	12.1929	11.5869	10.5178	9.6086
35	12.2725	11.6546	10.5668	9.6442
36	12.3465	11.7172	10.6118	9.6765
37	12.4154	11.7752	10.6530	9.7059
38	12.4794	11.8289	10.6908	9.7327
39	12.5390	11.8786	10.7255	9.7570
40	12.5944	11.9246	10.7574	9.7791
41	12.6460	11.9672	10.7866	9.7991
42	12.6939	12.0067	10.8134	9.8174
43	12.7385	12.0432	10.8380	9.8340
44	12.7800	12.0771	10.8605	9.8491
45	12.8186	12.1084	10.8812	9.8628
46	12.8545	12.1374	10.9002	9.8753
47	12.8879	12.1643	10.9176	9.8866
48	12.9190	12.1891	10.9336	9.8969
49	12.9479	12.2122	10.9482	9.9063
50	12.9748	12.2335	10.9617	9.9148

Rate %	7.50	8.00	9.00	10.00
51	12.9998	12.2532	10.9740	9.9226
52	13.0231	12.2715	10.9853	9.9296
53	13.0447	12.2884	10.9957	9.9360
54	13.0649	12.3041	11.0053	9.9418
55	13.0836	12.3186	11.0140	9.9471
56	13.1010	12.3321	11.0220	9.9519
57	13.1172	12.3445	11.0294	9.9563
58	13.1323	12.3560	11.0361	9.9603
59	13.1463	12.3667	11.0423	9.9639
60	13.1594	12.3766	11.0480	9.9672
61	13.1715	12.3857	11.0532	9.9701
62	13.1828	12.3942	11.0580	9.9729
63	13.1933	12.4020	11.0624	9.9753
64	13.2031	12.4093	11.0664	9.9776
65	13.2122	12.4160	11.0701	9.9796
66	13.2206	12.4222	11.0735	9.9815
67	13.2285	12.4280	11.0766	9.9831
68	13.2358	12.4333	11.0794	9.9847
69	13.2426	12.4382	11.0820	9.9861
70	13.2489	12.4428	11.0844	9.9873
71	13.2548	12.4471	11.0867	9.9885
72	13.2603	12.4510	11.0887	9.9895
73	13.2654	12.4546	11.0905	9.9905
74	13.2701	12.4580	11.0922	9.9914
75	13.2745	12.4611	11.0938	9.9921
76	13.2786	12.4640	11.0952	9.9929
77	13.2825	12.4666	11.0965	9.9935
78	13.2860	12.4691	11.0977	9.9941
79	13.2893	12.4714	11.0988	9.9946
80	13.2924	12.4735	11.0998	9.9951
81	13.2952	12.4755	11.1008	9.9956
82	13.2979	12.4773	11.1016	9.9960
83	13.3004	12.4790	11.1024	9.9963
84	13.3027	12.4805	11.1031	9.9967
85	13.3048	12.4820	11.1038	9.9970
86	13.3068	12.4833	11.1044	9.9972
87	13.3087	12.4845	11.1050	9.9975
88	13.3104	12.4857	11.1055	9.9977
89	13.3120	12.4868	11.1059	9.9979
90	13.3135	12.4877	11.1064	9.9981
91	13.3149	12.4886	11.1067	9.9983
92	13.3161	12.4895	11.1071	9.9984
93	13.3173	12.4903	11.1074	9.9986
94	13.3185	12.4910	11.1077	9.9987
95	13.3195	12.4917	11.1080	9.9988
96	13.3205	12.4923	11.1083	9.9989
97	13.3214	12.4928	11.1085	9.9990
98	13.3222	12.4934	11.1087	9.9991
99	13.3230	12.4939	11.1089	9.9992
100	13.3237	12.4943	11.1091	9.9993

Annuity £1 will purchase

Example:

Calculate the annual income (annuity) that could be purchased for £10,000 for five years at 10 per cent.

	£10,000
Annuity £1 will purchase for five years at 10 per cent	.263797
	£2,637.97

Note: This table is the reciprocal of the PV of £1 per annum table, so the proof can be found from

	£2,637.97
PV £1 per annum for five years at 10 per cent	3.7908
	£10,000.00

Example:

Calculate the annual repayment needed to repay a £10,000 loan or mortgage over five years at 10 per cent

	£10,000
Annuity £1 will purchase for five years at 10 per cent	.263797
	£2,637.98

Proof:

		Annual Payment	Interest at 10%	Capital repaid
1	£10000.00	2637.97	1000	1637.97
2	8362.03	2637.97	836.20	1801.77
3	6560.23	2637.97	656.02	1981.95
4	4578.28	2637.97	457.83	2180.14
5	2398.14	2637.97	239.81	2398.16

Annuity £1 will purchase

Rate %	7.50	8.00	9.00	10.00
1	1.075000	1.080000	1.090000	1.100000
2	0.556928	0.560769	0.568469	0.576190
3	0.384538	0.388034	0.395055	0.402115
4	0.298568	0.301921	0.308669	0.315471
5	0.247165	0.250456	0.257092	0.263797
6	0.213045	0.216315	0.222920	0.229607
7	0.188800	0.192072	0.198691	0.205405
8	0.170727	0.174015	0.180674	0.187444
9	0.156767	0.160080	0.166799	0.173641
10	0.145686	0.149029	0.155820	0.162745

Rate %	7.50	8.00	9.00	10.00
11	0.136697	0.140076	0.146947	0.153963
12	0.129278	0.132695	0.139651	0.146763
13	0.123064	0.126522	0.133567	0.140779
14	0.117797	0.121297	0.128433	0.135746
15	0.113287	0.116830	0.124059	0.131474
16	0.109391	0.112977	0.120300	0.127817
17	0.106000	0.109629	0.117046	0.124664
18	0.103029	0.106702	0.114212	0.121930
19	0.100411	0.104128	0.111730	0.119547
20	0.098092	0.101852	0.109546	0.117460
21	0.096029	0.099832	0.107617	0.115624
22	0.094187	0.098032	0.105905	0.114005
23	0.092535	0.096422	0.104382	0.112572
24	0.091050	0.094978	0.103023	0.111300
25	0.089711	0.093679	0.101806	0.110168
26	0.088500	0.092507	0.100715	0.109159
27	0.087402	0.091448	0.099735	0.108258
28	0.086405	0.090489	0.098852	0.107451
29	0.085498	0.089619	0.098056	0.106728
30	0.084671	0.088827	0.097336	0.106079
31	0.083916	0.088107	0.096686	0.105496
32	0.083226	0.087451	0.096096	0.104972
33	0.082594	0.086852	0.095562	0.104499
34	0.082015	0.086304	0.095077	0.104074
35	0.081483	0.085803	0.094636	0.103690
36	0.080994	0.085345	0.094235	0.103343
37	0.080545	0.084924	0.093870	0.103030
38	0.080132	0.084539	0.093538	0.102747
39	0.079751	0.084185	0.093236	0.102491
40	0.079400	0.083860	0.092960	0.102259
41	0.079077	0.083561	0.092708	0.102050
42	0.078778	0.083287	0.092478	0.101860
43	0.078502	0.083034	0.092268	0.101688
44	0.078247	0.082802	0.092077	0.101532
45	0.078011	0.082587	0.091902	0.101391
46	0.077794	0.082390	0.091742	0.101263
47	0.077592	0.082208	0.091595	0.101147
48	0.077405	0.082040	0.091461	0.101041
49	0.077232	0.081886	0.091339	0.100946
50	0.077072	0.081743	0.091227	0.100859

Year's purchase dual rate

Example:

Assess the price to be paid for a leasehold property. The lease has five years to run at £10,000 per annum and has been sublet at £15,000 per annum. The market is valuing such interests at 10 per cent with an allowance for recovery of capital by reinvesting in a sinking fund at 4 per cent.

Income	£15,000
Head rent payable	10,000
Profit rent	£ 5,000
YP dual rate for five years at 10% and 4%	3.5134
	£17,567

Proof:

Annual sinking fund to produce £17,567 in five years equals:

	£17,567
ASF for five years at 4% (from formula)	.1846271
	£ 3,243.34

Profit rent minus annual sinking fund equals investment income

£5,000 − £3,243.34 = £1,756.66

Rate of Return from investment equals

$$\frac{\text{Income}}{\text{Price}} \times 100$$

$$\frac{1,756.66}{17,567} \times 100 = 10\%$$

Year's purchase dual rate (no tax)
Sinking fund rate 4.00%

Rate %	7.50	8.00	9.00	10.00
Period				
1	0.9302	0.9259	0.9174	0.9091
2	1.7693	1.7538	1.7236	1.6944
3	2.5294	2.4978	2.4370	2.3790
4	3.2207	3.1697	3.0723	2.9807
5	3.8517	3.7789	3.6413	3.5134
6	4.4294	4.3335	4.1535	3.9878
7	4.9601	4.8400	4.6166	4.4129
8	5.4488	5.3043	5.0371	4.7955
9	5.8999	5.7309	5.4203	5.1416
10	6.3175	6.1240	5.7706	5.4558
11	6.7047	6.4872	6.0920	5.7422
12	7.0645	6.8235	6.3876	6.0041
13	7.3995	7.1355	6.6603	6.2444
14	7.7119	7.4256	6.9123	6.4654
15	8.0038	7.6958	7.1459	6.6693
16	8.2768	7.9479	7.3627	6.8578
17	8.5325	8.1834	7.5644	7.0324
18	8.7724	8.4038	7.7523	7.1946
19	8.9978	8.6104	7.9278	7.3455
20	9.2097	8.8042	8.0918	7.4861
21	9.4091	8.9863	8.2454	7.6173

Rate %	7.50	8.00	9.00	10.00
22	9.5970	9.1576	8.3893	7.7400
23	9.7743	9.3189	8.5245	7.8549
24	9.9417	9.4709	8.6515	7.9626
25	10.0998	9.6143	8.7710	8.0637
26	10.2493	9.7497	8.8836	8.1588
27	10.3908	9.8777	8.9897	8.2482
28	10.5249	9.9987	9.0898	8.3324
29	10.6519	10.1133	9.1844	8.4118
30	10.7724	10.2218	9.2738	8.4868
31	10.8867	10.3247	9.3584	8.5576
32	10.9952	10.4222	9.4385	8.6245
33	11.0983	10.5149	9.5144	8.6878
34	11.1964	10.6028	9.5864	8.7478
35	11.2896	10.6863	9.6546	8.8046
36	11.3783	10.7658	9.7194	8.8584
37	11.4627	10.8413	9.7809	8.9095
38	11.5431	10.9132	9.8394	8.9580
39	11.6197	10.9817	9.8950	9.0041
40	11.6927	11.0469	9.9479	9.0479
41	11.7623	11.1090	9.9983	9.0895
42	11.8287	11.1682	10.0462	9.1291
43	11.8920	11.2246	10.0918	9.1668
44	11.9525	11.2785	10.1354	9.2026
45	12.0102	11.3298	10.1768	9.2368
46	12.0653	11.3789	10.2164	9.2694
47	12.1180	11.4257	10.2541	9.3004
48	12.1683	11.4704	10.2901	9.3300
49	12.2164	11.5132	10.3245	9.3583
50	12.2624	11.5540	10.3573	9.3852
51	12.3064	11.5930	10.3887	9.4110
52	12.3484	11.6303	10.4186	9.4356
53	12.3886	11.6660	10.4472	9.4590
54	12.4271	11.7001	10.4746	9.4814
55	12.4640	11.7328	10.5008	9.5029
56	12.4992	11.7640	10.5258	9.5234
57	12.5330	11.7939	10.5497	9.5430
58	12.5653	11.8226	10.5726	9.5617
59	12.5963	11.8500	10.5945	9.5796
60	12.6260	11.8762	10.6155	9.5968
61	12.6544	11.9014	10.6356	9.6132
62	12.6816	11.9254	10.6548	9.6289
63	12.7077	11.9485	10.6732	9.6439
64	12.7327	11.9706	10.6909	9.6583
65	12.7567	11.9918	10.7078	9.6721
66	12.7797	12.0121	10.7240	9.6583
67	12.8017	12.0316	10.7395	9.6980
68	12.8229	12.0503	10.7543	9.7101
69	12.8431	12.0682	10.7686	9.7217
70	12.8626	12.0853	10.7822	9.7328
71	12.8812	12.1018	10.7953	9.7435
72	12.8991	12.1176	10.8079	9.7537

Rate %	7.50	8.00	9.00	10.00
73	12.9162	12.1327	10.8199	9.7635
74	12.9327	12.1472	10.8315	9.7729
75	12.9485	12.1612	10.8426	9.7820
76	12.9637	12.1745	10.8532	9.7906
77	12.9782	12.1874	10.8634	9.7989
78	12.9922	12.1997	10.8732	9.8069
79	13.0056	12.2115	10.8826	9.8145
80	13.0184	12.2228	10.8916	9.8218
81	13.0308	12.2337	10.9002	9.8289
82	13.0427	12.2442	10.9085	9.8356
83	13.0540	12.2542	10.9165	9.8421
84	13.0650	12.2638	10.9241	9.8483
85	13.0755	12.2731	10.9315	9.8542
86	13.0855	12.2820	10.9385	9.8600
87	13.0952	12.2905	10.9453	9.8655
88	13.1045	12.2987	10.9518	9.8707
89	13.1135	12.3065	10.9580	9.8758
90	13.1220	12.3141	10.9640	9.8807
91	13.1303	12.3213	10.9697	9.8853
92	13.1382	12.3283	10.9752	9.8898
93	13.1458	12.3350	10.9806	9.8941
94	13.1531	12.3414	10.9856	9.8983
95	13.1601	12.3476	10.9905	9.9022
96	13.1668	12.3535	10.9952	9.9060
97	13.1733	12.3592	10.9997	9.9097
98	13.1795	12.3647	11.0041	9.9132
99	13.1855	12.3700	11.0082	9.9166
100	13.1912	12.3750	11.0122	9.9198

Year's purchase dual rate adjusted for tax

Example:

As per pp. 217–18 but assuming tax on investment income is payable at 40 per cent in the £1 and on sinking funds such that the accumulations accumulate at 4 per cent net of tax

Profit rent	£5,000
YP dual rate for five years at 10% and 4% adjusted for tax at 40%	2.4527
	£12,263.50

Proof:
£12,263.50 (Price/Value)
£5,000 (Income)

Return on price at 10%	Return of purchase price at 4%
10% of £12,263.5 = £1,226.35	£5,000 less £1,226.35 = £3,773.65
Less tax at 40% = £735.81	Less tax at 40% = £2,264.19
735.81 × 100 = 6% (net of tax)	Amount of £1 p.a.
12,263.5	for five years at 4% 5.4163 (from formula)

£12,263.53

Thus with an adjustment for income tax the value is reduced to the point at which a 40 per cent taxpayer will obtain a 10 per cent gross return on the investment.

Year's purchase dual rate (taxed)
Sinking fund rate 4.00%
Income tax rate 40.00%

Rate %	7.50	8.00	9.00	10.00
Period				
1	0.5742	0.5725	0.5693	0.5660
2	1.1211	1.1148	1.1025	1.0905
3	1.6423	1.6289	1.6028	1.5775
4	2.1391	2.1165	2.0726	2.0305
5	2.6129	2.5792	2.5144	2.4527
6	3.0649	3.0187	2.9302	2.8468
7	3.4963	3.4362	3.3221	3.2153
8	3.9081	3.8332	3.6917	3.5602
9	4.3013	4.2107	4.0406	3.8837
10	4.6769	4.5700	4.3703	4.1873
11	5.0357	4.9120	4.6820	4.4726
12	5.3786	5.2378	4.9771	4.7411
13	5.7065	5.5482	5.2565	4.9940
14	6.0199	5.8440	5.5214	5.2325
15	6.3197	6.1261	5.7725	5.4575
16	6.6065	6.3952	6.0108	5.6700
17	6.8809	6.6520	6.2371	5.8709
18	7.1434	6.8971	6.4521	6.0610
19	7.3948	7.1311	6.6564	6.2410
20	7.6354	7.3546	6.8507	6.4115
21	7.8657	7.5681	7.0356	6.5732
22	8.0864	7.7721	7.2116	6.7265
23	8.2977	7.9672	7.3793	6.8721
24	8.5002	8.1536	7.5389	7.0104
25	8.6941	8.3319	7.6911	7.1418
26	8.8800	8.5025	7.8362	7.2668
27	9.0582	8.6657	7.9746	7.3587
28	9.2289	8.8218	8.1067	7.4988
29	9.3926	8.9713	8.2327	7.6065
30	9.5496	9.1144	8.3530	7.7091
31	9.7000	9.2514	8.4680	7.8069

Rate %	7.50	8.00	9.00	10.00
32	9.8444	9.3825	8.5777	7.9001
33	9.9828	9.5082	8.6826	7.9890
34	10.1155	9.6285	8.7829	8.0738
35	10.2429	9.7438	8.8787	8.1547
36	10.3650	9.8543	8.9704	8.2319
37	10.4823	9.9602	9.0580	8.3057
38	10.5947	10.0617	9.1419	8.3762
39	10.7027	10.1590	9.2221	8.4435
40	10.8062	10.2523	9.2989	8.5078
41	10.9056	10.3417	9.3725	8.5693
42	11.0011	10.4275	9.4428	8.6281
43	11.0926	10.5097	9.5102	8.6843
44	11.1806	10.5886	9.5748	8.7381
45	11.2650	10.6643	9.6366	8.7896
46	11.3460	10.7369	9.6959	8.8389
47	11.4238	10.8065	9.7526	8.8860
48	11.4985	10.8734	9.8070	8.9311
49	11.5703	10.9375	9.8952	8.9744
50	11.6391	10.9990	9.9091	9.0158
51	11.7053	11.0581	9.9570	9.0554
52	11.7688	11.1148	10.0030	9.0934
53	11.8299	11.1692	10.0470	9.1298
54	11.8885	11.2214	10.0893	9.1646
55	11.9448	11.2716	10.1298	9.1980
56	11.9988	11.3197	10.1687	9.2301
57	12.0508	11.3659	10.2059	9.2608
58	12.1007	11.4103	10.2417	9.2902
59	12.1486	11.4529	10.2760	9.3185
60	12.1947	11.4938	10.3090	9.3455
61	12.2389	11.5331	10.3406	9.3715
62	12.2814	11.5709	10.3709	9.3964
63	12.3223	11.6071	10.4000	9.4203
64	12.3615	11.6419	10.4279	9.4432
65	12.3992	11.6754	10.4547	9.4652
66	12.4354	11.7075	10.4805	9.4863
67	12.4703	11.7383	10.5052	9.5065
68	12.5037	11.7680	10.5289	9.5260
69	12.5359	11.7965	10.5517	9.5446
70	12.5667	11.8238	10.5736	9.5625
71	12.5964	11.8501	10.5946	9.5797
72	12.6250	11.8753	10.6148	9.5962
73	12.6524	11.8996	10.6342	9.6120
74	12.6787	11.9229	10.6528	9.6272
75	12.7041	11.9453	10.6707	9.6418
76	12.7284	11.9668	10.6878	9.6558
77	12.7518	11.9875	10.7043	9.6693
78	12.7743	12.0074	10.7201	9.6822
79	12.7959	12.0264	10.7354	9.6946
80	12.8167	12.0448	10.7500	9.7065
81	12.8366	12.0624	10.7640	9.7180
82	12.8558	12.0794	10.7775	9.7290

Rate %	7.50	8.00	9.00	10.00
83	12.8743	12.0956	10.7905	9.7395
84	12.8920	12.1113	10.8029	9.7497
85	12.9090	12.1263	10.8149	9.7594
86	12.9254	12.1408	10.8264	9.7688
87	12.9412	12.1547	10.8374	9.7778
88	12.9563	12.1680	10.8480	9.7864
89	12.9708	12.1809	10.8582	9.7947
90	12.9848	12.1932	10.8680	9.8027
91	12.9983	12.2051	10.8775	9.8103
92	13.0112	12.2165	10.8865	9.8177
93	13.0236	12.2274	10.8952	9.8248
94	13.0356	12.2379	10.9036	9.8316
95	13.0471	12.2481	10.9116	9.8381
96	13.0581	12.2578	10.9193	9.8444
97	13.0687	12.2671	10.9267	9.8504
98	13.0789	12.2761	10.9339	9.8562
99	13.0887	12.2848	10.9407	9.8618
100	13.0981	12.2931	10.9473	9.8671

Investment valuation of freeholds subject to leases

The method outlined in Chapter 3 is called a 'term and reversion valuation' as the expected income from the property is considered according to the period of time over which it is expected to be paid. This can be illustrated as:

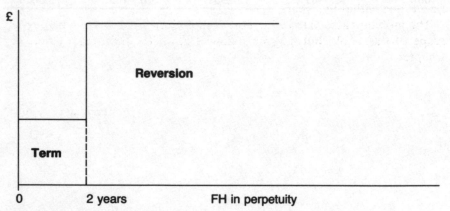

A popular alternative is the 'layer' or 'hardcore' method, which can be illustrated as:

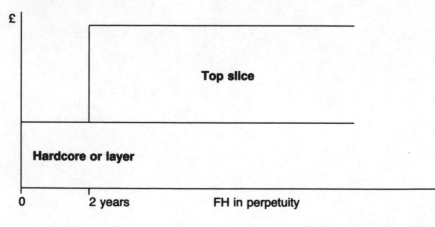

The example on p. 53 would be recalculated on the net incomes as:

Continuing income	£4,000	
PV £1 p.a. in perpetuity at 10%	10	£40,000
Top slice	£4,650	
PV £1 p.a. in two years at 10% 10		
× PV of £1 in two years at 10% .826	8.26	£38,429
		£78,429

The figure of 8.26 which is 8.2645 to four decimal places can also be assessed by deducting the PV of £1 p.a. for two years (1.7355) from the PV of £1 p.a. in perpetuity, 10 (10 − 1.7355 = 8.2645).

Some valuers may well decide to use different percentages for different tranches or layers of income to reflect any additional risk they see attaching to future income. This can lead to disastrous results, and the same yield approach is recommended for normal circumstances where the change in rent is due within five years.

The problems associated with more complex investments are outside the scope of this book, but may be followed up in the references given to Chapter 2.

Dual rate approach to the investment valuation of leasehold properties

A leasehold estate in property is less attractive than a freehold; it has a fixed duration created by the lease and it is further restricted by the terms and conditions of the lease. Thus within the property investment market it is considered more risky than an equivalent freehold in a comparable property.

During the early part of the nineteenth century valuers felt an increasing need to be able to demonstrate categorically that any capital paid out to buy a lease could be recovered in full before the end of the lease, when the lease would expire by effluxion of time and have no value. Initially this reduction in value over the life of the lease to £0 on the last day of the lease was thought to occur on a straight line basis, thus:

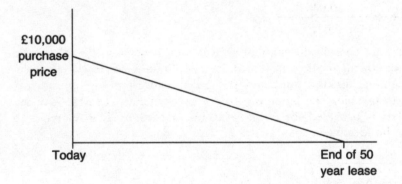

One arithmetically sound way of reflecting this in the valuation, and of providing assurance to purchasers that in fifty years' time they would be no worse off than they were today and indeed would be in a position to purchase another similar lease was to take into account the cost of creating a sinking fund with an assurance company which would accumulate over the length of the lease to recover in the fund exactly the sum paid out at the beginning to purchase the leasehold property. Such policies were available through insurance/assurance companies; they guaranteed at a very low safe rate the sum needed at the end of the lease. Thus the present value factors or year purchase multipliers on a dual rate basis provide both for the return on the investment and the return of the capital at two different rates of interest – the former is a market risk rate, the latter the safe insurance rate.

These multipliers can be calculated from the formula or from special dual rate valuation tables.

The formula is:

$$\frac{1}{i + ASF} \qquad ASF \qquad = \qquad \text{the annual sinking fund needed to replace £1 in } n \text{ years at a given rate per cent.}$$

$$ASF \qquad = \qquad \frac{i}{(1 + i)^n - 1}$$

Therefore the dual rate formula is:

$$\frac{1}{i + \dfrac{i}{(1 + i)^n - 1}}$$

Thus for fifty years with rates of 8% and 4% the substitution in the formula would produce:

$$\frac{1}{0.08 + \dfrac{0.04}{(1 + 0.04)^{50} - 1}}$$

However, to complicate matters it was felt necessary to adjust the calculation for the incidence of taxation, as both the income needed to set up the annual sinking fund and the accumulations in the fund were potentially taxable. The latter is solved by adopting a net of tax rate but the former is provided for by grossing up the sinking fund element to produce the formula.

$$\frac{1}{i + \left(ASF \times \dfrac{1}{1 - t} \right)}$$

The adjusted multiplier for fifty years at 8% and 4% adjusted for tax at 30% is 11.1910.

Example:

Value a leasehold property held on lease with fifty years to run at £5,000 per annum; the current market rental value is £15,000 per annum.

The leaseholder's income potential is	£15,000
Less rent payable	5,000
	£10,000
PV £1 p.a. for fifty years at 8%/4% tax 30%	11.1910
	£111,910

On these assumptions the investment value can be checked thus:

£111,910 (CV)
£10,000 (income)

Investment return of 8%	Sinking fund element p.a. = £10,000 − £8,952.80 =	£1,047.20
	Less tax at 30% =	314.16
		733.04
	Accumulating each year at 4% so multiply by the amount of £1 p.a. for 50 years at 4%	152.6671
	say	£111,910

This method of valuing leasehold investment properties has been used in the text as it is the standard market approach. It was and is the subject of considerable debate. The valuer must know the current dual rates acceptable to the market in order to use the method in practice.

Further reading: see Baum, A. and Mackmin, D. (1989) *The Income Approach to Property Valuation*, London: Routledge.

Appendix III

Check lists

CHECK LIST FOR SINGLE PROPERTY AUCTION SALE

Ten weeks prior to auction

Confirm instructions with client.
Check auction room/book room/ confirm in writing.
Reserve space for national advertising in *Country Life* etc.
Place preliminary advertisement announcing forthcoming auction.
Prepare, confirm and correlate preliminary details.
Arrange with solicitors to prepare conditions of sale etc.
Arrange for photographs, boards etc.
Arrange and prepare coloured plans for brochure.
Arrange for posters.
Arrange with printers for production of brochure.

Between ten and five weeks

Proof-read particulars, conditions of sale, check plans, photographs etc.
Agree brochure format and advertisements.
Place advertisements.
Order brochures.
Circulate brochures.

Between five and three weeks

Check that marketing is progressing.
Place auction reminder advertisements to appear 7–14 days before auction.
Advise police, if there are likely to be traffic or parking problems.

One week before auction

Check all arrangements for the day, including the room, car parking etc.

Check office arrangements for the day, *re*: final viewings, staff responsible for setting up the room, including all legal requirements.
Agree arrangements for formalizing the reserve price with the client.
Send reminder to all interested parties.

VENDOR'S CHECK LIST

Arrange for final meter readings to be taken on completion date with:

Electricity Board
Gas Board
Water Authority
British Telecom

Obtain estimates for removal, book removal men, and advise of new address for final account.
Agree terms with purchasers in respect of oil and solid fuel supplies.
Arrange for change of address cards to be forwarded on completion to:

Bank
Building societies
Share registrars
Insurance companies
DVLC
Employer
Doctor
Dentist
Friends
Clubs and associations

Arrange with Post Office for mail to be redirected.
Arrange change of schools for children.
Settle all accounts with local tradesmen including newsagent and milkman.
Make special arrangements for pets if necessary to avoid distress.

On the removal day

Prepare box of essentials, kettle, tea, milk, food, tools etc. and place in car or other safe place.
Do not hand over keys until sale is confirmed, or leave keys with agent with similar instructions.
Turn off all mains supplies before vacating the property.
Lock and secure the property.
Reclaim any overpaid council tax or water rates, insurance premiums, etc.

BUYER'S CHECK LIST

Confirm precise details regarding fixtures and fittings with the vendor, if not written into purchase contract.

Arrange details for collection of keys.
Book removal.
Inform:
  Electricity Board
  Gas Board
  Water Authority
  British Telecom
    of purchase completion date.
Arrange for Electricity Board or Gas Board to connect cooker, if necessary.
Arrange for change of address cards as for vendor.
Always arrive with simple tool kit, keys and light bulbs.
Make prior arrangements (where possible) with vendor for continuation of supply, if required, of milk, papers etc.
Ask vendor to leave details (in the case of a new location) of doctors, dentists, shops, schools etc.

Mortgage valuation – guidance notes for valuers

Mortgage
Valuation
Guidance for
Valuers
1 June 1992

THE ROYAL
INSTITUTION
OF CHARTERED
SURVEYORS

ISVA

GUIDANCE NOTES FOR VALUERS ON THE
VALUATION AND INSPECTION OF RESIDENTIAL
PROPERTY FOR MORTGAGE PURPOSES ON
BEHALF OF BUILDING SOCIETIES, BANKS AND
OTHER LENDERS.

These Notes are for the guidance of valuers and apply to
inspections carried out on or after 1 June 1992 and, in
respect of such inspections, supersede previous published
guidance. The Council of Mortgage Lenders and the
Building Societies Association were consulted during the
production of these Notes.

—

1.   The Valuer's Roles

1.1   The roles of the Valuer, who must have knowledge
       of and experience in the valuation of the residential
       property in the particular locality, are:

       1.1.1   to advise the Lender as to the open market
                value (not a forced sale valuation) (see
                section 4.4) at the date of inspection;

       1.1.2   to advise the Lender as to the nature of the
                property (see section 4) and any factors
                likely materially to affect its value;

       1.1.3   if required by the Lender, to provide an
                assessment of the estimated current
                reinstatement cost in its present form (unless
                otherwise stated) for insurance purposes
                including garage, outbuildings, site clearance
                and professional fees, excluding VAT
                (except on fees).

1.2   The Valuer should not make a recommendation as
       to the amount or percentage of mortgage advance or
       as to the length of the mortgage term. Nor is it the
       Valuer's responsibility to give advice as to the
       suitability of the property 'for second mortgage
       purposes'.

—

2.   The Valuer's Inspection

      Subject to the Valuer's judgement, a visual
      inspection is undertaken of so much of the exterior
      and interior of the property as is accessible to the
      Valuer without undue difficulty. Accordingly it is to
      include all that part of the property which is visible
      whilst standing at ground level within the
      boundaries of the site and adjacent public/
      communal areas and whilst standing at the various
      floor levels, as follows:

2.1   *Main Building – External*

Roof coverings, chimneys, parapets, gutters, walls, windows, doors, pipes, wood or metalwork, paintwork, damp proof courses, air bricks and ground levels.

2.2   *Main Building – Internal*

2.2.1   Parts not readily accessible or visible are not inspected, and furniture and effects are not moved, nor floor coverings lifted.

2.2.2   Subject to reasonable accessibility, the roof space is inspected only to the extent visible from the access hatch, without entering it.

2.2.3   Ceilings, walls, load bearers and floor surfaces are inspected except where covered or obscured. Readings should be taken with a moisture meter for rising dampness.

2.2.4   Cellars are inspected to the extent that they are reasonably accessible, but under floor voids are *not* inspected.

2.3   *Services*

The Valuer is to identify whether or not there are gas, electricity, central heating, plumbing and drainage services. Testing of services is *not* undertaken.

2.4   *Outbuildings*

Garages and other buildings of substantial permanent construction, and any structure(s) attached to the dwelling are inspected.

2.5   *Site*

The inspection should include the general state of boundaries, structures, drives, paths, retaining walls and the proximity of trees only to the extent that they are likely materially to affect the property's value.

2.6   *Neighbouring properties*

The nature, use and apparent state of repair of neighbouring properties in the immediate vicinity is considered only to the extent that they may materially affect the value of the subject property.

2.7   *Flats, maisonettes or similar units forming part of a larger building or group of related buildings*

The above provisions apply, but here 'Main Building' means the building containing the proposed security but not including other buildings physically attached to it.

2.7.1 *Main Building – External*: The exterior of the proposed security and sufficient of the remainder of the Main Building to ascertain its general state of repair.

2.7.2 *Main Building – Internal*: The interior of the proposed security, the communal entrance areas within the Main Building from which the proposed security takes access and the communal area on the floor(s) of the proposed security. The roof space will only be inspected (as defined in paragraph 2.2.2) where access is directly available from within the subject flat.

2.7.3 *Outbuildings*: Garaging, car parking, other buildings (excluding sports complexes) of permanent construction and any other structures attached to the Main Building or which serve the proposed security.

3.   **The Valuer's Report**

3.1   Subject to covering the matters referred to in section 1 above, reporting should be confined strictly to answering questions raised by the Lender.

3.2   If it is suspected that hidden defects exist which could have a material affect on the value of the property, the Valuer should so advise and recommend more extensive investigation by the intending Borrower prior to entering into a legal commitment to purchase or, in the case of a re-mortgage, as a pre-condition of the mortgage advance. It may be appropriate in exceptional circumstances to defer making a valuation until the results of the further investigations are known.

3.3   If it is not reasonably possible to carry out any substantial part of the inspection (see section 2 above) this should be stated.

3.4   Any obvious evidence of serious disrepair to the property or obvious potential hazard to it should be reported, as should any other matters likely materially to affect the value.

3.5   Where the Valuer relies on information provided, this should be indicated in the Report as also should the source of that information.

3.6   The Lender should be informed of the existence of any apparently recent significant alterations and extensions so as to alert the Lender's legal adviser to any enquiries to be made.

3.7 Where the proposed security is part of a building comprising flats or maisonettes, the Valuer's Report should identify any apparent deficiencies in the management and/or maintenance arrangements observed during the inspection which materially affect the value.

3.8 Where the apparent sharing of drives, paths, or other areas might affect the value of the subject property, the Valuer should inform the Lender.

3.9 The form of construction should be reported, and where non-traditional the Valuer should advise accordingly, stating the type of construction and the source of this information if it is not apparent from the inspection.

3.10 Where the Valuer decides to report a necessity for works to be carried out to a property as a condition of any advance and the Valuer identifies the property as being:

3.10.1 of architectural or historic interest, or listed as such; or

3.10.2 in a conservation area; or

3.10.3 of unusual construction

the Valuer should advise that a person with appropriate specialist knowledge be asked to give advice as to the appropriate works unless, exceptionally, the Valuer believes he/she is competent to give advice which if adopted would not be detrimental to the property's architectural or historic integrity, its future structural condition or conservation of the building fabric.

3.11 In the case of new properties or conversions where the Valuer is obliged to base the valuation upon drawings and a specification, this fact should be stated in the Report.

4. The Valuation

4.1 Unless it is made apparent by an express statement in the Report the Valuer will have made the following assumptions and will have been under no duty to have verified these assumptions:

4.1.1 that vacant possession is provided;

4.1.2 that planning permission and statutory approvals for the buildings and for their use, including any extensions or alterations, have been obtained;

4.1.3 that no deleterious or hazardous materials or

techniques have been used;

4.1.4 that the property is not subject to any unusual or especially onerous restrictions, encumbrances or outgoings and that good title can be shown;

4.1.5 that the property and its value are unaffected by any matters which would be revealed by inspection of the Contaminated Uses Land Register or by a Local Search (or their equivalent in Scotland and Northern Ireland) and replies to the usual enquiries, or by a Statutory Notice and that neither the property, nor its condition, nor its use, nor its intended use, is or will be unlawful;

4.1.6 that an inspection of those parts which have not been inspected or a survey inspection would not reveal material defects or cause the Valuer to alter the valuation materially;

4.1.7 that the property is connected to main services which are available on normal terms;

4.1.8 that sewers, main services and the roads giving access to the property have been adopted;

4.1.9 that in the case of a new property the constructon of which has not been completed, the construction will be satisfactorily completed;

4.1.10 that in the case of a newly constructed property, the builder is a registered member of the NHBC or equivalent and has registered the subject property in accordance with the scheme concerned; and

4.1.11 that where the proposed security is part of a building comprising flats or maisonettes, unless instructed or otherwise aware to the contrary, the cost of repairs and maintenance to the building and grounds are shared proportionately between all the flats and maisonettes forming part of the block, and that there are no onerous liabilities outstanding.

4.2 Among the relevant factors to be taken into account in the valuation are:

4.2.1 the tenure of the interest to be offered as security, and if known the terms of any tenancies to which that interest is subject;

4.2.2 the age, type, accommodation, siting, amenities, fixtures and features of the

property and other significant environmental factors within the locality; and

4.2.3   the apparent general state of and liability for
repair, the construction and apparent major
defects; liability to subsidence, flooding,
and/or other risks. (Particular care is needed
with non-traditional construction.)

4.3   Unless otherwise instructed any development value
is to be excluded from the 'open market valuation'
and the Valuer will not include any element of value
attributable to furnishings, removable fittings and
sales incentives of any description when arriving at
an opinion of the value. Portable and temporary
structures are to be excluded also.

4.4   The definition of 'open market value' is the best
price at which the sale of an interest in the property
might reasonably be expected to have been
completed unconditionally for cash consideration at
the date of the valuation assuming:

4.4.1   a willing seller;

4.4.2   that, prior to the date of valuation, there had
been a reasonable period (having regard to
the nature of the property and the state of the
market) for the proper marketing of the
interest, for the agreement of price and terms
and for the completion of the sale;

4.4.3   that the state of the market, level of values
and other circumstances were, on any earlier
assumed date of exchange of contracts, the
same as on the date of valuation; and

4.4.4   that no account is taken of any additional bid
by a purchaser with a special interest.

5.   Valuation for Insurance Purposes

In assessing the current reinstatement cost (see
paragraph 1.1.3) the Valuer should have regard to
the ABI/BCIS House Rebuilding Cost Index.

6.   The Valuer's Record of Inspection and Valuation

6.1   The Valuer is advised to make and retain legible
notes as to his/her findings and, particularly, the
limits of the inspection and the circumstances under
which it was carried out.

6.2   The Valuer is advised to keep a record of the
comparable transactions and/or valuations to which
he/she has had regard in arriving at his/her
valuation.

7.   **The Variation of Instructions**

All mortgage valuations should be in accordance with these Guidance Notes unless variations are notified to the Valuer in writing.

—

MODEL CONDITIONS OF ENGAGEMENT BETWEEN THE LENDER AND THE VALUER

1.   The Valuer will carry out for the Lender's current fee an inspection of the proposed security, and report, in accordance with the current RICS/ISVA Guidance Notes for Valuers on the valuation and inspection of residential property for mortgage purposes on behalf of building societies, banks and other lenders, subject to any variations specified by the Lender in the issue of instructions.

2.   The purpose of the report and valuation for mortgage is to enable the Lending Institution to assess the security offered by the property for the proposed loan and, where applicable, to enable the Directors to fulfil the requirements of Section 13 of the Building Societies Act 1986.

3.   The report and valuation will be presented on the Lender's prescribed form or other type of form as may be agreed.

4.   Before the Valuer proceeds, the Lender will take all reasonable steps to inform the Borrower as to the limitations of the inspection report and valuation, and will suggest that the Borrower commissions a more detailed inspection and Report before entering into a legal commitment.

5.   All disputes arising out of this agreement shall be finally settled under English Law and the parties irrevocably submit to the jurisdiction of the English Courts.

—

Published by RICS Books on behalf of

The Royal Institution of Chartered Surveyors
12 Great George Street, London SW1P 3AD

The Incorporated Society of Valuers and Auctioneers
3 Cadogan Gate, London SW1 0AS

First published May 1990   Revised May 1992
© RICS and ISVA May 1992 ISBN 0 85406 525 3

Alliance and Leicester – mortgage documents

MORTGAGE APPLICATION
PERSONAL DETAILS

MORTGAGE TYPE

IMPORTANT:
The 'Guidance Notes for Mortgage Applicants' that go with this form are an important part of it. Please make sure that you read them. If you do not have these notes, please contact your nearest Alliance & Leicester Branch. Our staff will be pleased to give you a copy.

Please return this form to:

Please answer in BLOCK LETTERS in the spaces provided or tick ✔ the relevant boxes.

See Guidance Note 1

	FIRST APPLICANT	SECOND APPLICANT
Title	Mr ☐ Mrs ☐ Miss ☐ Ms ☐	Mr ☐ Mrs ☐ Miss ☐ Ms ☐
	Other (please say what)	Other (please say what)
Surname		
First names in full		
Date of birth	Date Month Year	Date Month Year
Marital status	Please give details ☐ (e.g. single, married, divorced etc)	Please give details ☐ (e.g. single, married, divorced etc)
Dependent children	Number of dependent children ☐	Number of dependent children ☐
	Their ages	Their ages
Present private address (for correspondence)	Address _____ _____ _____ Postcode _____	Address _____ _____ _____ Postcode _____
How long have you lived at this address?	Years ☐	Years ☐
	Home telephone number ☐	Home telephone number ☐
	Work telephone number	Work telephone number
	Are you: the Owner ☐ Tenant ☐ Lodger ☐	Are you: the Owner ☐ Tenant ☐ Lodger ☐
	or living with relatives/friends? ☐	or living with relatives/friends? ☐
	If you are the owner, is your home mortgaged? Yes ☐ No ☐	If you are the owner, is your home mortgaged? Yes ☐ No ☐
Name, address and account number of present lender (or landlord if you are a tenant or lodger)	Name _____ Address _____ _____ _____ Postcode _____ Account number _____	Name _____ Address _____ _____ _____ Postcode _____ Account number _____
	Balance outstanding £ ☐ Monthly mortgage payment or monthly rent £ ☐	Balance outstanding £ ☐ Monthly mortgage payment or monthly rent £ ☐
	Have you had any other lender/landlord in the last 3 years? Yes ☐ No ☐ If yes give details on reverse of this form	Have you had any other lender/landlord in the last 3 years? Yes ☐ No ☐ If yes give details on reverse of this form
	Have you been 3 months or more in arrear with your mortgage or rent during the last 3 years? Yes ☐ No ☐ If Yes, give details on the reverse of this form	Have you been 3 months or more in arrear with your mortgage or rent during the last 3 years? Yes ☐ No ☐ If Yes, give details on the reverse of this form

ALLIANCE ✚ LEICESTER

G37A (9/91) [1220007]

FIRST APPLICANT	SECOND APPLICANT

Other mortgages

Are you responsible for a mortgage (residential or commercial) on any other property, either as a borrower or guarantor, solely or jointly? Yes ☐ No ☐

If Yes, please give details _____

Are you responsible for a mortgage (residential or commercial) on any other property, either as a borrower or guarantor, solely or jointly? Yes ☐ No ☐

If Yes, please give details _____

Previous private address(es) If less than three years at present address

Address _____
_____
_____ Postcode _____

(If more than one please give details on reverse of this form)

Address _____
_____
_____ Postcode _____

(If more than one please give details on reverse of this form)

Bankruptcy and debt

Have you ever been bankrupt or insolvent, made arrangements with creditors for debt, or been involved in Court proceedings for debt, or had any County Court Judgements registered against you? Yes ☐ No ☐

If Yes, please give full details, including any dates of discharge.
_____
_____
_____
_____

Have you ever been bankrupt or insolvent, made arrangements with creditors for debt, or been involved in Court proceedings for debt, or had any County Court Judgements registered against you? Yes ☐ No ☐

If Yes, please give full details, including any dates of discharge
_____
_____
_____
_____

Name and address of employer/business (If you are changing your job your answers should apply to your new job)

Name _____
Address _____
_____
_____ Postcode _____

Type of business _____
Position held _____
Length of service _____
Employee's number (if any) _____

Name _____
Address _____
_____
_____ Postcode _____

Type of business _____
Position held _____
Length of service _____
Employee's number (if any) _____

Please give the name and job title (position) of the person we should write to for confirmation of your employment (if self-employed enter accountants details)

Name _____
Address _____
_____
_____ Postcode _____
Job title or accountants name you are dealing with _____

If you have held your present job for less than 12 months, please give details of previous job on reverse of this form.

Name _____
Address _____
_____
_____ Postcode _____
Job title or accountants name you are dealing with _____

If you have held your present job for less than 12 months, please give details of previous job on reverse of this form.

Details of income (Please show whether weekly or yearly)

Basic income £ _____ wk/yr
Regular overtime £ _____ wk/yr
Regular bonus £ _____ wk/yr
Regular commission £ _____ wk/yr
Other income £ _____ wk/yr
Total earnings £ _____ wk/yr

Basic income £ _____ wk/yr
Regular overtime £ _____ wk/yr
Regular bonus £ _____ wk/yr
Regular commission £ _____ wk/yr
Other income £ _____ wk/yr
Total earnings £ _____ wk/yr

Regular monthly commitments

	Amount Owing	Monthly payment	Date final payment due
Bank overdraft(s)			
Unsecured loan(s)			
Hire-purchase balance(s)			
Credit Card(s)			
Other(s)			

Second applicant:

	Amount Owing	Monthly payment	Date final payment due
Bank overdraft(s)	£ _____	£ _____	_____
Unsecured loan(s)	£ _____	£ _____	_____
Hire-purchase balance(s)	£ _____	£ _____	_____
Credit Card(s)	£ _____	£ _____	_____
Other(s)	£ _____	£ _____	_____

	FIRST APPLICANT	SECOND APPLICANT

If self-employed, sole owner, partner or director

FIRST APPLICANT	SECOND APPLICANT
VAT number (if registered)	VAT number (if registered)
How old is the firm?	How old is the firm?
Are you:	Are you:
Self-employed ☐ Sole owner ☐	Self-employed ☐ Sole owner ☐
Partner ☐ or Director ☐	Partner ☐ or Director ☐
Yearly net income £ _____	Yearly net income £ _____
Drawings £ _____ wk/yr	Drawings £ _____ wk/yr

If limited company

What is the registered number?	What is the registered number?
How many Directors are there?	How many Directors are there?

Policies to be used with the loan

In the following boxes, please give details of any existing policies you have that you may wish to use with the loan or any new policy which is being arranged for you.
(If any of these are written under trust please tick ✔)

	1st Policy ☐	2nd Policy ☐	3rd Policy ☐
Type of policy and number			
Insurance Company and address			
Amount of life cover	£	£	£
End Date			
Whose life is assured?			
How much is the premium per month?	£	£	£

Investment accounts with Alliance & Leicester

Account number _____	Account number _____
Account number _____	Account number _____
When we give the loan we will change the address for these account(s).	When we give the loan we will change the address for these account(s).
Do you agree to this arrangement? Yes ☐ No ☐	Do you agree to this arrangement? Yes ☐ No ☐

Declaration

To the best of my knowledge the information given on this form is true and accurate. I will provide any further information that the Society may require.

I AGREE to tell Alliance & Leicester of any changes in circumstances relating to the purchase or mortgage before completion and authorise the Solicitor/Licensed Conveyancer acting for me to disclose such information to Alliance & Leicester.

I AGREE that Alliance & Leicester may give information about me and my mortgage arrangements to any credit reference agency at any time.

I AGREE that information given on this form can be used to help Alliance & Leicester, its subsidiaries or its agents to tell me about their other products and services.

I AUTHORISE Alliance & Leicester to make any enquiries or get references and allow any third parties to give them this information.

I have received and read the 'Guidance Notes for Mortgage Applicants'.

IMPORTANT: Reply to the above questions before signing.

I CONFIRM that I have carefully checked all the above answers and that they are correct.

Signature of first applicant		Date
Signature of second applicant		Date

FIRST APPLICANT   **SECOND APPLICANT**

ADDITIONAL INFORMATION   ADDITIONAL INFORMATION

Previous address(es)

1) Address _____
_____ Postcode _____
Dates: From _____ To _____
2) Address _____
_____ Postcode _____
Dates: From _____ To _____

1) Address _____
_____ Postcode _____
Dates: From _____ To _____
2) Address _____
_____ Postcode _____
Dates: From _____ To _____

Previous lenders/ landlords (Please give name, address and account number)

1) Name _____
Address _____
_____ Postcode _____
Account number _____
Dates: From _____ To _____
2) Name _____
Address _____
_____ Postcode _____
Account number _____
Dates: From _____ To _____

1) Name _____
Address _____
_____ Postcode _____
Account number _____
Dates: From _____ To _____
2) Name _____
Address _____
_____ Postcode _____
Account number _____
Dates: From _____ To _____

Details of any arrear (Use separate sheet of paper if necessary)

1) Name of lender/landlord _____
Details of arrear _____
_____
_____
_____
2) Name of lender/landlord _____
Details of arrear _____
_____
_____
_____

1) Name of lender/landlord _____
Details of arrear _____
_____
_____
_____
2) Name of lender/landlord _____
Details of arrear _____
_____
_____
_____

Previous job (Please give name and address of employer)

1) Name _____
Address _____
_____ Postcode _____
Dates: From _____ To _____
2) Name _____
Address _____
_____ Postcode _____
Dates: From _____ To _____

1) Name _____
Address _____
_____ Postcode _____
Dates: From _____ To _____
2) Name _____
Address _____
_____ Postcode _____
Dates: From _____ To _____

Alliance & Leicester Building Society,
Hove Administration, Hove Park, Hove, East Sussex BN3 7AZ. Tel: 0273 775454
Scottish Administration, Broughton Street, Edinburgh EH1 3SF. Tel: 031–557 2890

MORTGAGE APPLICATION
PROPERTY DETAILS

MORTGAGE TYPE

IMPORTANT:
The 'Guidance Notes for Mortgage Applicants' that go with this form are an important part of it. Please make sure that you read them. If you do not have these notes, please contact your nearest Alliance & Leicester Branch. Our staff will be pleased to give you a copy.

Please return this form to:

Please answer in BLOCK LETTERS in the spaces provided or tick ✔ the relevant boxes.

See Guidance Note 1

	FIRST APPLICANT	**SECOND APPLICANT**
Title	Mr ☐ Mrs ☐ Miss ☐ Ms ☐	Mr ☐ Mrs ☐ Miss ☐ Ms ☐
	Other (please say what)	Other (please say what)

Surname
First names in full

Present private address (for correspondence)
Address _____ Postcode _____   Address _____ Postcode _____

Address of property to be mortgaged (Give the plot number if the property is on an estate that is being built)

Address _____ Postcode _____

Is it a House ☐ Bungalow ☐ Detached ☐ Semi-detached ☐ Terraced ☐

Maisonette ☐ or Flat? ☐ Is it purpose-built ☐ or a conversion? ☐

Is there a garage? Yes ☐ No ☐ Roughly how old is the property? [ ] years

If it is not built of brick or stone with a tiled roof, please give details of the construction

Is it Freehold ☐ Feudal ☐ Leasehold? ☐ how many years does the lease have left? [ ]

How much is the Ground Rent/Rent Charge/Feuduty £ [ ] p.a. Can it be increased? Yes ☐ No ☐

If Yes, please give details of increases? [ ]

If there is any Maintenance or service charge, please say how much £ [ ]

If the property is yet to be built does the builder want paying by instalments? Yes ☐ No ☐

See Guidance Note 2

If the property is new is it being sold with the protection of either the:
- NHBC Buildmark Scheme   Yes ☐ No ☐
  OR
- Municipal Mutual Foundation 15 Scheme?   Yes ☐ No ☐

Living in and use of the property
See Guidance Note 3

Will you live in the property when the Loan is completed?   Yes ☐ No ☐

If No, will a dependant live in the property?   Yes ☐ No ☐

Will you or your dependant use the property for residential purposes only?   Yes ☐ No ☐

Please give the names of everyone aged 17 or over (excluding applicants) who will live in all or part of the property and how they are related to you

Tenancies
Will any tenancy be created? Yes ☐ No ☐ If you already own the property, to be mortgaged, is there any existing tenancy? Yes ☐ No ☐

If Yes to either of these questions, please give details

ALLIANCE ✚ LEICESTER

G37B (1/92) [1220009]

How much do you wish to borrow?
See Guidance Note 5

Amount £ [ ] for [ ] years If you are buying the property what is the purchase price? £ [ ]

What type of mortgage loan do you want?   Endowment [ ]   Pension-Linked [ ]   Repayment [ ]

Insurance
See Guidance Notes

With this application you will find details of HomeCover Extra, ContentsCover Extra and our Mortgage PaymentCover Schemes. If you would like us to arrange this cover, just tick the right box.

HomeCover Extra [ ]   HomeCover [ ]   ContentsCover Extra [ ]

Mortgage PaymentCover [ ]   Please give monthly benefit required £ [ ]

Improvements
See Guidance Note 4

If you are proposing to carry out immediate improvements alterations or repairs, please give details of the work and state if you are applying for a local authority Home Improvement Grant

[ ]

Is part of the loan to pay for this work?   Yes [ ]   No [ ]   If Yes, how much? £ [ ]

Are you using your own money to pay the full difference between the loan required and the total cost of the property?   Yes [ ]   No [ ]

If No, who is providing the rest of the money and what is the amount?

[ ] £

If you already own the property

What do you think the property is now worth? £ [ ]   Year you bought it [ ]

Why do you want the loan?

[ ]

Who is your Solicitor or Licensed Conveyancer?

Name of firm _____

Address _____

_____ Postcode _____

Name of Solicitor/Licensed Conveyancer you are dealing with _____

_____ Telephone number _____

Scotland only

What is the entry date? [ ]

Valuation of the property
See Guidance Note 7 for details of the various options then please tick your choice

Option 1 – Valuation/Limited inspection for Building Society purposes [ ]

Option 2 – House or Flat Buyers Report to suit your special needs as a purchaser [ ]

Option 3 – Building Survey: Please ask at your local branch before instructing a surveyor [ ]

Arrangements for valuer to visit the property

Name of seller [ ]   Telephone number

Selling agent's name [ ]   Telephone number

Which of the above should be contacted to arrange access to the property?   Seller [ ]   Selling agent [ ]

Declaration

To the best of my knowledge the information given on this form is true and accurate. I will provide any further information that the Society may require.

I AGREE to tell Alliance & Leicester of any changes in circumstances relating to the purchase or mortgage before completion and authorise the Solicitor/Licensed Conveyancer acting for me to disclose such information to Alliance & Leicester.

I AGREE that Alliance & Leicester may give information about me and my mortgage arrangements to any credit reference agency at any time.

I AGREE that information given on this form can be used to help Alliance & Leicester, its subsidiaries or its agents to tell me about their other products and services.

I AUTHORISE Alliance & Leicester to make any enquiries or get references and allow any third parties to give them this information.

I have received and read the 'Guidance Notes for Mortgage Applicants'.

IMPORTANT: Reply to the above questions before signing.

I CONFIRM that I have carefully checked all the above answers and that they are correct.

Signature of first applicant [ ]   Date [ ]

Signature of second applicant [ ]   Date [ ]

See Guidance Note 7   **ENCLOSURES**

I enclose a cheque for £ [ ] which is the Valuation charge.

I enclose MIRAS Form(s) 70, filled in and signed.   Yes [ ]   No [ ]

Alliance & Leicester Building Society,
Hove Administration, Hove Park, Hove, East Sussex BN3 7AZ. Tel: 0273 775454
Scottish Administration, Broughton Street, Edinburgh EH1 3SF. Tel: 031-557 2890

VALUATION FOR MORTGAGE ADVANCE
To: Alliance & Leicester Building Society

Applicant's copy

1. Applicant's name and address of property   Date

2. a) Age   b) Tenure

3. Description

4. Present occupier/existing tenancies

5. Accommodation and outbuildings

6. Construction of main structure

7. Any evidence of subsidence, heave, landslip or structural or flood damage?   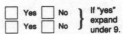 If "yes"
    Do you know of any such problems affecting properties in the vicinity?   expand
                                                                                   under 9.

8. Roads (including cost of any outstanding roadworks) and easements/rights of way

9. Condition/general observations (list any obvious essential repairs)

10. Floor area: (a) Main building   (b) garage   (c) outbuildings

11. Valuation for mortgage purposes

    a) £   in present condition   Insurance   ) £   (main buildings)
    b) £   with essential repairs and any recommendation) £   (outbuildings)
                      outstanding road works completed Any unusual hazard?

    On basis of Vacant Possession
                 Part Possession
                 Investment

**THIS REPORT HAS BEEN PREPARED BY A VALUER FOR THE BENEFIT OF THE SOCIETY AND
ITS DIRECTORS ACCORDING TO LAW. IT IS NOT A STRUCTURAL SURVEY. IT IS MADE WITHOUT LEGAL
RESPONSIBILITY TO THE APPLICANT OR ANY OTHER PERSON EVEN IF THE VALUER HAS BEEN
NEGLIGENT IN RELATION TO THE REPORT.**

IT IS PARTICULARLY IMPORTANT THAT YOU ALSO READ THE NOTES OVERLEAF.

ADV43 (8/90)

NOTES FOR APPLICANTS

This valuation has been carried out as required by the Building Societies Act for the sole purpose of enabling the Society to consider making a mortgage advance. A copy is provided for your information as a matter of courtesy and this should not be disclosed to anybody except your own professional advisers.

The Society is only interested in the property as security for the loan. Therefore, we need much less detailed advice about the property to make a decision on how much to lend than you need as a prospective owner and occupier.

The Society has not instructed the valuer to carry out a detailed building survey. Only a limited visual inspection of such parts of the interior of the property as are immediately accessible and of the exterior as are reasonably visible from ground level has been made. Furniture and the contents of cupboards and lofts have not been moved and floors beneath coverings have not been examined. Subject to reasonable access the valuer will look into but not enter the roof space and when a moisture meter is used only random tests for dampness will be made. Services will not be tested and drains will not be inspected. Cellars are inspected to the extent that they are reasonably accessible, but under floor voids are not inspected.

If any repairs are indicated in the report you should satisfy yourself as to the cost of this work by means of firm estimates from appropriate tradesmen. Any figures or retention shown either in the report or in the Society's offer of advance are for mortgage purposes only and are not intended as estimates of the actual cost of carrying out works.

YOU MUST NOT ASSUME, IF NO DEFECTS ARE MENTIONED IN THE REPORT, THAT ALL PARTS OF THE PROPERTY ARE FREE FROM DEFECT, NOR, WHERE YOUR ATTENTION IS DRAWN TO SPECIFIC DEFECTS, DOES IT MEAN THAT OTHER DEFECTS DO NOT EXIST.

If you do not satisfy yourself, independently of this report, of the condition of the property and the reasonableness of the purchase price or value of the property by consulting a suitably qualified surveyor you will be proceeding at your own risk.
The notes below further clarify the content of the report.

NOTES FOR VALUER - each note refers to the numbered questions overleaf.

1.   Include post code if possible.

2.   a.   Estimate age if not known.
     b.   State whether freehold, leasehold (and unexpired term) or feudal and details of charges such as ground rent, service charges etc.

3.   Description should state whether the property is a detached, semi-detached, terraced house or bungalow and if there is a garage. (Please indicate whether garage or space is on site or separately sited). Alternatively, if a flat or maisonette state whether it is purpose built or a conversion, give number of floors in block, number of flats in block, which floor the subject flat or maisonette is on and whether there is a lift and a shared or separate entrance and staircase.

4.   The name of the occupiers should be given if possible. Any tenancies or apparent tenancies should be reported.

5.   Accommodation should be recorded in outline normally without room sizes but indicating the number of floors. Central heating or other special features should be indicated.

6.   State materials and construction methods used.

7.   Indicate if there is any evidence of such problems in the property or properties in the immediate vicinity and elaborate as necessary under 9. Note any effect from flooding, mining, quarrying or any other extraordinary risk factor.

8.   State whether property abuts adopted or private roads. Refer to all apparent rights of way and draining rights etc. The cost of any outstanding roadworks should be estimated here.

9.   In the case of a property being built indicate the stage reached - related to normal building society stages. In all other cases the condition of the property should be indicated in general terms. A full list of minor repairs is not required but reference should be made to items of repair which materially affect your valuation for mortgage purposes. General observations should include comment on.

     a.   The character of the district and any matter likely to affect the value or market appeal of the security.

     b.   Any known planning proposals affecting the property or its immediate locality.

     c.   Whether the property lacks any of the normal services e.g. gas, electricity, water, mains drainage.

10. The gross external floor area should be stated.

11. a.   The valuation is for mortgage purposes. Please indicate the value of the property in its present condition and, if essential repairs are required, a valuation with repair works done should also be given.

     b.   The insurance recommendation figure should be on the basis of full rebuilding cost and any VAT payable, (an allowance for VAT should only be made in respect of professional fees), cost of demolition and removal of debris, architect's, surveyor's and legal fees, extra cost of rebuilding to comply with Local Authority requirements, drives, paths, fences, walls, swimming pools etc. The Society believes that the current edition of the RICS Guide to House Rebuilding Costs for Insurance Valuation forms a good basic guide.

     Please refer to any unusual insurance hazard e.g. close to cliff edge etc.

ADV43 (R)

GUIDANCE NOTES FOR MORTGAGE APPLICANTS

GENERAL INFORMATION

Interest

The interest calculated during the year in which the loan is given is from the date of completion to 31 December. Therefore payments, which are calculated on a calendar monthly basis, will not include all of the first year's interest. To ensure that no interest is outstanding at the end of the first year you will be asked to make a higher first monthly payment.

Mortgage guarantee

If you want to borrow a high percentage of the valuation of the property, the Society may have to arrange extra security in the form of a guarantee given by an insurance company. If you wish to have an idea of what the premium (which is a once only payment that cannot be refunded) is likely to be, our local branch office can help. The amounts of the guarantee and the premium are always shown in the Society's offer of loan.

The premium will normally be added to the loan and paid directly to the insurance company on your behalf at completion. Alternatively you may wish to pay the premium separately. If so, please arrange this with your solicitor or licensed conveyancer and tell the Society of your intentions.

It is important that you allow for this premium when budgeting your costs.

Note 1

a) Borrowers' voting rights

As a borrowing member of the Society you may be eligible to vote on "borrowing members' resolutions". In the case of joint members, only the first-named account holder is entitled to vote.

b) Joint purchase

If an applicant's spouse is to occupy the property the applicant should contact his/her solicitor to discuss including the spouse in the application. A late request to do this may cause delay.

Note 2

New Properties

Unless the construction of a new property is supervised by an architect or surveyor employed by you alone for the purpose, the builder must be registered with either:

a) the National House-Building Council and the Council's ten-year protection scheme known as Buildmark made available OR

b) the Municipal Mutual Insurance Limited and the Company's fifteen year guarantee scheme known as Municipal Mutual Foundation 15 made available.

Explanatory booklets are available from either the NHBC at 58 Portland Place, London W1N 4BU or the Building Guarantees Department of Municipal Mutual Insurance Limited at PO Box 71, Farnborough, Hants GU14 0NT.

Note 3

Who is a 'dependant'

A dependant is a relation of your family who is also maintained by you (regardless of how small the financial support may be). Several kinds of people can be said to be 'related' to the borrower. They include: your present partner or a former partner who receives maintenance from you; your brother, half-brother, step-brother, sister, half-sister, step-sister, parent, step-parent, grandparent, child, adopted child, step-child, or grandchild; your partner's brother, sister, parent, grandparent, child or grandchild; and the husband or wife of your relations.

Note 4

Mortgage interest relief at source (MIRAS)

If any of the cost of the proposed work is to be included in the loan, that part of the loan will not be eligible for MIRAS. On the form MIRAS 70, only show the amount of the loan that you will use to purchase the property.

ALLIANCE ✚ LEICESTER

Note 5

About repaying your mortgage

You can choose from three main types of mortgage; we have listed the differences and benefits of each below. If you are not sure which to choose, please come and talk to us. We are always available to help you choose the one which best suits your circumstances, for example there are flexible repayment terms of as long as 40 years for endowment and repayment and 50 years for pension-linked mortgages.

ENDOWMENT MORTGAGE

This is now the most popular way of repaying a mortgage. In effect it is a way of saving while buying your home. The Society provides the loan, and you pay us the interest only. This means that the capital balance on your mortgage will not reduce throughout the loan term. You also pay regular monthly premiums to an insurance company which are invested on your behalf. This investment builds up until the end of the loan term when there should be enough money to pay off your mortgage, and also leave you with a cash lump sum. Also with an endowment mortgage you get the added advantage of built-in life insurance, so that if you die during the policy term, the loan would be repaid in full. If you move you can take the policy with you and apply it to your new home. If you need to increase your mortgage or change the terms, we can arrange that too.

PENSION-LINKED MORTGAGE

If you are self employed or not in a company pension scheme you can link your pension to the mortgage. Under current tax laws there can be considerable advantages because tax relief is available on pension plan contributions as well as the mortgage interest payments, although the actual value of tax relief depends on your circumstances as a taxpayer. The Society provides the loan and you pay us the interest only. You also make regular contributions to a pension plan with an insurance company. At the end of your mortgage term the proceeds of the pension should be sufficient to repay the loan and also provide you with a pension for your retirement. The Society will be happy to take a suitable existing personal pension policy into consideration. If you do not have a pension arrangement, our mortgage advisers will be pleased to give you an example of the benefits and likely costs and discuss the details of the policy with you.

REPAYMENT MORTGAGE

With this method, you make a payment each month, part of which is the interest on the amount borrowed and the rest is repayment of part of the capital. Over the years the capital you owe gradually reduces, until at the end of your mortgage term it is completely repaid. However, unlike the endowment mortgage, life insurance is not included, so we can arrange a mortgage protection policy with Scottish Amicable, which will, provided you are up-to-date with payments, pay off your mortgage in full should you die during the policy term. If you select a repayment mortgage, we will write to you saying how you can protect your mortgage for a reasonably small cost. Our mortgage advisers will be pleased to discuss this in detail with you.

Note 6

Property insurance

Properties on which the Society lends money must be insured to our requirements and we will usually arrange this. Details of the amount to be insured will be provided with the offer of loan. Full details of the arrangements and premium payments will be provided then or soon after.

The amount to be insured is normally index-linked to the House Rebuilding Cost Index produced by the Royal Institution of Chartered Surveyors. The Society cannot be held responsible if the property is under insured during the term of the mortgage.

If at any time you consider the cover to be insufficient, please tell us what increase you require.

You should be aware of a standard exclusion clause that applies to all property insurance policies. No cover is given by insurance companies for defects that exist in the property at the time the policy is arranged nor does it cover any damage caused before the cover begins.

The Society's arrangements with its insurers do not require you to fill in a proposal form. However, a contract of insurance requires you to give any facts about yourself, your family or property which an insurer would regard as likely to influence the assessment and acceptance of an insurance proposal. Examples would be:

you or any person normally resident at your present address being charged with an offence, or having a criminal conviction (for example arson, theft or fraud); previous refusal by an insurer to provide you with householder's buildings or personal possessions insurance; a history of a high level of claims under these types of insurance; or defects specified in a private report on the property; that the property will be left unoccupied for any reason for more than one month at a time. If you consider that there are any facts which are, or might be, relevant, you should enclose a note with this application; if you do not, the insurance may not be valid.

With regard to these arrangements, Alliance & Leicester is an independent intermediary acting on your behalf, accepting responsibility for the advice provided and for the arranging of your insurance. The Society also undertakes to comply with the Association of British Insurers Code of Practice for the selling of general insurance, a copy of which is available on request.

Note 7

Valuation of the property

The Society is required by law to obtain a valuation report on the property. **The valuation may be carried out by a valuer employed by the Society, a valuer from a subsidiary company of the Society, or by an independent panel valuer not connected with the Society.**

The following options are available to you. The reports are very different and you should fully understand the scope of the report you choose. On the application form you will be asked which report you require and also to confirm in the declaration that you have read and understood the limitations of the Society's Option 1 report.

If you need further guidance, please ask your local branch office, solicitor or surveyor.

OPTION 1 - VALUATION/LIMITED INSPECTION FOR BUILDING SOCIETY PURPOSES

This report, a copy of which you will receive if an offer of loan is given, is undertaken for the Society's purposes only and is not a survey. It will be based on a limited visual inspection of such parts of the interior of the property as are immediately accessible and such parts of the

exterior as are reasonably visible from ground level. Furniture and the contents of cupboards and lofts will not be moved nor will floor coverings be lifted.

Services will not be tested neither will drains be examined. Subject to reasonable access the valuer will look into but not enter the roof space. When a moisture meter is used only random tests for dampness will be made. The Society's interest in the property is as security for your obligation to repay the loan with interest. We need much less detailed advice about the property to make a decision on how much we can lend, than you need as a prospective owner and occupier of the property.

There may be defects in the property which are not revealed in the valuation report, due to the limited nature of the inspection, which may not matter to the Society but which would certainly matter to you.

Neither the Society nor the valuer accepts any responsibility to you or any other person for the contents or adequacy of the valuation report. Nor does the Society or valuer guarantee that the purchase price is reasonable.

Any information about the state of the property or its value given to you or your agent before a copy of the report is supplied will also be subject to this disclaimer.

THE SOCIETY STRONGLY RECOMMENDS THAT YOU OBTAIN YOUR OWN MORE DETAILED REPORT ON THE CONDITION AND VALUE OF THE PROPERTY, BASED ON A FULLER INSPECTION. THIS WILL HELP YOU TO DECIDE WHETHER THE PROPERTY IS SUITABLE FOR YOUR PURPOSES BOTH AS AN INVESTMENT AND AS A HOME.

IT IS IMPORTANT THAT YOU SHOULD NOT RELY IN ANY WAY ON THE SOCIETY'S VALUATION REPORT IN DECIDING WHETHER TO GO AHEAD WITH THE PURCHASE.

The Society will be pleased to help you get a report suitable for your needs; details of the House or Flat Buyers Reports (Option 2) and Building Survey (Option 3) are set out overleaf. The fees for a fuller report are, of course, higher than for the Society's valuation report, because the surveyor will spend more time both inspecting the property and preparing a fuller report suitable for your needs.

OPTION 2 - HOUSE OR FLAT BUYERS REPORT

The House or Flat Buyers Report falls between the Valuation/Limited Inspection detailed above and the full Building Survey. There are two types of House Buyers Report – the RICS House Buyers Report and Valuation and the ISVA Home Buyers Standard Valuation and Survey Report, and both will be subject to the standard conditions of engagement issued by those organisations. These reports are intended to give you a reasonable assessment of both the general condition of the property and its approximate market value. A summary of the report will also be sent to the Society so we can decide how much to lend.

The inspection is only of those parts of the property which are uncovered and easily accessible – for example it may exclude part of the roof or floors covered by carpets. However, it should give enough information to help you decide whether to purchase the property on the agreed terms.

This type of report is designed for properties built after 1900 but can be used, at the surveyor's discretion, for some types of older property. The charges for all types of report are given in the scale shown and are payable to the Society with your application. **With these reports the Society will instruct, on your behalf, a suitably qualified surveyor who will write to you direct with the details of the Terms and Conditions of Engagement. The Surveyor will be responsible to you for the stated purpose of the report.**

OPTION 3 - BUILDING SURVEY

You may decide that you require a more detailed report than Option 2 provides. If you require a building survey it will normally be possible for the same surveyor to do the work and also undertake a valuation for the Society as described in Option 1. If you decide to choose Option 3, please make enquiries at our branch office when handing in your application **and before you instruct a surveyor.** If it is possible to use the same surveyor for both reports we shall still collect from you a valuation charge based on the Option 1 scale shown.

At the same time you should discuss with the surveyor the extent of the survey report you require and negotiate the additional fee which you will have to pay direct.

SCALES OF VALUATION CHARGE

Purchase Price*		Valuation Charge Option 1	Option 2
	£	£	£
Not more than	25,000	130	225
Not more than	50,000	130	250
Not more than	75,000	140	275
Not more than	100,000	155	325
Not more than	125,000	175	375
Not more than	150,000	190	375
Not more than	175,000	215	425
Not more than	200,000	220	425
Not more than	250,000	250	475
Not more than	300,000	280	525
Not more than	400,000	340	625
Not more than	500,000	440	725
Not more than	1,000,000	By negotiation	

The charges shown in the scales above include the Society's administration fee, and any Value Added Tax and travelling expenses that the Society has to pay the valuer, but exclude subsequent revisits to the property should these be necessary. This is usually £35 for each visit by the valuer.

Please note: *If you intend to do considerable improvement works or repairs the estimated cost of the work should be added to the purchase price and the valuation charge based on the total cost. Similarly, if the purchase price is reduced (for example sitting tenant purchase) or the property is already owned, the charge should be based on the estimated market value.

You may of course make your own arrangements for getting a suitable report on the property. If so, the Society will still require a valuation report for its own purposes and you will be liable to pay the cost of this valuation report.

RICS manual of valuation guidance notes – extracts

RICS MANUAL OF VALUATION GUIDANCE NOTES

Valuation guidance note VGN2A

This guidance note is reprinted in Appendix IVA in the leaflet format prepared jointly by the RICS and ISVA.

The manual contains a number of background papers which amplify parts of VGN2A. The topics covered include:

The valuer and the client
The Building Societies Act 1986
Liability to borrowers
The inspection
The form of the valuation report
Nature of the interest
Town planning and other regulatory matters
Other factors
Reinstatement cost assessment and exceptional risks
Model report form
Building Societies (Residential Use) Order 1987 SI 1987 and Appendices.

The RICS manual is the operational 'bible' for the residential mortgage valuer. It is regularly updated and has been recently amended to reflect some of the problems associated with the valuation of brand new houses. These changes may have been felt to be necessary because of the 'new build premium'.

The guidance now suggests that:

The valuation of a brand new property being sold by a developer should be approached in the same manner as any other valuation subject to VGN2A. It is the property as new which is to be valued, but comparable evidence can be drawn from both the sales and resales on the development.

Where there has been a satisfactory number of resales of adjacent similar new properties as the property being valued, this evidence is likely to be of greater importance.

However, where the valuer is not satisfied that this situation exists greater emphasis can be placed on prices realised recently for new property on comparable new developments and from within the second-hand market.

Adjustments are, of course, necessary to reflect any improvements in the design or layout of the subject property. The ease of maintenance during the early years and other factors which influence the decisions of purchasers, but excluding those matters for which guidance is given in paragraph 4.3 of the VGN2A.

Reprinted here are VGN2B, VGN2C, VGN2D.

VALUATION GUIDANCE NOTE VGN 2B

Reinspection of residential property for mortgage purposes

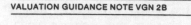

1

This Guidance Note covers 'reinspections' carried out for building societies, banks and other Lenders to which VGN 2A applies.

2

A 'reinspection' is a further visit to a property which has already been accepted by the Lender as suitable security for an advance of a specified amount so that the Valuer can advise:

(1) In connection with consideration of release of money on stage payments as to the stage of construction reached and as to the present value of the property, or whether the property as it stands is worth more than a quoted sum.

(2) As to whether the (new or newly converted or improved) property has been completed to the state assumed in the initial mortgage valuation report (a mortgage offer having been made in consequence thereof but no advance actually made).

(3) Part of the advance having been retained until specified works had been undertaken, as to whether those works have apparently been completed as assumed in the initial valuation report or as otherwise specified by the Lender to a standard satisfactory to justify lending on them and without significantly affecting adversely the value of the property.

3

3.1   In these cases the Valuer's duty is to inspect, to the extent described in VGN 2A, those parts of the property with which the service to be provided by the Valuer is concerned. It is not the task of the Valuer to inspect the whole property. The Valuer should, however, advise the Lender if in the course of the inspection:

(a) it is considered that the property may have been affected adversely by the works carried out; or

(b) new defects and/or repairing requirements and/or unsatisfactory workmanship are observed.

3.2   Unless asked to do so the Valuer has no duty to provide a new figure for reinstatement insurance purposes.

4

If no form is provided by the Lender, the Model Report form shown as an Annex to VGN 2B may be used to form the basis of the report. Attention is drawn to the caveats and warnings therein, and Valuers are encouraged to include caveats on these lines in their reports, whether or not the Lender makes provision therefor, and to recommend that copies of their reports are provided to Borrowers.

NOTE: The issue of further advice in respect of this type of work is under consideration following receipt of Counsel's advice.

MODEL REPORT FORM

REINSPECTION OF RESIDENTIAL PROPERTY FOR MORTGAGE PURPOSES

1.1 APPLICANT

1.2 LENDER'S REFERENCE

1.3 PROPERTY

1.4 DATE OF INSTRUCTIONS BY LETTER/FAX/TELEPHONE

1.5 DATE OF INSPECTION

Important notice to the Lender and prospective Borrowers: The purpose of this report is to give advice to the Lending Institution as a result of a further visit to a property which has already been accepted by the Lending Institution as suitable security for an advance, as to the stage of construction reached, or as to whether specified works have apparently been completed satisfactorily, and as to the value of the property at the date of the further inspection. This is to enable the Lending Institution to assess the security offered by the property for the proposed loan or further advance.

This report indicates the amount of work carried out at the property. It is based on a limited inspection, not a survey, of only part of the property. No guarantee is given that the works are of the standards specified for them or that there have been no breaches of statutory requirements. You should satisfy yourself that the standard of work is satisfactory for your purposes and your legal representative should confirm that all necessary consents and approvals have been obtained. You must not assume that, whether or not defects are mentioned in the report, all parts of the structure are free from defect. It is recommended that the Borrower is provided with a copy of this report.

2.0 WORKS

2.1 The works as described in your instructions/our report dated   appear to have been completed.

*2.2 The building works have progressed to those stages below where a cross appears in the box.

(i)	excavation for foundations	☐
(ii)	concrete in foundations	☐
(iii)	preparation for concrete floors or oversite concrete prior to floor laying	☐
(iv)	walls to damp proof course	☐
(v)	walls to ground floor window-cill height	☐
(vi)	walls to first floor level	☐
(vii)	walls to first floor window-cill height	☐
(viii)	walls to eaves level	☐
(ix)	roof timber fixed prior to laying roof covering	☐
(x)	building weather tight (prior to plastering)	☐
(xi)	drains (at test) prior to backfill (to the boundaries of the property)	☐
(xii)	practical completion	☐

This represents approximately   % of the cost of the works to be undertaken.

*3.0   ANY FURTHER ADVICE

I certify that the property the subject of this report has been inspected by me, that I valued the property and prepared this report, and that I am not disqualified from reporting on the property.

Signature of Valuer

Name of Valuer
(and professional qualifications)

on behalf of
(name and address of firm)

Telephone no: **Date of report:**

* delete if inapplicable or supplement if there are exceptions to the statements in paragraph 2.

VALUATION GUIDANCE NOTE VGN 2C

Revaluation of residential property for mortgage purposes

1 This Guidance Note covers a 'revaluation' carried out for building societies, banks and other mortgagees to which VGN 2A applies. It applies even if the original valuation was carried out by another Valuer, but only if the original report (or a copy) is made available to the Valuer.

2 A 'revaluation' is a report provided by the same organisation that provided the original valuation of the property, where the original report is available to the Valuer, and where the lending institution proposes to consider whether a further advance, usually of a specified sum, can be advanced on the security of the property or the repayment of a loan rescheduled. The revaluation may be of the property as it stands and/or with works proposed to it.

3 The Valuer's remit is to provide a report on:

(1) the current value of property;

(2) where defined works are contemplated, the current market value on the assumption that they have been satisfactorily completed, and a revised insurance valuation;

(3) any new factors likely to materially affect its value; and

(4) changes in the accommodation or its amenities since the previous inspection report.

4 The matters which a Valuer should consider in preparing the valuation and the extent of inspection are the same as those described in VGN 2A, to which reference should be made.

5 It occasionally happens that a Valuer is asked for an informal opinion on a revaluation without inspection. If such an opinion becomes available to a member of the public, including the Borrower, there is a danger of it being misunderstood or misquoted. When a Valuer does provide such an opinion (which should be expressed as approximate) it should be written or confirmed in writing, and the manner of valuation and the restrictions under which it is given should be clearly stated. The Lender must be informed that the value stated in such a fashion must not be quoted to the Borrower or any other party.

6 The presentation of the revaluation report will normally be dictated by the prescribed form provided by the mortgagee. In the absence of any such form the Valuer may wish to use the sample form shown in the Annex to VGN 2C.

NOTE: The issue of further advice in respect of this type of work is under consideration following receipt of Counsel's advice.

2c

MODEL REPORT FORM

REVALUATION OF RESIDENTIAL PROPERTY FOR MORTGAGE PURPOSES

1.1 APPLICANT

1.2 LENDER'S REFERENCE

1.3 PROPERTY

1.4 DATE OF INSTRUCTIONS BY LETTER/FAX/TELEPHONE

1.5 DATE OF INSPECTION

Important notice to the Lender and Borrower: The purpose of this report and valuation is to enable the Lending Institution to consider whether a further advance can be made on the security of the property or the repayment of a loan rescheduled.

The Client Lender has not commissioned a survey of the property, structural or otherwise. It must not be assumed, therefore, that if defects are not mentioned in this report, all parts of the structure are free from defect. Where your attention is drawn to some defects it does not mean that other defects may not exist. Moreover, services have not been tested. The report which follows has been prepared in accordance with inspection requirements and other assumptions, as applicable, as set out in the RICS/ISVA *Mortgage Valuation Guidance for Valuers* which were effective from 1 June 1992. Any exception is clearly stated below. No legal responsibility to the Borrower or any other person is implied or accepted by me as to condition or value of the property.

1.0 CHANGES

Since the last report, dated   , in my opinion –

1.1 The following new factors likely materially to affect the value of the property have arisen (if **NONE**, so state)

1.2 The following alterations have been undertaken to the property

2.0 PROVISOS, OR RETENTIONS RECOMMENDED (if NONE, so state)

3.0 PROPOSED WORKS

I am advised that the Borrower now proposes

4.0   VALUATIONS (assuming vacant possession unless otherwise stated)

4.1   Valuation in present conditions subject to completion of any works required under   4.1 £
       paragraph 2.0.

4.2   Valuation on completion of any works as described in paragraphs 2.0 and 3.0.   4.2 £

**5.0   BUILDING INSURANCE (this reinstatement figure must not be confused with the valuation
       at 4.0 above)**
       (This paragraph is only completed where works are noted at paragraph 3.0)

5.1   Estimated current reinstatement cost including garage, outbuildings, site clearance and
       professional fees, excluding VAT, except on fees, on the assumption that the works described
       at paragraphs 2.0 and 3.0 above have been completed.   5.1 £

Cover should allow for inflation during the term of the policy and any rebuilding period.

It should not be assumed that the present market value will be increased by an amount equal to the
quoted cost of works. If the property is old, of architectural or historic interest, or listed as such, or
is in a conservation area or of unusual construction, appropriate specialist advice should be sought
before carrying out works.

I certify that the property the subject of this report has been inspected by me, that I valued the
property and prepared this report, and that I am not disqualified from reporting on the property.

Signature of Valuer

Name of Valuer
(and professional qualifications)

on behalf of
(name and address of firm)

Telephone no: **Date of report:**

VALUATION GUIDANCE NOTE VGN 2D

Valuation of residential property in connection with possible mortgage foreclosure

1   This Guidance Note covers valuations carried out for building societies, banks and other mortgagees to which VGN 2A applies, where the lending institution is considering whether to foreclose on the mortgage.

2   An inspection and valuation and a report should be produced in accordance with VGN 2A.

3   Although not advocated by the Institution, it occasionally happens that a Valuer is asked for an informal opinion on a revaluation without inspection. If such an opinion becomes available to a member of the public, including the Borrower, there is a danger of it being misunderstood or misquoted. When a Valuer does provide such an opinion (which should be expressed as approximate) it should be written or confirmed in writing, and the manner of valuation and the restrictions under which it is given should be clearly stated. The Lender must be informed that the value stated in such a fashion must not be quoted to the Borrower or any other party.

4   If the lending institution requests a 'forced sale value', this should be taken and stated to mean Open Market Value as defined in VGN 2A with the proviso that the vendor has imposed a time limit for completion which cannot be regarded as allowing a 'reasonable period' as referred to in paragraph 4.4.2 thereof. If the time limit has not been specified by the Client/Lender, the Valuer should discuss and agree with the Lender what it is to be or, if this cannot be achieved, state what assumption has been made.

Home Buyer's Survey and Valuation

The Home Buyers' Survey and Valuation report is intended for use by a Member of The Royal Institution of Chartered Surveyors or a Member of the Incorporated Society of Valuers and Auctioneers only.

This edition of the report must only be used in conjunction with other material of the same edition.

HOME BUYERS'
Survey and Valuation

Page 1 of 9

- This report is provided on the terms set out in the enclosed RICS/ISVA Standard Conditions of Engagement. The report is provided solely for the named clients and their professional advisers and should not be relied upon by others.
- The purpose of the inspection described in the Standard Conditions is to provide a report on the general state of repair and condition of the property described below. The inspection is not a building/structural survey and this report is not intended to detail minor defects which do not materially affect value.
- The clients are advised to show a copy of the report to their legal advisers as it may affect investigations they will need to make.

A: INFORMATION

A1 Name and address of clients

A2 Property address

A3 Council tax band or rating assessment as applicable
(Verbal enquiry only.)

A4 Date of inspection

A5 Weather

A6 Limits to inspection
(Including to what extent the property was furnished and/or the floors were covered.)

SAMPLE

A7 Tenure

A7.1 Freehold

A7.2 Feudal

A7.3 Leasehold: unexpired term of years

A7.4 Amount of rent: ground/chief/ fixed/variable, etc.

A7.5 Maintenance/service charge (approximate)

A7.6 Other comments

A8 Apparent tenancies
(If any: details and rent(s).)

HOME BUYERS'
Survey and Valuation **2**

**B: GENERAL
DESCRIPTION
OF PROPERTY**

**B1   Description of
property**

B2   Accommodation

**B3   Outbuildings and
parking**

SAMPLE

B4   Approximate age
(Including date if available
of extensions and conversions
where applicable.)

B5   Orientation

**B6   Location and
amenities**

**B7   Summary of
construction**
(Some buildings may not
comply with the
requirements for today's new
buildings, and could include
harmful or hazardous
materials. This report will
include details of such
materials where their use is
apparent from the visual
inspection but with certain
types of building it may be
impossible to confirm the
details of construction.)

HOME BUYERS'
Survey and Valuation

Page 3 of 9

C: EXTERNAL CONDITION

C1   Chimney stacks and boiler flues
(Including associated flashings, etc.)

C2   Roofs
(Including valleys, flashings and soakers.)

C3   Rainwater goods
(Including parapet gutters.)

SAMPLE

C4   Main walls and damp proof course
(The foundations, cavity wall ties or other concealed structural elements have not been exposed for examination and therefore not all defects can be fully diagnosed. The adequacy of sub-floor ventilation is assessed only from the visible exterior surfaces.)

C5   Windows, doors and joinery

C6   External decoration

HOME BUYERS'
Survey and Valuation

C7 Garage(s) and outbuildings
(Comment is restricted to important defects, likely to have a material affect on value. Inspection of leisure facilities, etc., is excluded.)

C8 The site
(Only significant visible defects in boundary fences, walls, retaining walls, paths and drives are reported. Reference to potential hazards such as flooding and tree roots is included where these are readily apparent.)

C9 Drainage
(Inspection covers within the boundaries have been lifted where visible and possible [except in the cases of flats and maisonettes]. This is to facilitate a visual inspection. The drains have not been tested and it is not possible to comment on hidden areas. Where the drainage systems have not been traced, it is assumed that the drains are connected to the main sewer, or an alternative and acceptable means of disposal.)

SAMPLE

D: INTERNAL CONDITION
(Inspected from floor level only. Furniture, wall hangings, floor coverings, insulation material and stored goods have not been moved. *See* paragraph D5.)

D1 Roof spaces
(*See* paragraph C2. It should be noted that the inspection of the roof space is confined to details of design and basic construction. Individual timbers have not been specifically examined for defects although where defects have been observed as part of the general examination, such defects are noted in this report.)

D2 Ceilings

D3 Walls and partitions

HOME BUYERS'
Survey and Valuation

5

Page 5 of 9

D4 Fireplaces, flues and chimney breasts
(It is not possible to indicate the condition of flues or presence of flue liners. No assumption should be made as to the practicability of using the chimneys. It is recommended that any flues should be swept prior to occupation.)

D5 Floors
(Only the surface of floors which are not covered have been inspected but accessible corners of any coverings were lifted where possible to identify the nature of the surface beneath.)

D6 Dampness
(A moisture detecting meter has been used in selected accessible positions, without moving furniture, floor coverings, fixtures and fittings, to test for dampness.)

D7 Woodworm, dry rot and other timber defects

D8 Internal joinery including windows, doors, staircases, built-in fitments and kitchen fittings

D9 Internal decorations
(Furnishings have not been moved to confirm the state of covered or hidden decoration, which may be damaged or faded.)

D10 Cellars and vaults

HOME BUYERS'
Survey and Valuation

D11 Thermal insulation

D12 Services

(No tests have been carried out. Only significant defects and deficiencies readily apparent from a visual inspection are reported. Compliance with regulations and adequacy of design conditions or efficiency can only be assessed as a result of a test and, should you require any further information in this respect, it is essential that you should obtain reports from appropriate specialists before entering into a legal commitment to purchase.)

D12.1 Electricity

D12.2 Gas

D12.3 Plumbing and
heating

D12.4 Sanitary fittings

SAMPLE

D12.5 Other facilities

E: COMMON PARTS
AND SERVICES

E1   Extent of inspection

E2   Condition of
common parts

E2.1 External

E2.2 Internal

HOME BUYERS'
Survey and Valuation

Page 7 of 9

E3 Common services

E3.1 Water and heating

E3.2 Lifts

E3.3 Security system

E3.4 Fire escapes

(See paragraph D12. Your legal adviser should seek assurances that the undermentioned services have been regularly maintained and that there are adequate certificates available.)

F: FURTHER ADVICE AND VALUATION

F1 Road and footpaths
(Including side and/or rear.)

F2 Matters apparent from the inspection which should be checked by legal advisers

F2.1 Rights of way/ easements/servitudes/ wayleaves

F2.2 Road agreements

F2.3 In the case of flats, etc., a properly formed management company

F2.4 Drains/sewers liability

F2.5 Other
(E.g.: significant planning or highway proposals if known. Suspected contravention of building regulations, possibility of enforcement action and breach of likely planning permission.)

HOME BUYERS'
Survey and Valuation

Page 8 of 9

F3 Matters that might materially affect value, and any further advice

F3.1 In cases of flats, apparent management problems

F3.2 Obvious evidence of serious disrepair/ potential hazard to the property

SAMPLE

F3.3 Matters not included under F3.1 and F3.2 likely materially to affect the value, and any further advice

F4 Paragraphs referring to matters regarding the condition/hazards requiring immediate attention
(You are advised to obtain estimates of the cost of dealing with any matters referred to here before committing yourself to purchase.)

HOME BUYERS'
Survey and Valuation

F5   Building insurance

F5.1 Estimated current
reinstatement cost
in its present form
(unless otherwise
stated)

(This reinstatement figure must not be confused with the valuation at F6.)
(Including any garage and/or outbuildings, site clearance and professional fees, excluding
VAT, except on fees.)

F5.2 Approximate total
external floor area of
dwelling

F6   Open Market Value

(With vacant possession, excluding any development value unless otherwise stated, and
excluding the value of carpets, curtains and other sales inducements.)

F6.1 In its existing state

F6.2 As if any works
referred to at
paragraph F4 had
been undertaken
satisfactorily

SAMPLE

This report is provided on the terms set out in the Standard Conditions of Engagement for
The Royal Institution of Chartered Surveyors/Incorporated Society of Valuers and Auctioneers
Home Buyers' Survey and Valuation. I certify that the subject property has been inspected
by me, that I valued the property and prepared this report.

Signature of Surveyor ....

Name of Surveyor (and professional qualifications)...

....

On behalf of (name and address of organisation) ....

....

....

Telephone number ....

Date of report ....

HOME BUYERS'
Survey and Valuation

SAMPLE

RICS/ISVA Standard Conditions of Engagement

1. THE SERVICE

1.1 Based on an inspection as described below the surveyor/valuer, who will be a Chartered Surveyor or an Incorporated Valuer (hereinafter called 'the surveyor'), will provide in a standard reporting format which has been determined jointly by the RICS and the ISVA:

1.1.1 a concise report on the general condition of the property, identifying significant defects and repairs essential at the time of inspection and referring to readily apparent potential hazards;

1.1.2 a brief description of the property and any factors likely materially to affect its value;

1.1.3 the surveyor's opinion of the 'open market value' at the date of the inspection on the assumptions set out below and, if different, the value on the assumption that any essential repairs identified have been carried out satisfactorily;

1.1.4 usually an assessment of the estimated current reinstatement cost in its present form (unless otherwise stated) for insurance purposes including garage, outbuildings, site clearance and professional fees, excluding VAT (except on fees).

1.2 The report will not purport to express an opinion about or to advise upon the condition of uninspected parts and should not be taken as making any implied representation or statement about such parts; nor will it mention minor defects which the surveyor considers do not materially affect the value of the property. If the report does refer to some minor defects this does not imply that the property is free from other such defects.

1.3 The report is provided for the sole use of the named clients and is confidential to them and their professional advisers. No responsibility is accepted to others.

1.4 In preparing the report the surveyor will exercise the skill and diligence reasonably to be expected from a surveyor and valuer competent to advise on the subject property.

1.5 The report will not identify the existence of contamination in or from the ground, as this can only be established by other specialists.

1.6 If having arrived at the subject property the surveyor considers that it should not be reported upon in the RICS/ISVA Home Buyers' Survey and Valuation reporting format, the surveyor will be entitled not to proceed with the inspection and will report to the clients accordingly (*see* 6.2 below).

2. THE INSPECTION

2.1 The main building

2.1.1 The surveyor will undertake a visual inspection of so much of the exterior and interior of the property as is accessible with safety and without undue difficulty. Accordingly the report will cover all that part of the property which is visible whilst standing at ground level within the boundaries of the site and adjacent public/communal areas and whilst standing at the various floor levels. The surveyor will open trap doors where accessible and possible with safety and without undue difficulty. However he/she will be under no obligation to raise floor boards or to inspect those areas of the property that are covered, unexposed, or are not readily accessible with safety and without undue difficulty. Therefore furniture, floor coverings, fixtures and fittings will not be moved, but the inspection will include, subject to reasonable accessibility with safety and without undue difficulty, the roof space without moving insulation material. Inspection of the roof space is confined to details of design and basic construction; individual timbers are not specifically examined although, where defects are observed as part of the general examination, such defects will be noted in the report.

2.1.2 It is not possible to report on the condition of flues or the presence of flue liners, and the report will not advise upon whether or not any chimneys can be used.

2.1.3 The outer surfaces of the roofs will be inspected if they can be readily seen from a 3 metre (10 ft) ladder, set safely with its feet on the ground, or from any other accessible vantage point to which the surveyor is entitled to gain access.

2.1.4 A moisture detecting meter will be used in selected positions.

2.2 Services
The surveyor will provide an overall impression of the services, but will not test them and will not advise upon whether the property/services comply with regulations in respect of services. Drainage inspection covers will be lifted where visible and possible to facilitate a visual inspection, but drains are not tested.

2.3 Outbuildings
Garages and other outbuildings of substantial permanent construction and any structure(s) attached to the dwelling will be inspected. Leisure facilities within outbuildings will not be inspected.

2.4 Site
The boundary structures, retaining walls, paths and drives will be inspected to the extent that they are readily visible from positions to which the surveyor is entitled to gain access. Leisure facilities will not be inspected.

2.5 Flats, maisonettes or similar units forming part of a larger building or group of related buildings
The descriptions of the nature of the inspection given in paragraph 2.1 and paragraph 2.2 on services apply except that inspection covers will not be lifted and the condition or adequacy of lifts will not be investigated or reported upon. As to what will be inspected:

2.5.1 *External:* The exterior of the subject property, and sufficient of the remainder of the building in which it is situated and of the exterior of any other buildings of permanent construction, notified by the clients and agreed with the surveyor to be inspected, to ascertain their general state of repair.
(*Please note:* This is to enable the clients to arrange for inspection of that part of the exterior of the property to which a shared maintenance/service charge which would be payable by the clients applies.)

2.5.2 *Internal:* The interior of the subject property, and in a more superficial way, those communal areas within the building from which the subject property takes access and on the floor(s) of the subject property plus such other communal areas/roof/ roof spaces notified by the clients and agreed with the surveyor to be inspected.
(*Please note:* This is to enable the clients to arrange for inspection of other communal parts which are the subject of shared maintenance/ service charges which would be payable by the clients.)   ◊

© The Royal Institution of Chartered Surveyors August 1993

HOME BUYERS'
Survey and Valuation

Conditions of Engagement (continued)

3. THE REPORT

3.1 If it is suspected that hidden defects exist which could have a material affect on the value of the property, the surveyor will so advise and recommend more extensive investigation prior to entering into a legal commitment to purchase. It may be appropriate in exceptional circumstances to defer making a valuation until the results of the further investigations are known.

3.2 If it is not reasonably possible to carry out any substantial part of the inspection (*see* section 2 above) this will be stated.

3.3 Any obvious evidence of serious disrepair or potential hazard to the property will be reported, as will any other matters apparent from the inspection which are likely materially to affect the value.

3.4 Where the surveyor relies on information provided, this will be indicated in the report, with the source of the information.

3.5 The report will state the existence of any apparently recent significant alterations and extensions so as to alert legal advisers.

3.6 Where the subject property is part of a building comprising flats or maisonettes, the report will identify any apparent deficiencies in the management and/or maintenance arrangements for the whole building observed during the inspection which the surveyor considers materially to affect the value.

3.7 Where the apparent sharing of drives, paths or other areas might affect the value of the subject property, the surveyor will so report.

4. THE VALUATION

4.1 Unless it is made apparent by an express statement in the report the surveyor will have made the following assumptions and will have been under no duty to have verified these assumptions:

4.1.1 that vacant possession is provided;

4.1.2 that planning permission and statutory approvals for the buildings and for their use, including any extensions or alterations, have been obtained;

4.1.3 that no deleterious or hazardous materials or techniques have been used and that the land is not contaminated;

4.1.4 that the property is not subject to any unusual or especially onerous restrictions, encumbrances or outgoings and that good title can be shown;

4.1.5 that the property and its value are unaffected by any matters which would be revealed by inspection of any register or by a local search (or their equivalent in Scotland and Northern Ireland) and replies to the usual enquiries, or by a statutory notice and that neither the property, nor its condition, nor its use, nor its intended use, is or will be unlawful; and moreover that the value of the property would not be affected by the possibility of any entry being made in any register;

4.1.6 that an inspection of those parts which have not been inspected would not reveal material defects or cause the surveyor to alter the valuation materially;

4.1.7 that the property is connected to main services which are available on normal terms;

4.1.8 that sewers, main services and the roads giving access to the property have been adopted;

4.1.9 that in the case of a newly constructed property, the builder is a registered member of the NHBC or equivalent and has registered the subject property in accordance with the scheme concerned;

4.1.10 that where the subject property is part of a building comprising flats or maisonettes, unless instructed or otherwise aware to the contrary, the cost of repairs and maintenance to the building and grounds are shared proportionately between all the flats and maisonettes forming part of the block, and that there are no onerous liabilities outstanding.
(*Please note:* As no formal enquiries will be made by the surveyor the clients' legal adviser should have sight of this report and be asked to verify:

(i) the assumptions given above;

(ii) any information provided to the surveyor which is set out in the report;

(iii) in respect of leasehold properties the details and adequacy of the lease;

(iv) matters relating to town planning, statutory or environmental factors, mining, roads or services or contravention of building regulations.)

4.2 Unless otherwise instructed any development value is to be excluded from the 'open market valuation' and the surveyor will not include any element of value attributable to furnishings, removable fittings and sales incentives of any description

when arriving at an opinion of the value. Portable and temporary structures will be excluded also.

4.3 The definition of 'open market value' is the best price at which the sale of an interest in property might reasonably be expected to have been completed unconditionally for cash consideration on the date of valuation assuming:

4.3.1 a willing seller;

4.3.2 that, prior to the date of valuation, there had been a reasonable period (having regard to the nature of the property and the state of the market) for the proper marketing of the interest, for the agreement of price and terms and for the completion of the sale;

4.3.3 that the state of the market, level of values and other circumstances were, on any earlier assumed date of exchange of contracts, the same as on the date of valuation;

4.3.4 that no account is taken of any additional bid by a purchaser with a special interest.

5. VALUATION FOR INSURANCE PURPOSES

5.1 In assessing the current reinstatement cost (*see* paragraph 1.1.4) the surveyor will have due regard to the Association of *British Insurers/ Building Cost Information Service House Rebuilding Cost Index.* The assessment will not include loss of rent or cost of alternative accommodation for the reinstatement period.

5.2 In the case of a flat or maisonette the figure will be for the flat or maisonette only and it will be necessary for the clients' legal adviser to establish and advise whether the insurance arrangements relating to the remainder of the block or building are satisfactory.

6. CHARGES

6.1 The clients will pay the surveyor the fee agreed in writing for the report and valuation and expressly agreed disbursements.

6.2 Before agreeing the fee the clients are expected to give a fair indication of what is to be inspected, including the size of the main building in which a flat/maisonette is situated; in the event of the inspection being substantially more extensive than described by the clients, the surveyor shall be entitled to an additional reasonable fee. In the event of the surveyor acting in accordance with paragraph 1.6 above, his/her reasonable travelling costs shall be payable by the clients.

SAMPLE

© The Royal Institution of Chartered Surveyors August 1993

The Domestic Property (Valuation) Regulations 1991

The Domestic Property (Valuation) Regulations 1991 S.1 1991 No. 1934 specifies the basis of valuation for the purpose of the Council Tax in the following terms:

Basis of valuation

2.–(1) For the purposes of the valuation under section 3 (valuation of domestic properties) of the Act, the value of any domestic property shall bc takcn to bc thc amount which, on thc assumptions mcntioncd in paragraph (2) below, the property might reasonably have been expected to realize if it had been sold in the open market by a willing vendor on 1st April 1991.

(2) The assumptions are –

(a) that the sale was with vacant possession;
(b) that the interest sold was the freehold, or in the case of a flat, a lease for 99 years at a nominal rent;
(c) that the property was sold free from any rent charge or other encumbrance;
(d) that the size and layout of the property, and the physical state of its locality, were the same as at the time when the valuation of the property is made;
(e) that the property was in a state of reasonable repair;
(f) in the case of a property the owner or occupier of which is entitled to use common parts, that those parts were in a like state of repair and the purchaser would be liable to contribute towards the cost of keeping them in such a state;
(g) in the case of a property which has a room to which this sub-paragraph applies, that the room was not included in the property;
(h) in the case of a property which contains (otherwise than as part of a room which, by virtue of sub-paragraph (g), is assumed not to be included in the property) fixtures to which this sub-paragraph applies, that the fixtures were not included in the property;

(i) that the use of the property would be permanently restricted to use as a private dwelling; and

(j) that the property had no development value other than value attributable to permitted development.

(3) Sub-paragraph (g) of paragraph (2) applies to any room of one of the following descriptions, namely, kitchen, bathroom and lavatory. which has features which –

(a) are substantially different from those of ordinary rooms of the same description; and

(b) are designed to make the room suitable for a use by a physically disabled person;

but nothing in that sub-paragraph shall require it to be assumed that there was not included in any property at least one room of each of those descriptions.

(4) Sub-paragraph (h) of paragraph (2) applies to any fixtures which –

(a) are designed to make the property suitable for use by a physically disabled person; and

(b) add to the value of the property.

(5) In paragraph (2) –

'common parts', in relation to a property, means any part of a building comprising the property and any land or premises which the owner or occupier of the property is entitled to use in common with the owners or occupiers of other premises in the immediate locality;

'flat' has the same meaning as in Part V of the Housing Act 1985(a);

'permitted development' means development –

(a) for which planning permission is not required; or

(b) for which an application for planning permission is not required;

'rent charge' has the same meaning as in the Rent Charges Act 1977(b); and

'state of reasonable repair', in relation to a property, means such state of repair as might reasonably be expected by a prospective purchaser, having regard to the age and character of the property and its locality.

Further reading

CHAPTERS 1 AND 2

Aldridge, T.M. (1986) *Boundaries, Walls and Fences*, 5th edn, London: Oyez.

Bloom, G.F., and Harrison, H.S. (1978) *Appraising the Single Family Residence*, AIREA.

Building Research Establishment publications on Precast reinforced concrete housing.

Card, R., Murdoch, J.R. and Schofield, P. (1986) *Law for Estate Management Students*, 2nd edn, London: Butterworths.

Evans, A.W. (1985) *An Introduction to Urban Economics*, Oxford: Blackwell.

Harvey, J. (1981) *The Economics of Real Property*, Basingstoke: Macmillan.

Marshall, D. and Worthing, D. (1990) *The Construction of Homes*, London: Estates Gazette.

RICS (1987) *Property Doctor Book*, London: RICS Books.

TRADA (1981) *Introduction to Timber Frame Housing*.

CHAPTER 3

Baum, A.E. and Mackmin, D.H. (1989) *The Income Approach to Property Valuation*, 3rd edn, London: Routledge.

CHAPTERS 4, 5, 6 AND 7

Carpenter, Clive, and Harris, Susan (1988) *Property Auctions*, London: Estates Gazette.

Murdoch, J.R. (1979) *The Estate Agents Act 1979*, London: Estates Gazette.

Murdoch, J.R. (1984) *The Law of Estate Agency and Auctions*, 2nd edn, London: Estates Gazette.

Perkins, D. (ed.) (1989) *The Estate Agents Factbook*, London: Professional Publishing Ltd.

RICS (1990) *Code of Measuring Practice*, London: RICS Books.

RICS (1984) *Practice Notes for Estate Agents*, London: RICS Books.

RICS (1991) *Putting the Estate Agents Act and its Orders and Regulations into Practice*, London: RICS Books.

Scott, B. (1981) *Skills of Negotiating*, Aldershot: Gower.

Stephens, N. (1981) *The Practice of Estate Agency*, London: Estates Gazette.

Thelwell, N. (1982) *This Desirable Plot*, London: Methuen.

Vivian, M.J. (1975) *The Art of House Agency*, ISVA.

CHAPTER 8

'Building Societies Act 1986', HMSO.
Byron, R.J. (1979) *The Building Society Valuer*, London: *Estates Gazette*.
Property Valuation Handbook B3, Valuations for Loan Purposes, College of Estate
  Management.

CHAPTER 9

Bowyer, J. (1988) *Guide to Domestic Building Surveys*, 4th edn, London:
  Butterworth.
Hollis, M. (1986) *Model Survey Reports*, London: Henry Stewart.
Hollis, M. (1988) *Surveying Buildings*, London: RICS Books.
RICS (1988) *Conditions of Engagement for Building Surveying Services* London:
  RICS Books.
Ross, M. (1986) *Negligence in Surveying and Building*, London: *Estates Gazette*.
TRADA (1981) Structural Surveys of Timber Frame Houses.

CHAPTER 10

Legal side to Buying and Selling a House, London: Consumers Association.
Moeran (1988) *Practical Conveyancing*, London: Oyez.
Storey, I.R. (1987) *Conveyancing*, 2nd edn, London: Butterworths.

CHAPTER 11

Baum, A.E. (1990) *Statutory Valuation*, 2nd edn, London: Routledge.
Hubbard, C. and Williams, D. (1987) *Handbook of Leasehold Reform*, London:
  Sweet & Maxwell.
Property Valuation Handbook C3: Leasehold Enfranchisement, College of Estate
  Management.

CHAPTER 13

Catt, R. and Catt, S. (1981) *The Conversion, Improvement and Extension of
  Buildings*, London: *Estates Gazette*.
Spain, B.J.D. and Morley, L.B. (1987) *Home Improvement Price Guide*, London:
  E.F. & N. Spon.

CHAPTER 14

Yates, D. and Hawkins, A.J. (1988) *Landlord and Tenant Law* (Part II, Residential
  Tenancies), London: Sweet and Maxwell.

CHAPTER 15

Baum, A.E. (1990) *Statutory Valuation*, London: Routledge.
Guide to House Rebuilding Costs for Insurance Valuation (Annual), BCIS.
Property Insurance (1985), 3rd edn, London: RICS Books.

All RICS and RICS/ISVA publications may be purchased from the Surveyors
  Bookshop, RICS, 12 Great George Street, London SW1P 3AD, who are also
  able to supply most of the books referred to in this list.

Index